D1084620

Lessons of War

The Civil War in Children's Magazines

Lessons of War

The Civil War in Children's Magazines

Edited by James Marten

A Scholarly Resources Inc. Imprint
Wilmington, Delaware

Scholarly Resources Inc.
104 Greenhill Avenue
Wilmington, DE 19805-1987

Library of Congress Cataloging-in Publication Data

Lessons of war : the Civil War in children's magazines / edited by
  James Marten.
      p.   cm.
   Includes bibliographical references and index.
   ISBN 0-8420-2654-1 (alk. paper). — ISBN 0-8420-2656-8 (alk.
paper)
      1. War—Literary collections.   2. United States—History—Civil
War, 1861–1865—Literary collections.   3. United States—History—
Civil War, 1861–1865—Juvenile literature.   4. Children—United
States—Books and reading—History—19th century.   5. American
literature—19th century.   6. Children's periodicals, American.
7. Children's literature, American.   I. Marten, James Alan.
PS509.W3L47   1998
810.8'0358—dc21   98-15798
                                                                            CIP

To Brandon

About the Editor

James Marten is associate professor of history at Marquette University, where he teaches courses on the Civil War era, childhood, and African-American history. He is the author of *The Children's Civil War* (1998) and *Texas Divided: Loyalty and Dissent in the Lone Star State, 1856–1874* (1990).

Contents

Acknowledgments

Although I was born nearly a century after the Civil War, the children's literature I grew up with projected more than a little of the certainty about what good little boys and girls were made of that figures so strongly in the stories and poems of this collection. One of my favorite childhood authors, Laura Ingalls Wilder, memorialized the mostly hardworking, thrifty, and reliable pioneers of her little town on the prairie—which happened to be the county seat of one of the South Dakota towns in which I lived—and similar virtues were applauded in the *Weekly Reader* we read at school, and in the *Jack and Jill* magazines we received at home. The message may have been secularized and modified and even camouflaged behind mysteries and adventures, but it was still fairly clear that we would do well to mind our p's and q's, just like the real and fictional characters who populated our books and magazines. It may be a long way from Oliver Optic and Louisa May Alcott to Maurice Sendak and Richard Scarry, the Berenstain Bears, and *Goosebumps*—favorites of my daughter, Lauren, my son, Eli, and my nephew, Brandon—but there is a thread that at least tenuously connects writing for children over the generations: the insistence by our society that certain types of behavior are more acceptable than others.

My deepest thanks go to work-study students Keri Lindemann and Alexandra Richardson, and to Jane Gray, administrative assistant in the Marquette University history department, who completed the time-consuming work of putting the stories, poems, and articles on disk. During a briefly tense hour in the Marquette computer lab, Lauri Czolgosz helped translate the files from a Windows to a Mac format. Joel Jaecks assisted with the illustrations, and Gregory Eiselein provided a helpful reading of the manuscript and offered useful suggestions for expanding my inadequate knowledge of the latest critical studies of children's literature. Matthew Hershey at Scholarly Resources showed immediate and encouraging interest in publishing a reader of these neglected examples of children's literature; I appreciate his enthusiasm, professionalism, and practical advice. Michelle Slavin at Scholarly Resources was a cheerful and responsive editor.

I "discovered" these stories and articles, poems and games, letters and editorials, while researching a book on children's experiences during the Civil War. Since it is difficult to know exactly when work on one project left off and work on the other began, I would like to express my appreciation to the Office of Research Support at Marquette University and the Bradley Institute for Democracy and Public Values for their financial support, and also to acknowledge the research assistance of James Bohl, Annie Chenovick, Brian Faltinson, Patricia Higgins, and Frank Keeler. Finally, I would like to thank Julie Gores and Joan M. Sommer in the interlibrary loan office at Marquette University's Memorial Library.

Introduction

"The Great Importance of Little Things"

> You know that, if you break a small wheel in a cotton-mill,
> the entire machinery will stop; and if the moon—one of
> the smallest lumps of matter in the universe—shall fall
> from its orbit, the whole planetary system might go reeling
> and tumbling about like a drunken man. So you see the
> great importance of little things,—and little *folks* are of
> much greater importance than little *things*.
> —Kirke, "The Boy of Chancellorsville," 600.

Readers of "The Boy of Chancellorsville" were assured by Edmund Kirke that they were indeed important, not only to their parents and friends but also to the
larger community—to the whole world. The hero, Robert, survives the epic Battle of Chancellorsville, during which he saves
a life, eases the last moments of a dying man, befriends a dog,
scolds a haughty Confederate general, and brings out the best
in the men who care for him during his long months in a
Confederate prison. These "little things" amount to a great deal,
Kirke shows. Children should never feel unimportant: If they
do their best and stay true to themselves, they can contribute
mightily to their family's well-being, to their society, and to
their country's war effort.

"The Boy of Chancellorsville" is only one of the selections from children's magazines included in this volume. These
stories do not offer a history of children during the Civil War.
Rather, they provide samples of how children experienced the
war as well as demonstrating how authors of children's literature adapted their genre to the conflagration threatening to tear

apart the United States. The editors and authors included in the selections in Chapter One carefully constructed a literary community that provided sympathy and encouragement for children facing the challenges of war. Chapter Two highlights the efforts of a single editor, Oliver Optic, to rally children to the political ideals that inspired the Union war effort. The ways in which the war influenced childhood play is the subject of Chapter Three, while Chapter Four shows how children's magazines portrayed the sacrifices that the war forced onto many children. Chapter Five describes the special relationship that developed between children and soldiers, both in fiction and in real life. The readers were expected to translate these stirring tales and letters into action. Chapter Six shows how children contributed to the war effort and the lessons they learned from their war work. The handful of articles and stories on the war taken from Southern publications are presented in Chapter Seven. Finally, Chapter Eight suggests several ways that children were encouraged to think about the war after it had ended.

Even as it introduced more highly politicized—not to mention entertaining—themes and styles, children's wartime literature continued the antebellum tradition of promoting "family values." The antebellum United States, seized with restless expansionism, political uncertainty, and a diversifying population, already had begun lurching toward a "modern" era of industrialization and urbanization. These powerful changes caused even the most optimistic Americans to wonder how traditional assumptions—those ideals that had helped the United States take the moral high ground among the corrupt and stagnant monarchies of the world—could be maintained. One way was to ensure that future generations learned the importance of those seemingly peculiarly American ideals. A leading historian of children's literature, Ann Scott MacLeod, has argued that nineteenth-century Americans, including authors for children, viewed childhood as a time of preparation for adulthood, a crucial period for "learning, becoming, forming a worthy character for the future."* To that end, children's magazines had for decades sought to cultivate principles designed to ensure order

---

*Ann Scott MacLeod, *American Childhood: Essays on Children's Literature of the Nineteenth and Twentieth Centuries* (Athens: University of Georgia Press, 1994), 23. Claudia Nelson suggests that writers for children in Victorian England actually promoted these rather "feminine" qualities as "masculine" ideals in books for boys. *The Feminine Ethic and British Children's Fiction, 1857–1917* (New Brunswick: Rutgers University Press, 1991).

and social responsibility: hard work, obedience, generosity, humility, and piety. They showed close-knit, God-fearing families surmounting difficulties, and broken families lapsing into poverty and failure. Works of fiction and nonfiction alike stressed character and framed the world in moral terms, assuring readers that patriotism and unselfishness together would guarantee individual success and national honor.

Amid the anxiety-driven and sometimes heavy-handed moralizing in children's literature during the decades before the Civil War, politics was all but ignored, as writers tended to focus instead on self-control and self-improvement rather than on politics. American Anti-Slavery Society pamphlets, periodicals such as *The Slave's Friend*, and even mainstream novels (for example, the immensely popular *Uncle Tom's Cabin*) thrust the increasingly controversial issue of slavery into children's reading material. Nevertheless, an overwhelming majority of Northern publishers of juvenile books, magazines, and textbooks assiduously avoided racial issues. This trend changed, however, when the Civil War erupted. Although many antebellum ideas and

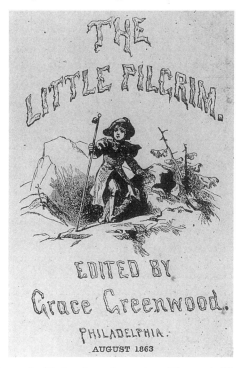

The Little Pilgrim *aspired to be a juvenile version of Bunyan's* Pilgrim's Progress. *From* The Little Pilgrim.

Inspired by the Union war effort, this martial-looking little boy invited readers into the patriotic world of The Little Corporal. *From* The Little Corporal.

themes would continue to appear in children's wartime literature, the magazines and novels written for Northern children during the war embraced politics, issued scathing critiques of slavery, and promoted a vigorous prosecution of the Union war effort. A whole new set of war-related topics infused the familiar forms and comfortable assumptions of Northern children's magazines, as writers provided accounts of battles and of life in the army, short biographies of leading generals and politicians, and military trivia and statistics. Authors also would encourage children to take part in the Northern war effort by inspiring them with tales of bravery and patriotism and by explaining the causes and history of the war in its political and moral contexts.

More than a half-dozen magazines for children had been founded during the several decades before the Civil War, and a platoon of them were already circulating when Confederates fired on Fort Sumter in April 1861. Others soon appeared. The war, in one way or another and at some time or another, would affect all of these magazines. But a few monthlies dominated the effort to make children aware of the causes and costs of the war. *The Little Pilgrim*, for example, published by Grace Greenwood—the pen name of Sara J. C. Lippincott—had already had an eight-year run when the war broke out. Adapting its title character from John Bunyan's *Pilgrim's Progress*, *The Little Pilgrim* was sometimes harsh in its pervasively Protestant moral sense, including in its pages fairy tales, European travelogues,

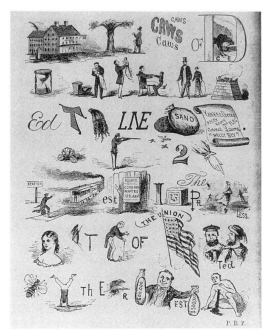

An "illustrated rebus" whose pictures and symbols, when put together, said "In the cause of independence our forefathers sacrificed their lives and fortunes. Let us aim to hand down to latest posterity the priceless heritage of the Union, cemented by their richest blood." From Our Young Folks.

and pious obituaries of deceased readers. Less obviously religious in tone—but still devoted to instilling proper morals in its readers—was *The Student and Schoolmate*, created in the mid-1850s by the merger of two juvenile magazines. Its editor, Oliver Optic (William T. Adams), pushed many of the same themes as his competitors, but he also included original songs and what were referred to as dialogues (brief playlets) and declamation pieces, all of which provided ample encouragement for youthful patriotism after the war began.

A few months before the end of the war, Ticknor and Fields, publisher of the notable journals *The Atlantic Monthly* and *The North American Review*, entered the children's market with *Our Young Folks*, which quickly became a children's classic and whose circulation eventually exceeded 75,000. Edited by Lucy Larcom, John Townsend Trowbridge, and Mary Abigail Dodge, the magazine attracted the talents of Louisa May Alcott, Harriet Beecher Stowe, Henry Wadsworth Longfellow, and John Greenleaf Whittier. *The Little Corporal* appeared just after the

Confederate surrender, and it was closely associated with the war. It grew out of a campaign organized in the spring of 1865 by Chicagoan Alfred L. Sewell to mobilize children to raise money for the Northwestern Sanitary Fair. He formed the Army of the American Eagle and awarded military ranks to children who sold pictures of "Old Abe, the War Eagle," the famous mascot of the 8th Wisconsin Regiment. The $16,000 that the children collected went to the U.S. Sanitary Commission. Frequently using military terms—Sewell called longtime readers "veterans" and urged them to "re-enlist" when their subscriptions lapsed—*The Little Corporal* was the only children's magazine directly related to the experiences of war.

Many other commercial and sectarian magazines were published in the North that shared the characteristics of their better known competitors. In the South, however, few children's magazines were published; hence the paucity of Southern selections in this volume. Southern children had often subscribed to the popular "juveniles," but once the war began, sectional pride and the blockade brought that to an end. In addition, Confederate publishers, plagued by shortages of ink, paper, and skilled printers, generally ignored magazines and novels in favor of instructional literature, producing more than two dozen catechisms and hymnals. Nearly three-fourths of the children's volumes published in the Confederacy were schoolbooks designed to make children aware of the issues that caused the war and to muster Southern youngsters' support for the Confederate war effort. The few children's magazines that did appear in the Confederacy occasionally presented patriotic narratives and images. Samuel Boykin's *Child's Index*, a hard-shell Baptist Sunday school paper, and the *Deaf Mute Casket*, published by the North Carolina Institution for the Deaf and Dumb and the Blind, were the longest running Confederate juveniles. The Presbyterian *Children's Friend* and the Methodist *Children's Guide* each lasted for about two years. Shorter lived was *The Child's Banner*, a religious publication from Salisbury, North Carolina. Although far more theologically oriented than typical Northern magazines—and less likely to include war themes—they, too, explained the war to children and encouraged their involvement. As a Confederate newspaper declared in announcing the first issue of *The Child's Banner*, these papers would meet "as nearly as possible . . . the wants of the children in these days of evil."[*]

---

[*]Raleigh *Daily Confederate*, December 22, 1864.

Whether it was seen as an evil or as an inspiration, the Civil War penetrated, invigorated, and politicized children's magazines, North and South. The motto of *The Little Corporal*, "Fighting against Wrong, and for The Good, the True, and the Beautiful," combined perfectly the moral and patriotic urgency of publishers' campaigns to educate and mobilize children. The content of the magazines reflected the real-life experiences of children: their fears over loved ones fighting in the war, their enthusiastic support for the war effort, and their hardships and losses. The stories in these magazines were meant to inspire children to greater courage, patriotism, and endurance, and to show them how to bear up in the face of adversity and to overcome their doubts and faults. Young readers were introduced to the relevant political issues of the day, exposed to the sacrifices made by gallant soldiers, and shown how they could help their country win the war. At the same time, these publications continued to educate and motivate their readers and to celebrate virtuous behavior and useful knowledge. Values such as obedience, determination, piety, and loyalty—all promoted long before the war—were even more vital during the nation's greatest crisis.

Several themes were prominent in the magazines' response to the war. First was the necessity of informing children about the causes and conduct of the war, as well as about the incredible hardships that the war brought. Many articles also used the war as an opportunity to teach important moral and ethical lessons; it was a valuable—if tragic—chance for self-improvement. A third common denominator was the implicit—and often explicit—recruitment of children to work for the Union or Confederate war effort. Underlying all of these themes were common assumptions about gender roles and race. Boys and girls had different parts to play in the crisis; even more stark was the magazines' often stilted and patronizing portrayal of African Americans.

In exploring the Civil War for children, Northern magazines offered a fairly narrow look at the state of American society, from a white, middle-class, and generally small-town (although not necessarily rural) vantage point. In these stories, poor people appear as victims or as noble charity cases; servants, who do most of the hard work when children undertake good deeds, are almost invariably Irish and often named Bridget; African Americans are earnest in their colorful, uneducated way. All the characters stick to their expected roles. Boys play at being soldiers and girls pretend to be nurses—when they are not giggling at the boys. Scoffing boys or wise adults frequently remind girls of the limitations of their future choices. The people in these stories are incredibly serious, although in a bow to traditional literary convention, youngsters' overweening niceness is tempered with just a dash of naughtiness. Both children and adults in Civil War stories remain totally unself-conscious in their condescension toward people of other classes and races. Physical appearance means a lot in these stories, and a "noble countenance" goes a long way in establishing a person's character. Even the size and characteristics of the families written about are standardized, give or take a child or two. The oldest son, fourteen, perhaps, struggles to retain his dignity; a daughter on the verge of puberty displays hints of her maternal instincts; a mischievous nine- or ten-year-old boy caroms through most stories; a toddler spouts cute phrases; and a baby burdened with a cloying nickname coos in the background. Certain plot devices created a few variations. Widowed mothers usually have only one or two children, and sometimes even the most genteel families are temporarily poor because the man of the house is off fighting the Rebels.

Children clearly immersed themselves in the Civil War, and tales of virtually all of their activities and experiences appeared in children's magazines. For instance, in a number of the following selections, children talk in their memoirs about "picking lint," the scraping of cloth into soft piles for packing around battlefield wounds. The U.S. Sanitary Commission is frequently referred to. This great philanthropic undertaking raised money for the benefit of soldiers, buying and distributing medical supplies, blankets, and extra food; delivering mail; and maintaining field hospitals for the Union armies. Sanitary Commission wagons—labeled S.C.—were familiar sights on all the major battlefields. Millions of dollars to fund the commission were raised at the giant "Sanitary Fairs" held throughout the North, in which thousands of children participated.

For these "little things" and for the larger themes they examined, these magazines are important historical artifacts, reflecting, even over a century later, and albeit in sometimes stereotyped, exaggerated, or sanitized versions, what children knew about the war convulsing their world, and how they acted on that knowledge. As such, the following selections help us to understand the roles that children played in mid-nineteenth-century American society and reveal the contours of their wartime experiences.

J.M.

1

Chats with Readers "Round the Evening Lamp"

◆━━ ⊰◈⊱ ━━◆

Creating a Literary Community

Father Brighthopes could have been every child's favorite uncle. The retired fictional clergyman made regular appearances in *Our Young Folks* as a wise, kindly, and cheerful soul who surrounded himself with children eager to discuss pressing moral issues. Each month, with earnest goodwill and gentle prodding, he engaged a half-dozen or so youngsters in meaningful but relaxed conversation. Asking just the right questions, calmly suggesting and sometimes exhorting, the good old man managed to coax his young friends into discovering important moral truths. "Always making the best of things" was the simple lesson a few months after the Civil War ended. One should not make too much of little hardships, especially considering the trials that "our noble heroes" had endured without complaint during the war. Make the best of "favorable conditions," he urged his listeners, but minimize the effects of unhappy "little crosses and privations."

Although Father Brighthopes did more than a little preaching in his conversations with the children, he and they undertook this process of discovery together. The children were never scolded and rarely corrected; rather, they searched with their elderly mentor for the truth with the aid of mutual respect and shared assumptions. In fact, most Civil War-era children's magazines tried to create similar "communities" with first-person editorials that spoke directly to readers, correspondence from or even between children, and letters from adults with interesting bits of information or appeals for charitable causes. Oliver Optic's *The Student and Schoolmate* featured didactic editorials from the "Teacher's Desk," while *Forrester's Playmate*

*All children's magazines encouraged youngsters to consider the editors and other
subscribers as a kind of extended family, gathered in a cozy parlor.*
From Our Young Folks.

shared a monthly "Chat with Readers and Correspondence,"
and *Our Young Folks* gathered children cozily "Round the
Evening Lamp." Content sometimes varied to include games
or brief notices on new children's books, but all were devoted
to creating an intimate family of readers. Most editors responded directly to readers' queries, commented on the solu-
tions to puzzles sent in by children, and sometimes—notably in
The Little Pilgrim—encouraged readers to submit their own
writings. This format was obviously good for circulation: How
could a child forsake such a comforting extended family when
it came time to renew the subscription? It was also a useful
method of communication.

      These features may have been especially effective dur-
ing wartime, when shared patriotism, sacrifice, and sympathy
further cemented the usual bonds of affection and common interest found in these literary communities. Articles, editorials,
and letters involved children in the war effort, helped to explain the cataclysm threatening their country, their families,
and themselves, and provided a kind of mediation between
readers and the war. A cynic might call this indoctrination, a
social scientist would call it socialization, but Civil War children called it literature.

THE EDITOR AS TEACHER

Oliver Optic—the pen name of William T. Adams—refused to talk down to his juvenile readers. His monthly column in *The Student and Schoolmate*, "Teacher's Desk," emphasized political and military issues. In 1863, Optic berated the "cheap patriotism" of drum-beating and flag-waving that had appeared early in the war and applauded the sincere patriotism more recently displayed by both the army and the public. This seriousness was reflected in the patriotic editorials and articles that he included in every wartime issue of *The Student and Schoolmate*.

The prolific Optic was the author of the most popular juvenile novels about the war. His pair of trilogies, known collectively as the "Army and Navy Stories," followed the adventures of two brothers, Tom and Jack Somers. Seventeen when the war began, the boys rush to join the Union army and navy, respectively. Optic emphasized the creative courage and steadfast patriotism of both boys, who operate more or less alone, relying on their own skills, only a few close friends, their courage and patriotism, and their virtue—qualities found in virtually every story and novel for children during the middle third of the nineteenth century. Their escapades showed what it meant to be a "true soldier," to be someone "who loves his country, and fights for her because he loves her; but, at the same time, one who is true to himself and his God."*

Optic urged his young readers to look inside themselves for just that mixture of faith, patriotism, and "war spirit." In a December 1862 column, Optic encouraged them not only to "shout for the Stars and Stripes, for the Union, for the Constitution" but also to carry that loyalty—that obedience, discipline, and respect—into the house and the schoolroom. In these ways, home-front children could prove just as loyal and worthy as the heroic Somers boys.

"Teacher's Desk"
The Student and Schoolmate 12 (February 1863), 61

Never since the days of the Revolution, have the courage and fortitude of the American people been so severely tried as at the

---

*Optic's books, all published by the Boston publisher Lee and Shepard, were *The Soldier Boy* (1863), *The Young Lieutenant* (1865), and *Fighting Joe* (1866); and *The Sailor Boy* (1863), *The Yankee Middy* (1866), and *The Brave Old Salt* (1867).

present time. We seem to be making no real progress in the suppression of the rebellion. Defeat and disaster follow defeat and disaster so rapidly, that we are not permitted to recover from the effects of one, before we are confronted by another.

And yet, though there is a feeling of disappointment and discouragement, there is no general despondency. The people still have faith in the triumph of the great principles which led them to take up arms. "Truth is mighty and must prevail," is the sentiment which animates the adherents of an undivided Union. Though borne in defeat and disaster, the Old Flag still, and more than ever before, means freedom. We know that we are battling on the side of freedom, against the combinations of slavery and aristocracy. We believe now, as in 1775, that "all men are created equal"; we believe He is the Father of all men, and that through our present tribulations, He will lead us to a more holy and perfect peace than we have ever known before.

We have often reminded our young readers of the fact that they live in historic times; in a period whose every day will be a page for future ages to read. This year, even more than the last two, promises to be full of great events. With the Happy New Year came that Proclamation which inaugurates a mighty change in the policy of the government. Tremendous consequences must follow in its train.

The days that try men's souls are upon us—may we be equal to the occasion! As yet, we have been called upon to endure but little positive suffering. We know not the meaning of the word, as it is understood in the cities and villages of the misguided South. Except that our young men leave their happy homes for the battle-fields of the Union, and our hearts are occasionally wrung by the tidings of their loss, we should not know that we were engaged in the mightiest contest the world has ever known. We may be called upon to endure more, to make great sacrifices of comfort and plenty; if we are, let us show our devotion to the great cause by suffering without a murmur. Above all, let us be true to God, true to ourselves, true to the historic character our fathers bequeathed to us.

"Teacher's Desk"
The Student and Schoolmate 11 (December 1862), 428–29

Some little boys and girls think it is degrading to be obedient. They seem to have an idea that they are magnificent little people, and that nobody ought to expect them to mind; to be gentle and submissive as they should be. This is a great mistake. There is nothing mean and degrading in obedience. If there was we should all be mean and degraded, for we are all obliged to obey our superiors.

The only difficulty just now with the Southern States is, that they will not acknowledge the legal authority of the President; they will not obey him; they will not observe the laws of the land,—laws which they helped to frame and promised to obey. Jeff. Davis, the arch rebel, is only like a bad boy who will not mind his parents or his teachers. We commend the Northern States, and call them loyal, simply because they are obedient.

What is good for States and nations is certainly good for little boys and girls. If the loyal States are worthy of praise because they are obedient, there can be nothing degrading in obedience. A little boy or girl who does not obey his parents or teacher is just as much a rebel in principle as Jeff. We like to see children who shout for the Stars and Stripes, for the Union, for the Constitution, carry the same idea into the family and school-room. Let them be loyal always and everywhere; not only to the country, but to their parents and teachers—to God and themselves.

Obedience is the first lesson we learn as citizens. We must obey the laws, rather than our own inclinations, and children should feel that it is right and honorable to yield entire obedience to those who are placed over them for their moral and intellectual well-being. Discipline is necessary in the school and in the family, as well as in the army, and the boys who expect to make good soldiers, must remember that obedience is the sum total of the soldier's duty. Without it our great army could not hold together a single day. Therefore, always keep it in mind, that obedience is right and honorable.

"Teacher's Desk"
The Student and Schoolmate 12 (March 1863), 93

The war has increased our vocabulary, and words which are now used and understood by all, would have been unintelligible two years ago. And the work of coining new words still goes on. Every month or two we receive an addition to our language, and if the war lasts a few years longer, the English tongue will be as copious as any other in the world.

The last new word we have to record, is "copperhead"—an epithet applied to those who desire to make peace with the rebels on any terms; who are willing to submit to all the demands of the traitors of the South, and we respectfully suggest to

Worcester and Webster that, in subsequent editions of the
Quartos, "copperhead" shall be defined as simply "a traitor."*
Any long and elaborate explanation of the meaning of the term
would be superfluous.

We like this word for the class to whom it has been applied. The copperhead is a snake, quite as dangerous as the rat-
tlesnake. It has no rattle to warn the passerby that he means to
strike a deadly blow; and we find the political copperhead lurk-
ing in the dark places of the land, ready to strike at the National
existence whenever an opportunity is presented. The copperheads are just as much the enemies of their country, as the
Southern rebels who rattle before they bite.[†]

"Teacher's Desk"
The Student and Schoolmate 15 (May 1865), 158–59

Yes, a brighter day has dawned; Richmond is ours. The
Confederate forces have not only been scattered, but their chief
army has surrendered. The leaders in secession have sought
safety in ignominious flight. Under this state of things, can the
rebellion long exist? We think not.

The time is near at hand, when a reunited country will
once more place this nation in a position vastly in advance of
what it could have been, but for the severe ordeal through which
it has been passing.

Slavery is no more! They who sought to perpetuate it
have failed in their unholy work, and the game they played to
win has been lost to them.

Yet our danger is not wholly passed. As Gov. Andrew
has well said in a recent speech in New York, "There are questions to be agitated that now will shake society to its founda-
tion. There will be more peril at the close of the war than
before it. On the possibility of bad statesmanship more dam-
age is to be apprehended than in the mishaps of the battle-
field. The fault of the American people is to trust men whom
they know are untrustworthy."[††]

---

*Joseph Worcester and Noah Webster were the authors of the most prominent dictio-
naries in antebellum America.

[†]Republicans frequently labeled Northern Democrats who opposed the Lincoln administration's war aims—especially emancipating the slaves—"copperheads."

[††]John A. Andrew, an abolitionist, was Republican governor of Massachusetts from
1860 to 1866.

We have hope that these possibilities may vanish away, and that those who are now holding responsible positions in our National councils will prove as true, as loyal, as discreet and efficient as those who have led on our brave armies in their recent encounters.

Our young readers have an interest in this matter, and hence we claim to bring the subject to the Teacher's Desk. A knowledge of our country's history from its earliest days to the present time is of the greatest importance. Boys and girls of to-day will, it is true, affect all future time. But, even if mistakes should be made, a knowledge of the principles on which our government is founded may enable those thus educated to overcome the evils that would otherwise ensue.

Let the youth of our land claim as a part of their education such information as will fit them either to be intelligent legislators themselves, or at least qualify them to make a judicious use of their privilege as voters by placing the most competent and trustworthy men in official positions.

Let the sad news which reaches us just as we are going to press, render the above more important in our eyes. Had the people of the South enjoyed the blessings of an education, such as we refer to, the rebellion would never have had existence. Had the principles of liberty inspired every heart, never would there have been those cowardly enough to strike a blow at the nation's heart in the murder of President Lincoln and the contemplated murder of his Secretary of State.

But the assassins were not alone—others must have aided and abetted, but more cowardly than they that struck these blows, they conceal themselves from the public eye. But the eye of a just God is upon them, and, while we bow to this National bereavement, may we live to learn our duty to God, our country, and ourselves.

All eyes are now turned to Vice-President Johnson, who, under the Constitution, becomes President of the United States.

May he be equal to the demand of the place and the hour. When we reflect upon his early history, the struggles he made to secure an education, and his more recent experience in Tennessee, we are impressed with the belief that while we mourn the one, we may rejoice that we possess the other.*

May God be with him to guide his counsels, direct his action and lead him and us into the enjoyments of that happy

---

*Andrew Johnson of Tennessee, the only representative of a southern state not to resign his seat in the U.S. Senate, had no formal schooling and was essentially a self-educated and self-made man. He was military governor of his home state from 1862 to 1865.

Earnest children surround the kindly Father Brighthopes, who regularly dispensed wisdom and affection to readers of Our Young Folks. *From* Our Young Folks.

future that seemed to be opening when our beloved leader, his predecessor, was so rudely slain.

"IT WOULD MAKE YOUR HEARTS ACHE TO SEE THEM"

Part of the political creed put forth by Northern children's magazines reflected the growing interest in and concern for the plight of the people over whom the war was being fought: the African Americans recently freed or still enslaved in the South. Children were guided toward a much more liberal attitude toward blacks than most Americans—even Northerners—displayed toward the nearly four million slaves and one million free blacks living in the United States. Editors showed the degradation of slavery and the unfairness of double standards for even free blacks, and promoted the government's decision to begin the process of ending slavery via the Emancipation Proclamation.

In children's magazines, most references to blacks were to "contrabands"—slaves who fled to Union lines and received their freedom as "contraband of war"—living and attending school in the relative safety of Union lines. Publishers tried to focus children's attention on the challenges facing these African Americans, particularly those former slaves who clustered by the thousands in the pestilent, dangerous, hopeless contraband "camps" that sprang up near Union army posts. Freedmen, women, and children huddled in old packing crates, tobacco barns, and sod huts; from one-fourth to one-half of the residents of those grim camps died.

As is so often the case, children bore the brunt of the hardships faced by the contrabands. A visitor to a freedmen's camp in Washington in the spring of 1865 described the helplessness and degradation of families without food and babies without diapers or clothes. A nine-year-old girl supported her mother and younger siblings by selling rags. The dozen freed slaves huddled in a stable included a young girl with consumption, a motherless boy with pneumonia, and an infant dying of malnutrition. Another group, six children ranging in age from one to twelve, lived in a shed in a sea of mud with no fire or food and wearing only rags.

Northern children rarely read these heartbreaking truths in their magazines. Instead, they enjoyed colorful and optimistic accounts of newly freed black children attending the hundreds of schools sponsored by Northern missionary societies. White women and army officers from the North as well as black men and women served as teachers. In letters to families back home, they told of teaching the former slaves the names of the days and months, counting, personal hygiene, and sewing, in addition to reading, writing, and arithmetic. Teachers also filled their letters home with entertaining and sometimes poignant glimpses of the lives of newly freed African Americans. Similar stories and letters appeared in the pages of wartime children's magazines.

The letters that follow were written by women working with the black children who crowded into crude schools throughout the South. Like other stories and articles about African Americans written for children during the war, they seem condescending and at times even racist. They emphasize that black children were really not so different from whites after all, and take pains to describe the light skins of many of the children, a delicate but direct reference to the sexual liberties taken by masters with their female slaves. The tone of these public letters resembles closely the tone of the private letters written by white women who traveled into the South as missionaries to the newly freed black men, women, and children. Some of the most charming—and patronizing—passages in those private letters concern the women's relationships with the little black children they came to know. A New Englander named Lucy Chase remarked that the children she encountered at Norfolk, Virginia, "would fain worship us, the little things." They "like to handle us, to pull at our hoops, and hang about us." Some teachers noted the close bond formed between the white women and their black students. After teaching in a New Bern, North Carolina, school for several months after the end of the war, Nellie Stearns exclaimed, "I declare I never think but I am black too when I am with my scholars."*

"Dear Pilgrim"
G. N. Coan
The Little Pilgrim 11 (June 1864), 81–82

I was much pleased when you visited me, last month, way down in this secesh city, and thought I should write you a letter immediately; but I have so much to occupy my time that it seemed as if I could not spare any for you; and yet I want to tell you something about these little colored children we have come down here to teach. But first let me tell you that many of these children are as white as any of you are, with blue eyes and straight hair, or pretty auburn ringlets. It is not their color that has made them slaves, but it is because they have African blood in their veins. So these dear children, as bright and fair as you, have been slaves, put up on the auction block to be sold far away from their mothers. And this has been done for many years; mothers and children torn asunder by their cruel masters, never to see each other's face again. Oh! the horror of slavery, who can tell? God alone, who has heard the groans and cries of these oppressed ones for so many years, can fathom it. But the day of deliverance has come, and the children enjoy their freedom far more than you can imagine, for you have never been deprived of this precious boon.

Some say that this people cannot learn, that they are stupid and dull; oh! if you could see our schools you would not think so: they learn very rapidly, so much so that they astonish us by their progress in geography, arithmetic, reading, etc. We have in our Sabbath-school over six hundred, and my infant class numbers one hundred and fifty. Some of them are dressed very neatly, while others are ragged and dirty, shivering with the cold—their

---

*Lucy Chase to "Dear ones at home," April 1, 1863, in *Dear Ones at Home: Letters from Contraband Camps,* ed. Henry L. Swint (Nashville: Vanderbilt University Press, 1966), 61–62; Nellie F. Stearns to "Lizzie," November 5, 1865, Nellie F. Stearns Letter, Perkins Library, Duke University, Durham, N.C.

little bare feet, looking as if they never saw a fire; and yet, could you see their eyes sparkle and their faces shine with delight, as they sing their little songs (such as you sing), and hear them answer questions from the Bible, I am sure you would be delighted, and think they were anything but stupid.

Their love for their teachers is unbounded, and they are continually bringing flowers, apples, and bits of candy, and sometimes they bring a bit of cake or an egg when they have nothing else to bring. And if we meet them on the street they always have a pleasant smile and "howdy" for us.

The name of Mr. Lincoln is a household word with them, for they feel that they owe their freedom to him. A few Sabbaths since a gentleman asked them if they could vote for the next President who it would be? With one accord they shouted out, "Abraham Lincoln." "But if Mr. Lincoln should die, who then?" "Abraham Lincoln." "No, if he were dead who would you vote for?" The unanimous cry was, "Uncle Sam." And if you could hear them sing, "Uncle Sam is rich enough to send us all to school," you would think that he was the greatest man living.

Many of these children have suffered a great deal from cold and hunger this winter, and it would make your hearts ache to see them around my door asking for old clothes, their only garment an old brown tow-cloth frock, all rags and patches of different colors, bare-footed and bare-headed; and then to go with them to their homes, which are, perhaps, wretched hovels, the cold wind piercing through every crevice, their beds the floor, with old bits of blankets to cover them; you would not surely think they had much to make them happy, and yet they are as full of their fun and frolic as any children can be.

Now, readers of *The Little Pilgrim*, I could tell you a great deal about these children if I had the time. I have spent nearly a year among them, and I think it has been one of the pleasantest of my life; and yet there is much to make one sad, for these children have not had the good teaching you have had, but have been taught to lie, and steal, and strike and throw stones at each other, besides much more that is bad, and these things are a great trial to their teachers, yet they do not feel discouraged, for they already begin to see the fruit of their labors in their pupils' efforts to do right.

Now, dear children, can you not do something for these poor little ones? There are still hundreds of them who cannot go to school for want of comfortable or decent clothing: will you not send them some of your old dresses, quilts, sacks, or shoes, so that they may be able to go to school, and learn to read the word of God, and thus become good men and women? And then, perhaps, sometime I will tell you something more about them.

"My Dear Young Friends"
Clara C. Clarke
The Little Pilgrim 9 (June 1862), 93

You have never seen my name in your much-loved little paper as a writer, for I seldom write; but as a worker, you have so often seen it, that you doubtless feel a good deal acquainted with me. And you probably think I am a great friend to the little folks. Yes, I am. I love them dearly, and wish for their happiness and improvement, or I, now more than fifty years of age, should not work so hard for them every winter. And I believe the little folks love me. I judge so by the many very pleasant greetings I receive, when they meet "The Pilgrim woman," as some call me; or, as others call me, "Little Pilgrim's mother." I think they love me a great deal for Little Pilgrim's sake.

I know the little folks pretty well, too, and know that they love to be useful. Certainly they do, if they wish to be like their dear Saviour. You know how He sought the poor, the blind, the lame, the sick, and the friendless, to do them good. Now, I don't expect you can do much while you are little, to cure the sick, or the lame, or deaf, or dumb, though I know that little folks sometimes are excellent nurses for a dear father or mother, brother or sister. But there are those who are in one sense blind, and lame, and dumb, whom you can help to see, and to walk, and talk; yes, and sing, too, for joy. And now I write to you, children, to urge you to do just this kind of work, and I know that in doing it, your little hearts will be made very happy. Christ says, "Ye have the poor always with you"; and the assurance is given, too, that "he that hath pity on the poor, lendeth unto the Lord; and that which he hath given, will He pay him again"; and "He that hath mercy on the poor, happy is he." Doubtless, you, many a time, after giving or doing some kind deed to some one—poor, forlorn and heart-broken—have felt so happy that you could jump, and sing, and laugh, and perhaps even cry, for very joy.

> "One God reigns in the heavens—there is no other,
> And all mankind are brethren—thus 'tis spoken;
> And who so aids a sorrowing, struggling brother
> By kindly word, or deed, or friendly token,
> Shall win the favor of our Heavenly Father,
> Who judges evil, and rewards the good,

And who hath linked the race of man together
In one vast universal brotherhood."

Very likely many of you and your parents have already been helping the class of poor which I wish to introduce to you. You have heard of the great number of colored people now collected at Fortress Monroe, Va., who have, till lately, been slaves, but are now free.* Yes, free! And who does not wish that every slave may soon be free? There are thousands there; and "still they come." Let me tell you, Little Pilgrim makes his monthly visits there, and the children love him and his pretty stories very much. They are just beginning to read, as they or their parents have had no chance to learn before; but are now very eager to learn. Almost their first inquiry after arriving is for a spelling book, and their highest ambition, to learn to read; and they learn very fast. Some are earnest Christians. Most of them, however, on their arrival, are ignorant and debased, but show themselves anxious for and capable of great improvement. There is seldom found among them one who uses strong drink, or swears, or uses tobacco. Uncle Sam (you know who Uncle Sam is) hires those who can work, and pays them; for they are generally industrious when they are paid for their labor. They all are provided with food, and nearly all with some clothing, by the United States government, though the need of clothing is yet very great, and must be relieved by the charitable. Their moral and religious wants must entirely be ministered to by the benevolent people of the North, through General Wool, Mr. Wilder, their superintendent, and others, who have command at the Fortress, do what they can to improve their condition. The American Missionary Association have sent them a missionary, Rev. L. C. Lockwood, and others have gone there to instruct them and do them good.† Now, children, are you not glad for all this? Their missionary informs me that they are very much in need of more money, as well as clothing—for these folks must

---

*Located on the tip of the Virginia peninsula, Fortress Monroe was a Union stronghold that was never taken by Confederate forces. As early as the summer of 1861, escaped slaves were streaming into Union lines for refuge.

---

†Most of the "contraband" at Fortress Monroe and in other parts of the South—men, women, and children—worked as servants for U.S. Army officers, as laborers on fortification, or as workers on occupied plantations. Children often worked half days, the other half being devoted to attending schools operated by the army, by individuals, or by the American Missionary Association, which sent scores of white and a few black teachers into the South to teach blacks of all ages. Gen. John Wool commanded the Department of Virginia, headquartered at Fortress Monroe, in 1861 to 1862.

have school-houses and churches, teachers and books, and the missionary well knew that the little folks, who know how good it is to go to school and learn, would be just the ones to help get the money; so he wished me to put this request into Little Pilgrim's budget, to be delivered to every child and every parent where he visits. The cry is, "Come over and help us."* Money will help. The Bible says—"Money answereth all things, but the love of money is the root of all evil." Do you say—"Where shall I get the money to send?" Some of you have parents who could send a great deal of money; and the parents of others are not very rich, but could spare some. And have you not a rich uncle or aunt, who loves to please you? Now, just whisper a sweet, pleading whisper in the ear of each and every dear friend, asking them to send all they can spare, and soon the spiritually blind will see, and the lame walk; the dumb will talk, and will sing, too, heartily their thanks to you, and to their Heavenly Father, for the great benefits bestowed upon them. Is not money often given to you to buy toys and candy?—and would you not rather give that money to so good a cause? I think you would, and feel much better than to use it for yourself.

Now, Charlie, and Mary, and Carrie, and Willie, and all other darling children, of whatever name, just be busy bees a few days, and gather, not honey, but money, for that will give to those poor people that which is far sweeter than honey. Remember, "where there is a will, there is a way," and go to work in earnest. . . .

Good-by, dear children, good-by, with much love from your friend, Clara C. Clarke.

Syracuse, N.Y., May, 1862.

"A Letter from Arkansas"
Cullen
The Little Corporal 2 (February 1866), 23

My dear little boys and girls:

I want to say a few words to you who fly kites, and trundle hoops, and skate, and slide down hill, and play with balls and marbles and dolls. Look up, now, and listen. Before many years are gone, you know, your fathers and mothers and older friends, who now build the cities, and make the railroads; who dig tunnels, to give you pure water to drink; who govern the

---

*The seal of the Massachusetts Bay Company featured an American Indian saying "Come Over and Help Us."

world; and, above all, who teach you, and make homes for you, will be laid away in their graves; and then—(did you ever think of it?)—you will have all this, and so much else to do. If you have thought, I shall not need to tell you that you have to learn a great many things; especially such things as will help you, by and by, when you have this great world to take care of, to make happy homes, and a prosperous country.

You have all heard of the wicked rebellion of our country, and of its cause, which was slavery. I am sure, no brave and unselfish child likes slavery; and so, you are glad it is done away with. Here, where I write, and all over the Southern States, there are crowds of people—boys and girls, and men and women—who were slaves; but who are now free. How glad and thankful they are, and we too; but, in our rejoicing, there are many sad things to remember. Many of these freed people have no homes now, and no clothes nor food, and do not know how to take care of themselves. Slavery has crippled their powers, and they are like children, as we would be if we had lived as they have. Now, I think it will be plain to you, as it is to me, that since the white people made them slaves, these same white people are bound to teach them, and help them, till they can take care of themselves. Besides, these freedmen have fought bravely and nobly for our country; and we owe them more than I can describe.

Some of us are here to teach these freedmen, and it has occurred to me, that you ought to know something about them, and that you would like to; so, with the permission of The Little Corporal, who wants to know and teach all useful things, I am going to tell you something of what I have seen and heard during nearly a year that I have been here.

The colored people have all the time been very zealous in the pursuit of knowledge. They are best pleased with those teachers who are most strict with them. "I want you to be mighty tight on my test," is their most frequent request. Our schools are very large, but by some way, most of our pupils manage to come comfortably and neatly dressed. We sometimes have those who are so old they have to wear spectacles; but they are very patient and diligent in the First Reader, hoping, by and by, to be able to read the Bible, which is their great ambition. We find the older people very ignorant of many things which they need to know very much; and we cannot do anything like so much as we want to do. Schools are needed to teach the women and girls to mend and make clothes, and cook, and take care of houses. Nothing would delight these dark fathers and mothers more than to have their daughters taught to sew, as well as to read and write. They want their children to be trained as white children are. I have heard them talk a great deal about it.

The freedmen crowd into the cities, where their cabins are crowded in clusters with only very narrow alleys between them. The schools are the great attraction; but much sickness is the consequence of all this crowding. Small pox is now raging to an extent that would be considered alarming in a northern city; but we have learned not to mind it much.

Last Saturday evening, in company with other teachers, I went to the house of one of our colored friends, to hear some music. It was what had formerly been the home of a wealthy white man, whose rebellion had left a place for his former slaves. A cheerful fire was blazing on the hearth when we entered, throwing its light over as pleasant and interesting looking group as one would often see. In a warm corner sat the grandmother, a benevolent looking mulatto woman, wearing a black turban. Her face showed scarcely a wrinkle, and her teeth were good, though her great-grandchildren were playing about her feet. Several of her grandsons were present, and two of them, at least, would pass in our northern towns without exciting any suspicion that they were negroes. They were accompanied by their wives— noble looking women, with splendid hair and eyes. Two young children played about the floor; one of them, the sprightliest little fellow of ten months I ever saw, came climbing over the arm of the chair in which I sat, to steal a banjo out of my hand. His rosy cheeks and fair, broad brow would have gladdened the heart of any white mother. How glad I was to know our noble martyred President had made freemen of this boy and all those about me. Forming a kind of background to the group I have described, and looking as unlike them as possible, were two genuine negroes, in soldier dress, who seemed to feel that, because of their darker hue, they should keep the fires burning, and perform any other similar service which might be needed.

The music we thought very fine. First, there was playing on the guitar, and singing, by a brother and sister; then a few tunes on a French harp; and lastly, the brothers, ranging themselves in order, with violin, violoncello, and other instruments, gave us national anthems, war songs, and old home-hallowed melodies, closing with "Home, Sweet Home," which they seemed to like best of all.

"We used to play that almost every night last summer, when we were out South," said one of the brothers, "and my old mistress would often send out to have us stop, it made her feel so bad to think of her own old home."

We were amused on our way home, by one of the teachers, who had just come, remarking, with an air of great incredulity, "I wonder if any of these people were really slaves!"

I should like to tell you of many interesting children I have met here, but my letter is already too long, and I will mention only one—that of a little girl of mine, named Fanny.

She is a delicate brunette, and looks out of place in a colored school. She is very sensitive, and possesses few of the peculiarities of colored people. I taught her through the spring and summer, and found her always punctual at school, and faithful in preparing her lessons. I fear she will be unhappy if left to grow up here. She certainly will never be likely to become what she is capable of being. Her mother, a young quadroon, of only twenty-three, is very anxious for Fanny's advancement.

Such children have poor advantages, for our schools are crowded with those just commencing to read; and the teachers are few, and there is danger that even these may have to leave; for the old slaveholders are bitter against us; and we fear, when they are again established in power, we shall not be allowed to go on; beside, our funds are failing.

Think of us, dear children, in your happy homes and schools, and consider if there is anything you can do for us.

CHRISTIAN SOLDIERS

A striking form of correspondence in children's magazines— especially those with well-developed traditions of editor and reader interaction—appeared when young soldiers wrote letters from the army to their fellow readers. *Forrester's Playmate* actually encouraged long-time readers who had enlisted to alert the editor to where they were and how they were doing. Aside from the first-hand information from the front that some of the letters provided, they were also useful from a patriotic editor's point of view for the moral lessons they offered. If even soldiers could remember to be temperate, to think of their families first, and to live clean, Godly lives in the midst of the corruption and disease and dangers of army life, then children should certainly be able to do the same in the safety of their homes and nurseries. Even more important, perhaps, was the human face that letters from soldiers gave the heroes fighting for the Union. The "Uncle Mark" to whom some of the correspondents refer is Mark Forrester, editor of *Forrester's Playmate*.

"Chat with Readers and Correspondents"
Forrester's Playmate 22 (February 1864), 160

I should like to know how many of our old Playmates are in the army of the North at the present time. [I shouldn't like to know how many are fighting in the rebel army, if there be possibly a single one, for fear of accidents—to my inkstand, or my pen. I feel sure there are not a great many, any how.] But, I repeat, I should like to know how many there are in arms against rebellion and treason. It was only last week that I learned of one, who went out a private in the "44th," soon became a lieutenant, accepted a captaincy in the 54th (colored regiment), was present and severely wounded at the assault on Fort Wagner, and is now senior captain in the regiment, although less than twenty years old! He, too, belonged to our circle. And I hear of them on all hands, and am only sorry that I cannot give an extended list of the heroes. Perhaps I can do so, at some future time. For this purpose I shall be thankful for any information, in regard to the exploits of "our boys," that may be forwarded. One lady partly agreed (?) to send me a picture of her son, in his "court suit," but I suppose she has forgotten it. If she is a constant reader, now-a-days, this will be a reminder. A photograph of the young patriot will be doubly valuable.

"Chat with Readers and Correspondents"
Forrester's Playmate 22 (March 1864), 184

7th Maine Battery, Vet. Vol.,
Camp Berry, Washington, D.C.
(January 7th, 1864).

Dear Uncle and Cousins:
      Believing that a change of climate will not serve to make me any less a member of your circle, I write you at this time and from this place. My reasons for not writing of late are, that I have been engaged in the service of my country, where I am still at work, and hope that my feeble efforts will be the means of doing a little good. I have joined a company of artillery, and I know that Uncle Mark, and all my good cousins, will approve of the act and wish me God speed. I see that my cousins are sending you their faces [photographs], (I wish they would send me some,) you shall have mine if I can get a good one. Would it not be a good pass, for some of my cousins to write sometimes to me? What an enjoyment it would be amid the hardships of camp

life. Come, cousins, write to Frank with the address as above. He will get it and write you in return. Now for the Prize Puzzle. I do not expect I have got it all right; but no matter, I am willing to abide by the terms.

One place I cannot get ahold of; the rest may be all wrong, but I always want to try.

I am, truly yours,

Frank, 2nd.

"Chat with Readers and Correspondents"
Forrester's Playmate 23 (June 1864), 92–93

Bethel, Me., June 2, 1864

Dear Uncle Mark:

You see by this I have, to use a military expression, "changed my base of operations." Soon after writing to you from Washington, it was my misfortune to contract a disease, which, for a time, threatened to take me from the number of our circle. But our good "Uncle Sam," thinking that the air of my own native hills might accomplish that which all else had failed to do, kindly allowed me to return home; and here I am, where, as "Bertha" says, I am "needed very much just now." I am yet an invalid, but so much improved, that, God willing, I shall soon return again to my brothers in the field; hoping yet to be able, if necessary, to lay some willing sacrifice upon the altar of my country.

Cousin Bertha has my thanks for her kind wishes in my behalf. Every expression, kindly uttered, serves to strengthen the resolution of the soldier, making him feel that, in defending his country, he is also protecting his home, loved ones and friends, from the machinations of those who would despoil us of all that is worthy the name of an American citizen. God is our leader, and the time cannot be far distant when our blood-washed country shall rise again to its place at the head of nations, and our glorious old banner wave in triumph over every portion, not a stripe erased, nor a star blotted out.

No, Bertha, I shall not forget to write to Uncle Mark, and, perhaps, if I knew some of my cousins by their right name, I should be tempted to give them a specimen of my letter-writing, for friendship's sake. I trust that when next you hear from me, I shall be again at my post, and have a lot of good news to tell.

So you are going to have an enrollment of your "warrior boys." How glad I am! Although I feel that, as yet, I do not deserve the name, still I hope that the future will be more charitable. I will send you my photograph, since my cousins are doing the same, but I am afraid you will think it but a poor addition to the pages of your album.

I have studied upon the "hard nut" which you gave us, and think I have strained, if not fully cracked it. I sent you my answer yesterday, and you shall be the judge. Wouldn't it be funny if I should get that ten-cent piece? I assure you it would be a great curiosity in these parts. But there, I shall not, so I will congratulate the lucky winner.

Then we are to have another "puzzle" to work upon? All right. Send it along. I believe I have tried to answer them all so far, and although I have not succeeded so well as many of my cousins, still I am not in the least discouraged, but am more than ever ready to "try, try again." Hoping, this month, to hear from more of my cousins, and also that I may at some time have the privilege of beholding the beauties of that album,

I am, dear Uncle and cousins, yours, etc.

Frank, 2nd.

"Letter from Camp Hamilton"
Uncle Sam
The Children's Friend (Dayton) 3 (June 1, 1861), 1

"Uncle Sam" raised a company of volunteers, was elected captain, and is now in Camp Hamilton, Ohio, ready for duty. "Captain Sam," as we may now call him, is a warm friend of the children; and a strong advocate of the Sabbath-school cause. He promised to send us an occasional communication, giving the readers of the Friend a description of camp-life. Here is his first letter:

Camp Hamilton, Ohio, May 8th, 1861

RESPECTED EDITOR, OF THE FRIEND:

I desire to say to the Sabbath-school with which I was connected, and especially to members of my class, that I have not forgotten the children, though I am now in a military camp. The songs of the Sabbath-school, and the pleasant faces are not heard or seen here. Our camp is on the Butler County Fair-grounds; and now, since it is cleaned up, is a very pretty place. "Uncle Sam" was the officer of the day on yesterday, and concluded to have the grounds cleaned up; so, after dinner, he set seven hundred strong men to work, and in about two hours everything was in nice order, and looked right pleasant. But, in the evening we had another "cleaning out." The Canal runs close by our camp, about three hundred yards off; and some days ago, several bad men tied a boat up at the nearest point, and have been selling the volunteers "rifle-whisky" ever since we have been here. My company, the "Buckeye Guards," were on duty yesterday; and when one of the fellows from the boat tried to slip past the guard, with a big coat on, and two bottles of whisky in his pockets, the guard caught him and took him to the guardhouse. At dusk the men of the camp concluded to stop the sale of whisky from that direction—and a mighty shout was raised, the men rushing forth from the gates of the camp, toward the boat—and soon the barrels, kegs, and jugs were bursting and flying in all directions. The canal was covered with the fragments; and, the work accomplished, the men returned to the camp and to their quarters. Some of the men who assisted in this work of destruction were those who, heretofore, had been made drunk with this whisky, but were perfectly sober when they destroyed it.

Farewell, dear readers of the Friend. I hope to meet you again some time. Be early at the Sabbath-school, study your lessons well, and be obedient to your teachers and parents.

"Mr. Sewell, Dear Friend"
The Little Corporal 1 (August 1865)), 30

I received your beautiful little Paper last week, and would like to get up a club, but fear I shall not be able. My mamma has been to Wisconsin to see my soldier papa's grave. She thinks if you will send a copy to my aunt, she will raise a club of six or more. I should like so much to have the paper, but we are poor and mamma don't think she can pay for it for me. Our home is very lonely since dear papa went away. How our hearts ache to think he can't come back any more.

Your friend,

Jennie S.

How darkly the picture passes before my mind's eye. The father grandly fighting under the shadow of the starry flag, battling for you children, and for me, shot down by a traitor's bullet—now sleeping till the resurrection morning. While we enjoy the peace he bled for, little Jennie and her mamma weeping bitterly—too poor to pay now since their home is left so "very lonely"—their hearts aching "to think he can't come back any more." This is only one in many thousand. I never saw Jennie, but she is one of the soldiers, and I want her to have the paper she likes so much, and shall send it to her at my own expense, but who will send it to the others who would like it as well as she. I would if I was rich enough, but I show you a way in another column by which the work can be done, and only be a pleasure to us all.

"Josie's Letter"
The Little Pilgrim 12 (December 1865), 162–63

Dear Little Pilgrim—

Now that I have returned to our city home again I thought I would write you another little letter. I have commenced to go to school for the first time, and I am so pleased with it that I don't want to stay at home a single day. I often hear of little boys and girls playing truant, that means running away from school without leave, but I think if they loved their teachers, and wished to learn as they ought, they wouldn't do such a naughty thing.

And now that the war is over, I do not see soldiers marching about the streets as I used to, with drums beating, and flags flying; it seems strange too, not to have any more soldiers' funerals to go out to look at. There is a hospital in our street, that used to have a great many sick and wounded soldiers in it, and almost every day I would hear the drum beat, and I knew by the sound that it was a soldier's funeral. Then I would run up to the corner of the street where I could see it pass. Often there would be but one ambulance, with the coffin in it covered with a flag, and only a few soldiers following, with guns to fire a salute over the grave. Once I saw the funeral of a general that was brought here to be buried; he was killed in a battle before Petersburg. Oh my! what a sight it was, such a long train of carriages that followed, besides several hundred soldiers that came up from Fort Delaware to attend his funeral. There were three bands of music and a great many people on foot, some carrying flags and banners; some were "Odd Fellows," and had queer looking white aprons on.* There were two large cannons in the procession, drawn by four horses. The general's war-horse followed close to the hearse, with his sword fastened to the saddle. It took the procession a long time to pass, and it was very interesting to look at.

I often think how much the poor soldiers have suffered to put down the Rebellion. Once when I was out playing, I saw a sol-

---

*Odd Fellows were among the many fraternal and benevolent organizations popular during the nineteenth century.

dier lying on the grass by the road-side, looking so sick and weary; so I ran home to ask my mamma to fill one of my little dishes with some nice rice pudding she had baked for dinner, then I carried it over and gave it to him. He seemed much pleased and thanked me, saying I was a good little girl.

I wondered if there was any little girl in the south, that would carry pudding to dear Uncle Bernard, who was a prisoner at Salisbury, North Carolina?* Alas no! He lay in prison for several months, then died far away from us all. It makes me feel so sad whenever I think of him; yet I love to talk about him, and want always to remember him. I expect the most of the little boys and girls that read The Little Pilgrim have lost some one they loved by the war, perhaps a dear papa or brother. I know they must feel very sad. My uncle was a young man, and when the war came, was among the first to enlist as a soldier and go to it; the first time he was taken prisoner, he was put in the Libby Prison, at Richmond.

After he had been there a long time he was exchanged, and came home nearly worn out; but as soon as he got better he returned to his regiment. I have heard him tell how they suffered in prison, some dying from starvation; their last words were bread! bread! Now isn't it dreadful to think of?

My Uncle Bernie was very fond of little children, and always had something pleasant to say to them. He was so funny too; he used often to play with us little girls, and we liked to have him with us very much.

But sometimes he would play Big Bear, and would chase us all about the house on his hands and feet, growling just like a real bear. Then we would all run as fast as we could to get out of his way, you might be sure. One time I remember he was at grandma's and we cousins were there too, on a visit. So we had a play at Big Bear, but oh my! he was so savage, that we all scampered upstairs to Aunt Annie's room to get away from him. Aunt Annie took us in and locked the door to keep him out. We were safe now, so we thought, but suddenly the window was thrown up and in jumped Big Bear; he had gone around to the back part of the house and climbed up the bower to the roof, then came into the window; so we girls set up a great shout and tried to get away, but it was no use, he had us sure enough; now it was real fun, and I cannot help feeling very bad, when I think we can never have any more plays with dear

*Opened in an abandoned cotton warehouse in 1861, by 1864 the Confederate prison camp in Salisbury, North Carolina, held over 10,000 Union prisoners of war. More than a third of them died between October 1864 and the end of the war.

Uncle Bernie. When I heard he was taken prisoner the last time, I used to remember him in my little prayer every night; before I went to sleep I would say, "I pray the Lord to bless papa and mamma and little Nellie, and all our friends, and bring Uncle Bernie safe home from the Rebels"; but he never came, and mamma said the good Father thought best to take him to his own home in Heaven, away from the horrors of war. I will love him, and remember him always; for my Aunt Annie says "he was a brave soldier, and truly patriotic, and died for the good of his country."

Good by.

Josie.

COSTS OF WAR: LETTERS FROM HOSPITALS

Two final selections show, in extended form, the way that correspondents drew children into the war for the Union. Both are written as letters describing military hospitals. Between them, they introduce a number of topics common to wartime articles: the sacrifices of the soldiers (including drummer boys), the experiences of Southern blacks, the nuts and bolts of fighting a war, the weakness of the Southern cause, the mix of piety and patriotism that even the youngest soldiers demonstrated. Children were clearly not shielded from the bloody reality of war; as the preceding letters and articles have shown, they were starkly aware that fathers and brothers could be taken from them at any time. But, given the state of medical knowledge in the midnineteenth century, so could adults and children living far from the fighting. It is not surprising that so much of the content of wartime children's periodical literature frankly confronted death. Writers for children—especially in sectarian magazines—had always tried to prepare readers for the end of their earthly existence. Life was short and full of uncertainty; piety could leaven the fear and sorrow that characterized young lives in peace and in war.

Obviously, the only way that most Northern women could see the effects of war directly was by becoming army nurses. By doing so, Carrie Vernon and "Cousin Mabelle" took on responsibilities and saw sights that most antebellum women would have been expected to avoid as too jarring for their delicate sex. As nurses, however, they tempered the audacity of their decisions to go to the front by fulfilling the traditionally feminine role of caregiver. As such, the authors of the letters that follow are both sources of dramatic and interesting information and noble role models for girl readers.

"Pencillings—Hospital Life"
Carrie Vernon
The Little Pilgrim 11 (November 1864), 144–45

Well, children, I'm wondering if any of you have missed Pencillings, at all, this year. I've missed The Little Pilgrim, I assure you, and have resolved and re-resolved, every month, to write something for you, and let Grace* know where I was, so I could have a glimpse of that sturdy Little Pilgrim with his staff again.

But I've had a better excuse than many people have for breaking so many good resolves. Do you wonder what it is? Listen, then. Uncle Sam has had some work for me to do in a hospital. He set me to taking care of some of his sick boys; and I have tried and tried to find the time to write to you something about them, but couldn't.

And now that I have, I'm wondering what I'd best tell you first; whether about the arrangement of the hospitals, or just scenes and incidents. You'd of course like best to read those, but wouldn't it be best for some of you northern little folks, especially, who live so far away from a hospital that you never saw one, to know something first of the inside arrangement and regulations, so that you will be better able to see just how everything looks. And as I wish you to make it a rule always to do what is best, first, rather than what pleases you best, I will do the same myself, and try to show you the inside of a hospital.

To make you see this plainer, I think I will take you with me to visit one, if you would like the trip. It will cost you nothing except a little exercise of that very funny part of you which physiologists call the brain. Let me introduce you to that city which is "set upon hills," that beautiful capital of Tennessee, Nashville. These two large buildings on Spring Street, known as the Masonic Hall and First Presbyterian Church, now constitute Hospital No. 8. Let us enter the first. Here a "blue coat" at the door, with sword, rifle and bayonet, is the guard, but he steps aside and lets us pass. Just in front is a broad flight of stairs, [on] which, while ascending, we can read this caution inscribed upon the wall in evergreen:—"Remember you are in a hospital, and make no noise." Let us pause at this door, and I will introduce you to the matron.

"Miss J., allow me to introduce the little readers of the Pilgrim; they wish to visit the hospital, if convenient."

---

*Grace Greenwood—Sara J. C. Lippincott—was editor of *The Little Pilgrim*.

"Certainly," says the lady, "I was just starting on my usual daily visit through the wards, and shall be happy to have their company."

Up another broad flight and other cautions meet our eyes, in evergreen, such as "Keep away from the wall," "No smoking here." This last is, of course, unnecessary for this company, as we do not propose taking any smokers along, if we know it; and if they try to hide it, they'll not dare to come very near, else their disagreeable breath will betray them.

We ask the matron of her duties; and throwing open a door which has "Linen Room" printed above it in large letters, we see huge piles of clothing for the soldiers and their beds upon the shelves, and two clerks who are sitting at a table.

"This department comprises all the work assigned to me," she says; "whatever else I do is voluntary and gratuitous; but I usually visit through the entire hospital once a day. But today," she adds, laughingly, "it would be difficult to define my duties. I think I might properly be called Commandant of the Black Squad, or Chief of the Dirty Brigade," and she explains by saying that she has seven black women and two men, subject to her orders, who are engaged in cleaning the building.

"They are fumigating this room," says our usher, throwing open the doors of a large room with something of a smoky appearance, and she adds, "They have had a few cases of small-pox here, which have been sent to the proper hospital." But we perceive that some six or eight patients are here, together with some three or four men in the middle of the room, who are talking. We pass to another. "There is one very sick man in this ward," says the lady, "and a young boy who is but little better." We enter, and find there are three rows of the single iron army beds, or cots, which are so close to each other as to give only room to walk between, while the space between the rows is about the same as the aisles in a church, or somewhat wider. One row is placed with the heads of the beds against each wall, and one through the centre of the room.

In the first row upon the right we find the "very sick man," who seems suffering very much from fever and pneumonia. His face is flushed and swollen, and his breathing difficult, but he tells the nurse he feels better, while she scans his features and takes note of his hard breathing with an anxious face, but with encouraging words.

We turn now to the "young boy" of whom she had spoken. He is a slight boy of only fifteen, and with delicate girlish features, and has been anxiously watching her coming.

"Sit down here, mother, on the side of my bed," he says. She does so, when he asks her to bend her head down so he can tell her something. This she does, when he says with difficulty, but loud enough for us all to hear, "There's some money under my pillow; I want you to get it and buy me some dried peaches."

"I don't want your money," she says, "but you shall have the peaches if I can find them"; and before leaving the building, we see her write a note and dispatch someone for the fruit. "This boy always calls me mother," says Miss J. to us, "and the first day he was brought here he sent his nurse down to ask if I would come up and kiss him. He has been his mother's pet, and now I correspond with her on his account."

His fever is very high, and we pass our cold hand soothingly over his forehead, and try to speak words of comfort; and as we turn to leave, he looks up pleadingly and says:

"Can't you kiss me?"

"Yes, indeed, I can—am glad to do so," and we press our own to his burning lips, and receive his feverish, unpleasant breath; not a disagreeable task, though, for all, when we remember that he is the pet of a mother whom he misses so very much, and who may never look upon her boy again.

We bid him good-by, promising to call again, and pass to another ward. Here is one who is dressed and sitting upon the side of his bed, which is neatly made up. His face is towards us as we approach, but instead of raising his head to look at us we perceive that it is bent in a listening attitude. We stand by his side and are pained to discover that his eyes are closed as smoothly and tightly as for the last slumber, and that he has no power to open the lids or move them; but there is a pleasant, contented look upon his broad brow and calm features, and his story is something like this:

"It's a fact that I was gettin' to be a mighty bad boy before I came into the army, and afterwards I got in bad company, and was fast learning to gamble, swear, and drink with the worst of 'em. I just nearly broke my mother's heart with my bad ways. My mother is a right good Christian woman, an' I don't s'pose there's a single day that passes over her head but that she prays for me. And I reckon the Lord's heard some of her prayers for me, lately, if not before, for I'm not the same boy, by a long shot, that I used to be."

Then we tell him we believe it may be one of the best schools he was ever in; and also that he must not look forward to a life of idleness, even if he is blind, and we tell him of the labors of the blind poet Milton, of the historian Prescott, and of that blind author and divine, Professor Henry, who said he never knew what happiness was, until after he became blind. We now leave him, looking really happy, and with a promise to comply with his urgent invitation to visit him again.

Now we pass downstairs and into a large, pleasant, cleanly room, large enough to contain some four or five rows of beds. Upon a rostrum at one end is a desk and table for the use of the wardmaster, clerk or steward, while keeping the books or writing letters.

Here is a pale, sallow visage, the owner of which asks piteously, if we "have any oranges?" "No," but we provide means so that he has some purchased.

"I'm from North Carolina," he says. "I hid in the woods and mountains, lived on roots and berries, and swam rivers to get away." In reply to our query as to whether he would like a letter written home, he says no, and informs us that his wife and father arrived in town only a few days ago.

"Then you have seen them?" we ask.

"Yes, they've both visited me, but my wife comes the oftenest."

Just now, his nurse—the young man who takes care of him—who should know better, but doesn't, interrupts him by telling us that "it isn't so," that "his family are all in North Carolina," and that he is "out of his head."

"That's just the way," said the patient, turning to us with a flushed and angry look, "that they're talking to me all the time, and trying to make me think I'm crazy. I reckon I know whether I've seen my wife or not!"

"Of course you do," we say, quietingly; "does she bring you anything nice to eat?" and add that we wish she would come while we were there so we can see her.

"Well, she don't bring me much to eat," he says, in a faint, drawling voice; "she don't understand fixin' up things for sick folks like you do, you know; and then she's weakly like; but then she does what she can, you know—she's allays willin', for she's got a right gude heart. She don't dress and look like you do, you know," he added, "for she's sort o' torn to pieces like, by this war."

Yes, we can understand it. Upon inquiring of the wardmaster, we are surprised to learn that this man is really a monomaniac upon this subject, persisting in the declaration that his wife and father visit him often, though no one sees them.

"He can't live," says the wardmaster; "he's lost all heart and is worn out. There isn't over one-fourth the chance for a Southerner to live, after coming to a hospital, there is for our own men. They will do more fighting with less food, when in the field, than our Northern boys, but when the excitement is over, if sick or wounded, they lose heart and die."

When we learn of the wardmaster that the man must die, we feel glad, as we glance back to him, that he is comforted by these imaginary visits from father and wife.

But, children, my line of communication with you narrows, and must be closed for the present, but if Grace thinks best, it will probably be open next month. A good day to you.

"The Drummer Boy at Gettysburg"
Cousin Mabelle
The Little Corporal 1 (November 1865), 67–68

You have all heard of the battle of Gettysburg? Well, as soon as the news reached us, I determined to go and do what I could for the brave men who had sacrificed so much for our country. So, on the morning of the 4th, before a ray of sunlight had lighted up the hills, and while the birds were still sleeping in the trees, I was hurrying along over the iron road—"rushing through the mountain, rattling over bridges, whizzing through the valley, puffing over ridges," towards Gettysburg. At every stopping place we received fresh news from the battle; sometimes "The Union army was retreating in confusion!" sometimes "Lee's army was beaten and our forces driving them back!" but all agreed that a terrible battle was going on and help for the wounded was needed; so, without stopping for refreshments, we hurried on. It was late in the afternoon when we stopped and were told the train could go no further. After a long search, and longer dispute with an avaricious old man, we took a horse and buggy, and partly by threats and partly by promises, succeeded in getting our baggage and a boy into it and set off. I will not tell you about the long ride and tiresome walk, or of all the trouble we had in finding a place to put our baggage and eat a luncheon; of the impossibility of finding a quiet corner to rest a moment, and the difficulty of getting anything for the suffering soldiers, who were every moment being brought in—because I don't want you to think the people were all heartless and ungrateful, and because I want to tell you the story of a Sabbath School Scholar in the Hospital, or a long store room, which, before the night was over, we had cleared of rubbish and filled with beds. Before it was day there was only one empty, and about ten o'clock that was filled by a wounded boy.

He was only thirteen, but about as you are, Charlie, or even Georgie, there, who is at most fifteen; and had been in the army almost nine months, and "never got a scratch before," he said, though he had been in three big battles and some skirmishes. But now his right arm was shattered, and minié ball had lodged in his left leg. Poor boy! The surgeons had taken out the ball and bound up the wound, but the arm would have to be cut off. They had told him so, and though he trembled and the great tears stood in his eyes, he said, "I was afraid it would, but I'll try to bear it." Just then an assistant came up where the chief surgeon was standing, and said something in a low tone. The surgeon told him to telegraph immediately for supplies; then he beckoned me to follow, and went straight to the drummer boy's cot, and said, "My dear boy, your arm ought to be amputated and dressed immediately, but our chloroform is all gone. Can you stand an operation without?" He turned deadly pale, his lip quivered, and large tears rolled slowly over his face. I went to him, and taking his well hand in mine, talked to him a moment, and then he said, "If you will stay right here by me, I will try."

Now, I had never seen anything like that done, and the very thought made me shudder and turn sick, as perhaps you do, little girl, in reading this; but I could not hesitate long, with those brown eyes, brim full of tears, looking straight into mine so *pitifully*, and I said, "Yes, dear, I will stand right here." Then he turned his face toward me, away from the doctor, and said, "I will try. Go on." He endured it all patiently, and, when it was over, looked up in my face and murmured, "Won't you kiss me once, just as mother would?" The tears choked me so I could not speak, but I bent over him and kissed his white lips. "My brave boy," said the surgeon, "many a man to-day has borne an operation less heroically. Keep up your courage; you will be well enough to go home and see your mother soon, I hope. Only keep up your spirits." "I'll try to," he murmured, patiently. Then I was called away, and when I returned, an hour afterwards, he was asleep.

In a few days he was able to sit up and talk some. Then he told me his mother was a widow, and had a son older than he, who was a sergeant in the army, and a daughter, two years younger than he was, at home. He said his name was Edwin Grant, his sister's, Hattie, and his big brother's, Charlie. Then, with a promise of writing to his mother and sister that night, telling them how and where he was, and finding out where his brother was, if I could, I left him again.

You see, there were hundreds and hundreds in the town too badly hurt to be moved, and it seemed a long time before we could get much to do with. Then there were a great many who wanted to do a great deal and did not know how to do anything; many ladies who would scream and faint when they ought to be quiet and self-possessed; many gentlemen who would upset a bottle or drop a bandage just as one was ready to use it; many of both sexes who seemed to do nothing but make a noise and get in the way. Learn to be quiet, orderly, and thoughtful now, children, and no one can say that of you when you are men and women.

I thought I had a large supply of papers and magazines with me, but soon found I had not half enough. The men wanted something to think of besides their aching bodies and sorrowing friends, and stories and pictures were just the thing. Eddie thought so as he lay on his narrow cot in that one position—for it was many days before he could be moved at all, while the hot sun and fiery fever made the room seem warm and close, although we tried hard to keep it cool and pleasant. Some of the poor fellows would talk in their delirium about the "cool spring down in the lot," or "the brook up in the mountains," while others would moan and mutter, and sometimes scream outright in their pain. Often when one would begin talking of home, and call out for a mother or sister, I would go to him and lay my cool, moist hand upon his forehead, answer him kindly and quietly, then laying a cloth, wet with ice water, on his head, in a few minutes soothing him to sleep.

But through it all—the heat, and noise, and dust—Eddie, the drummer boy, grew steadily better. On the sixth day after the arm was taken off, he called me as I was passing by his little bed, and asked if I would please to come and stay with him a little while when I got time. I told him I would after I had gone around the room, given the fever patients their medicine, and attended to the supper of all. In about half an hour I came back to Eddie. He put out his left hand, and said, with a smile, "I'm so glad you've come; you're very kind; but don't you get awful tired sometimes?" "Not as tired as you do, dear, lying still all the while; if all were as comfortable as you we would not mind the steps we take. What is it, Eddie, that keeps you so constantly quiet and patient?" "Well," he answered, musingly, "two years ago, before I 'listed, I went to Sunday School, and had the best kind of teacher, and she used to talk to us about reading the Bible, and praying, and doing our duty; and if ever a fellow tried to be good, I did. But 'twas awful hard work, and sometimes I would get ugly; I couldn't help it. And sometimes I had a mind to give it up. But just then there was a revival in the Sunday School, and I made up my mind I would enlist under the banner of King Emmanuel. So I just offered myself, and He accepted me. I knew He would, because He said, 'He that cometh unto me I will in nowise cast out!' So, after that, whenever I got into trouble, I just went to our Captain, Jesus, and told him all about it;

and 'twould all come right pretty soon. You know He said, 'Cast thy burden on the Lord, and He will sustain thee, and strengthen thee, and comfort thee!' Well, when I went to war, I just made up my mind that I would stick to it, and I have! I promised mother I wouldn't drink nor swear, use tobacco nor play cards; and I haven't. I promised myself that I wouldn't be afraid to tell the truth or do what I knew was right any time, and I haven't. But I couldn't have helped it sometimes if I hadn't known that 'Jesus is my Captain.' I've prayed to Him ever since I've been sick, and He has helped me all the time. I couldn't have borne the pain, or the weariness, or anything else, if Christ hadn't a helped me. And, do you know," he said, with a glow of affection in his dark eyes and over his pale face, "do you know I believe He sent you here to help us? The doctor told Jim (the man in the next cot) that he knew of more'n twenty who'd a died if you hadn't a watched 'em so night and day. Yes'm," he said again, "I do believe God sent you." And as I thought of all the sickening sights and sounds I had seen and heard unmoved, how without sleep, and almost without food, I had for days and nights worked on, I, too, believed it was God who had sent me and strengthened me. After Eddie had rested a few minutes, he asked me to read a little in his Testament. So I read part of the fifteenth chapter of St. John, and then, kneeling by his cot, prayed that Christ would keep His brave little soldier all through the battle of life, and at last take him up on high. Then I kissed him good night, and left him. But I heard the man in the next cot say to himself, "'Twas better'n a sermon any how"; and another mutter, "Well, I wish I felt as good as he does."

In a few days more Eddie's mother and sister came. I had been in another part of the town to visit other "brave boys," and as I opened the door of our hospital, a sweet girlish voice sang out:

> "We've 'listed for life, and will camp on the field,
> With Christ as our Captain, we never will yield;
> The sword of the Spirit both trusty and strong,
> We'll hold in our hands as we're marching along."

And as the voice rose sweet and clear on the chorus, Eddie's joined, "Marching along, we are marching along." I wish you could have seen them, and heard the poor dear fellows all around beg for "one more like that"; and every day after, little Hattie Grant spent hours singing to the soldiers. If our Young Corporal would let me, I'd like to tell you more about her and her two brothers, for we finally found Charlie; but I have told you enough for this time.

2

Patriotism and Perseverance

━━◆━━

Oliver Optic's Civil War

"What has been gained by all the fighting?" asked a boy named William in a story from *Our Young Folks* published just after the war ended. "Why," said his sister Susie, "Cousin Primly has got a commission, and Mr. Shoddy has got rich, and Tom Noddy has got a wooden leg, which they say he can skate and dance with, and the Rebels have got whipped!" But these rather flip answers failed to satisfy either curious child, and they appealed to their Uncle Rodman to explain exactly "what the fighting was for, what brought it about, and all that."

In Father Brighthopes fashion, Uncle Rodman articulated a decidedly Northern view of the conflict. Not surprisingly, he lay the blame squarely on the evil Slave Power bent on destroying the Union, leading the ignorant Southern masses blindly into war. "The Rebels took up arms and attacked us," he explained, "and there was nothing left for us to do, if we would preserve our rights, our self-respect, and the respect of the world, but to fight in self-defense." The stakes were unimaginably high: It was a fight between the "dark ages" and the "brightest blessings of freedom." Finally, in its death grasp, the Slave Power had murdered President Lincoln, "perhaps the most humane and forbearing ruler, as well as one of the kindest-hearted men, that ever lived."

In Uncle Rodman's hands, the war became a parable of good versus evil: madly ambitious slave owners, gullible poor Southern whites, rightfully indignant Northern Republicans attempting to eradicate slavery peacefully, long-suffering Southern Unionists, and the ultimate victory of "the noblest, strongest government in the world." The "rebellion," he

—33—

*Oliver Optic, the most prolific author and publisher for children during
the Civil War. From* The Student and Schoolmate.

declared, "was a stupendous piece of folly, as well as stupendous wickedness." But "now we turn over a new leaf of history," where there is "no more war; no more human bondage, liberty, and love for all." He called on the children to let this golden future "inspire you now with high aspirations, noble motives, and all generous thoughts and hopes!"

In a phrase recalling New Testament scenes of Jesus teaching his disciples, the story closed with William and Susie "seriously pondering what he had said."* And well they should have. Their beloved and knowledgeable uncle had, in a few paragraphs, offered the entire political gospel preached in children's magazines. Coming just two months after the collapse of the Confederacy, it was a powerful punctuation point to the literary war in the North.

Our Young Folks, however, which did not appear until January 1865, came late to the campaign. The man who provided the most intense coverage of the war for children, especially for boys drawn to the martial atmosphere and masculine values of wartime, was Oliver Optic (William T. Adams), whose *Student and Schoolmate* beat the drum for the Union war effort in monthly articles, stories, declamation pieces, dialogues, and poems. His friendly but unrelentingly patriotic

---

*J. T. Trowbridge, "The Turning of the Leaf," *Our Young Folks* 1 (June 1865), 398–401.

"Teacher's Desk" editorials have already been featured. The war infused every facet of his magazine., and although Optic tackled other subjects in his long career as a children's writer and editor, he found his most prominent niche in war stories. His 1870s successor to *The Student and Schoolmate, Oliver Optic's Magazine,* occasionally revisited the Civil War long after most of its competitors had gone on to other things. His "Army and Navy" trilogies remained popular for the rest of the century and were given brand-new editions in the 1890s. Optic focused on the war more than any other author or editor, convinced that knowledge about the causes and conduct of the war would nurture patriotism in young Yankees. As a result, no other magazine exhorted its young readers to rally behind the Northern war effort as consistently and insistently as *The Student and Schoolmate.*

LIFE IN THE ARMY

Readers consumed large helpings of military jargon, news, and trivia from children's magazines throughout the war. They learned, for instance, that a single army division had sent 98,000 letters during one two-month period, that the government paid $16 each for rifled muskets, and that a girl living near Boston knit one hundred pairs of mittens for soldiers. Biographies of generals and descriptions of military insignia and armaments appeared very early in the war. Civil War children could not get enough information about the conflict raging in far-off Virginia or Tennessee; as adults, they remembered rushing downstairs to check out the latest news from the front and to follow the movements of Union armies in the maps of ongoing campaigns printed almost daily. Editors of juvenile magazines eagerly tapped into this lively interest.

Oliver Optic's *Student and Schoolmate* devoted two six-part series to the "life in the army" genre of articles. Charles C. Coffin's "Letters from the Army" showed the daily life of soldiers in camp. Two years later, another series, called "Campaigning"—much of which appears below—focused on the organization, administration, and even deployment of military units ranging in size from a regiment to an entire army. In an era when the peacetime army of the United States rarely reached twelve thousand men, the size of Civil War armies, which often climbed above one hundred thousand soldiers, must have seemed incredible to children and adults alike. Articles like these helped make the unimaginable scale of the war more comprehensible, but they also gave Northern children a new vocabulary—pickets, flank attacks, foraging, the Sanitary Commission—which they eagerly applied to their play.

Other elements of magazines' indoctrination of children into the Union war effort also surfaced in "Campaigning." The last two installments show a picket guard of Yankees fighting a skirmish with Confederate cavalrymen. Despite the strategic insignificance of the affair, readers witness vicious Rebels looting bodies and attacking wounded, defenseless Yankees, and meet an intelligent and helpful African-American contraband. Even more important, however, was the application of prewar ideas to the war—the importance of order, hierarchy, and admiration and respect for legitimate authority. The army, in a phrase that cynical veterans would no doubt have scoffed at, provides "a lesson of system," of efficiency, that will ultimately lead to victory. Furthermore, the officers in these articles function coolly and courageously, despite "all the tumult, confusion, slaughter, and sacrifice" that surround them. All of this would inspire confidence among youngsters back home, especially those worried about fathers and brothers in the army, and encourage their patriotism.

"Campaigning"
The Student and Schoolmate 14 (July 1864), 21–22

As the active campaign of spring is now working out such glorious results for the Union and liberty, this may perhaps be the fitting time for my promised word. And in order to make that word intelligible, I offer the first papers on the organization of an army. I do so because many read about Regiments, Brigades, Divisions, Corps, etc., without having any distinct idea of either.

A Regiment is composed of ten companies, each company commanded by its Captain, and all the companies, or Regiment, by the Colonel, and two other field officers, Lieut.-Colonel and Major. But what is the object of three field officers? Why could not one command?

One does command, the others serve under him. If the Colonel should be killed in an engagement, the Lieut.-Colonel takes his place. If he should fall, the Major succeeds him, and then the senior Captain follows.

But this is not the only object in having three field officers. When the old 15th Mass. first went into active service, it had to perform a great deal of picket duty. Yes, but what does picket duty mean? That I will tell you by and by. Now we must settle the question of organization. Our first posts lay along the

Potomac River. Well, some parts of the river needed but little guarding; it was so deep it required just enough to see that no boats attempted a crossing. Other points, called fords, where people could wade across, these had to be watched with greater diligence, and a large number of men.

To accomplish this, three companies would be sent from camp under command of the Major. He would distribute his men as the emergency demanded; and the three Captains would send in their reports to him, of what they had seen, heard, or done, every morning. And he would send a report of the whole to the Colonel at the camp. Three other companies could be sent away on a similar duty under the Lieut.-Colonel, the Captains under him reporting to him, and he in his turn sending a report every morning at an early hour, to the Colonel. Then if either of these forces should be attacked by the enemy, the Colonel would have four companies to advance with and render them assistance.

In this way, you can break your Regiment up into smaller bodies, and yet have so much system that the Colonel can tell every morning just where his entire command is, what it has been doing, how many are sick, how many fit for duty—in a word, the entire history. It is necessary for him to have this, because he has to tell somebody else. This opens the question of organization of a brigade, of which we will speak in our next; and after giving you an insight into the organization of an army, we hope to speak to you of the position of the different officers commanding during a fight, the movement of an army from one point to another, and then if you really want them, a few reminiscences from camp and prison.

"Campaigning, No. 2: A Brigade, and a Division"
The Student and Schoolmate 14 (August 1864), 47–48

In speaking of a Regiment, I showed you how easily it could be divided and sent to different points, while the Colonel, commanding the whole, would have regular information of its movements. Now a Brigade is a larger body of men, under the control and direction of one mind. It is generally composed of four Regiments, but when these are much reduced by sickness and losses in battle, others are added, so as to increase the number of men. In this organization the Colonels forward their reports to the General commanding the Brigade, so every morning at eight A.M., he can tell where his entire command is, and what it has done for the past twenty-four hours, learns how many men have been killed or taken prisoners, and just how many he has in his command to throw against the enemy, or to resist any movement which they may make.

Now if a place is captured requiring about four thousand men to hold it securely, instead of taking four Regiments that have never moved together nor seen each other, they appoint such a Brigade to occupy the place, and you have a small army, all its officers familiar with each other and their duties. A Brigade Quartermaster, to see to rations, Surgeon, to meet the demands of the regimental surgeon, teams and teamsters, ambulances and drivers, everything making it perfect and complete, so that it can move to any position, entirely independent of the army from which it was detached.

Now for a Division. This is a body of men three times as large as a Brigade. Three Brigades brought together, each of the Brigadier Generals being responsible to the General commanding the Division, so that he, sitting in his tent at nine A.M., can learn from the reports of his three Brigade Generals, the exact condition of his command. Now if it requires ten or twelve thousand troops for any given work, here is a body of men, knowing each other, accustomed to moving together, their relations and positions distinctly understood, so that they can be sent under that one mind as easily as a company can be detached and sent from a Regiment. But when a Division is sent on such duty, or a Brigade, they have a certain number of Cavalry, and so many Batteries of Artillery, so that every branch of the service is represented, and ready to meet its kind in an engagement. The Cavalry hold the outposts on most distant picket points, because they can travel faster to warn of the enemy's approach; and when they are driven in, it gives the Infantry outposts time to get into position to meet the coming foe. If the Infantry pickets are outnumbered and driven in, too, then the Artillery, which is always posted so as to sweep all the approaches to the town or fort where our pickets have all fallen back, pour in grape and canister upon the advancing foe, the Infantry being drawn up in the line of battle just behind the Artillery, ready to meet the enemy as he rushes up with the purpose of capturing the pieces.

What a lesson of system. In a Regiment the ten Captains each reporting the condition of his company. In a Brigade, the Colonels that of their Regiments. In a Division, Generals giving an exact account of their Brigades, so that the General of the Division handles twelve thousand men, knowing all the facts, as the Captain his hundred, or the Colonel his thousand.

"Campaigning, No. 3: A Corps and an Army"

The Student and Schoolmate 14 (October 1864), 108–10

In conversing, some time since, with a gentleman who had little appreciation of system, we referred him to the army for an illustration of its power. "Oh, yes!" he replied, "but where is its value without a military genius at its head?"

Its value *without* marked military ability at its head is *unquestioned*. It makes a *weak* general *strong*; while one of *ability* is made *mighty* through the increased strength, knowledge, and confidence which it imparts.

The General of a Division, through the reports of his three Brigade commanders, is thoroughly conversant with the condition of his twelve or fifteen thousand men. After a short experience in the field, he knows the character of each regiment, whether it will do to trust it in a charge, or commit to its custody some important position where the utmost vigilance is demanded. We wonder at this—one mind controlling the movements of so many, familiar with its organized worth, and confident of its ability for any given task. We recall a dialogue between Maj.-General Sumner and one of his Brigade commanders, on the battle-field of Fair Oaks. Observing what he conceived to be a weak point in the line of battle, he suggested the wisdom of strengthening it. The Brigadier replied, "*That, sir, is the ____ Mass., and will hold its position.*" The regiment had established its character, and was in this way widening its reputation. Having never failed, it was leaned upon for hard positions and hazardous points.

If we wonder, then, at the organization of a Division, giving to one mind so much control, what when we advance to the Corps? In this you have three Divisions, under the authority and orders of a Corps commander. Multiplying our fifteen thousand by three, gives us forty-five thousand men. And yet this vast number is so completely organized, that the history of the three generals commanding the Division enables the Major-General commanding the Corps, to master all the details on every morning, knowing the strength of his Corps, the Division to be entrusted with any hazardous expedition, the Brigades and Regiments for any minor operations.

Passing from the Corps to the Army, its organization requires but a few words. A Corps in itself is an army—for instance: the forces holding Western Virginia, and co-operating with those in the Valley of the Shenandoah, may not, except in case of a raid by the rebels, number more than thirty or forty thousand men, and be made an army by itself for that specific duty, under one department commander. But when we take the vital points in Virginia and Georgia, Richmond and Atlanta,—at these we mass our troops for the capture, and they theirs to defend. So that an army there may be composed of six Corps, of more or less as the emergency may demand, or the ability of the Government supply.

To wield these Corps, we have one mind. Maj.-General Meade learns every morning from his Corps commanders the positive condition and strength of his entire force. He allots each Corps its position, imparts his plan and the part which each of these Corps are to play in the conflict.

The Corps commanders take their work, and divide it among their Divisions. The Division commanders theirs to distribute among the Brigades: so that the one mind at the head, reaches down through the Corps, Divisions, and Brigade commanders, to the Regiment and Company, and a hundred or a hundred and fifty thousand men move to carry out the plan, under the complete control, and subject to the order of one mind. Consequently one mind, in the midst of a terrific conflict, can move his Corps to suit the emergencies, to check an unexpected advance, or break through a weak point discovered in the enemy's line. From his position and the reports brought to him from the Corps commanders during the fight, he changes or modifies his plan. This Corps may be very much pressed, and in want of assistance. The Corps commander states his want, in written communication, forwarded by an Aid. The General commanding the Army meets the demand from some Corps not hardly pressed, sending to its commander an order to send a Brigade or a Division to the relief of such a General. The troops thus sent report to the Commander of the Corps whom they go to assist, and receive from him their work and orders, until the emergency is over and they returned to their rightful command. If the whole line is engaged, then assistance must be drawn from the reserve, a body of troops kept for just such a pressure. If he has no troops to send, the Corps commander is ordered to hold his position with the promise of a demonstration for his relief.

This demonstration may be made by a vigorous charge upon the enemy's line by some other Corps, compelling him to withdraw from his attack, to check our supposed advance.

It is in such a position that true military genius reveals itself. Cool, calm, and self-possessed in the midst of all the tumult, confusion, slaughter, and sacrifice that surround him, reading the enemy's purpose from his mode of attack or defense, changing his plan and making new combinations, while orders and reports are continually coming to claim his attention and going forth at his dictation.

The usual military routine can be mastered by a mind of average ability; but to read and conquer an enemy's purpose in the midst of such surroundings, to change a plan by a few judicious moves, and turn an apparent defeat into positive victory— that requires all the help coming from thorough military education, experience, and genius.

"Campaigning, No. 5"
The Student and Schoolmate 15 (February 1865), 39–42

"Well, well, that beats old possum! You don't mean to say that you gave him your real name, Joe?" "Yes, I do mean to say so. You don't suppose I would do the mean thing *there*, Jim, do you?" "Do the mean thing, no! I call it a grand joke to fool a strange sutler." "Sutler, you coon! that was no *sutler*; that was the Sanitary Commission, and I gave them my name, Regiment, and Company,—that was all they would take for the shirt and socks I so much needed." "I reckon you'll miss the charity part of that move, Joe. They'll make returns, and the cost with profits will turn up on your clothing account. You don't catch me in any

An image of valor and patriotism in the "Campaigning" series.
From The Student and Schoolmate.

such trap as that. If they have things to *give away*, why don't they do it without getting your name, Regiment, and Company? You are a little green, yet, Joe."

The above dialogue took place between a new recruit and an old skeptical veteran. The latter having been in the service *six months*, the former some five weeks. Joe perhaps merited the term *green*, as he had succeeded in losing his entire outfit on his way to camp. He could obtain no clothes from the Quartermaster's department for weeks, and having left what little means he had with his widowed mother, found himself in rather straitened circumstances. Passing from guard duty in the center of ————-town, on the outskirts of which his Regiment was encamped, he saw—what is known to all in the army *now*— U.S. SAN. COM. stuck up on the door of an old wooden building. He obtained permission from the Sergeant of the guard to step in—where stating his case, the agent of the Commission met his demands, taking his name, Regiment, and Company, to show what disposition he, the agent, had made of the things committed to his care. Jim, being on guard with him and knowing the low state of his finances, supposed he had obtained them on credit, never intending to pay, from the fact of his getting them as he supposed, from a sutler establishment in the town, rather than the sutler of the Regiment. Joe happened to know the object and purpose of the Sanitary Commission, because his mother was a member of a branch society in her own town, while Jim had gone from home ere much publicity had been given to its efforts at the commencement of the war. I want to tell you how Jim's doubts about the Sanitary Commission were cured. Some six weeks after this, in one of the many cavalry skirmishes of that period, when the enemy were so much better in their Cavalry organization and tactics than we were, the Company with which Joe and Jim were connected were out on a foraging expedition, or at least near enough to support some Cavalry who were in quest of hay and grain for their horses. The Infantry were stationed at a point where two roads crossed, to prevent the enemy from cutting our Cavalry off, they being about quarter of a mile in advance. The large old-fashioned Virginia residence, against which the expedition was planned, was in plain view from a fork of a tree on the right of the road over which our Cavalry had gone. The Captain of the Company had taken his position in the above mentioned fork, so as to be prepared for any emergency which the movement of foragers might suggest, when the picket on the road leading to the left sent in to the Company Head-Quarters a curious specimen of a Virginia contraband. The old fellow had been noticed some time previous to his arrest, moving with the *utmost caution*; this the picket interpreted as a desire on his part to collect information for the enemy. In order, therefore, to make sure work, a little Yankee strategy was devised, and two of the squad, one of whom proved to be Joe, were ordered to move toward the negro, one on each side of the road, sheltered by the woods through which the road passed; getting on their hands and knees they succeeded with a little caution in getting between their prey and his home, then clearing the Virginia fence at a bound, Joe and his comrade commanded a halt! Seeing the force in his rear, the contraband concluded to "clar out ob dat on a right smart git," when to his utter dismay the picket held the road in his front. "De good Lord save dis here nig—" and down he went in the middle of the road on his knees. Sam, for that proved to be the name of the contraband, soon discovered that he had been arrested. "Fus' rate—jus where dis chile was gwine." His caution was used for the sake of avoiding the rebel picket. Somewhat disappointed in the character of their game, Joe and his companion returned to the picket post, having transferred Sam to the custody of the First Lieutenant.

While this was transpiring below, the Captain had noticed our Cavalry moving off to the left of the house at quite a brisk pace. Just at this point the First Lieutenant made his appearance with Sam, from whom the Captain obtained information which seemed to be of importance, and promising busy times. As the Captain was ascending the tree after his conference with Sam, and the hasty departure of the Lieutenant to the picket on the left, the clear sharp ring of a rifle quickened his movements and sent its peculiar thrill over all. The Company immediately fell in, examined their pieces, put on their haversacks, etc. Before this was accomplished, several reports were heard and the distant echo of the Cavalry bugle. After making a hasty reconnaissance the Captain descended, called in the pickets from the right and left hand roads, and posted one half of his Company behind the fence on each side of the road over which our Cavalry would have to return, First Lieutenant in command on the right, Second Lieutenant on the left, with orders to keep cool, letting our own Cavalry pass, reserving their fire until the rebels were right up to the cross roads, then to fire, and with an unearthly yell, charge. This plan had been arranged with our Cavalry; they if attacked were to lead the enemy into this ambush—that being the military name for a force concealed in this way; then they, the Cavalry, were to turn and follow up whatever advantage might arise from the fire and charge, or yell of the Infantry.

The Captain had hardly got his position at the *front*—for this was a movement where risk on his part was demanded—when the Cavalry came at break-neck speed along the road; our men were all hid; the unsuspecting Johnnies were bringing up the rear in splendid style, having already unhorsed four of our poor fellows who now lay bleeding in the road behind them; when all of a "suddin" as one of the rebs afterward remarked, our Captain's clear commanding voice struck upon their nerves—"By Company fire—Battalion prepare to charge," then the cheer and yell broke them in utter confusion, some taking the right, others the left, the largest portion retreating on the double quick over the ground of their recent splendid charge. Two of the wounded cavalry men had so far recovered from their shock as to be returning when this masked charge took place; anxious to avoid imprisonment they were trying to clear the fence when these chivalrous representatives of tyranny charged up to the fence, and upon these unarmed and wounded men. Joe with five of the company rushed upon the hacking fiends, and for a few moments they were pretty generally mixed up. The indignation of our men at the cowardly act gave nerve to every blow, three of the Johnnies being unhorsed, and two captured. Joe and two others were wounded, the first it was feared seriously, two sabre cuts in the head and a bullet through the right arm near the shoulder. Having lifted him from the ditch, secured their prisoners, and turned to retrace their steps, a new dilemma opened upon them,—our forces had fallen back, owing to the appearance of some fresh rebel Cavalry over the road on our left—over which Sam had come—and of whose presence he had made the Captain aware. A few moments sufficed to turn the tables upon our heroes; their prisoners were unloosed; they bound; Joe being left for dead upon the side of the road near the fence where the sympathy of his comrades had laid him; left there, but not until he had been nearly stript by his merciless foes.

"Campaigning No. 6"
The Student and Schoolmate 15 (April 1865), 117–18

The sun was hid behind the long mountain range known as the "Blue Ridge," some time ere the skirmish was closed; heavy clouds had been gathering on the horizon, promising one of those severe and sudden storms, so familiar in our Southern States.

The forces had hardly reached the cover of their old positions, ere the storm was upon them in its fury. Each party felt entire security, and sought whatever shelter they could, dis-

cussing in all the various shades of gloom or hope the movements of the day.

Had any one been posted in Capt.—'s observatory (the
tree by the cross roads,) they might have seen a movement near
the bank, where the supposed remains of Joe had been placed. It
might have been a piece of timber floating, for the water had ac-
cumulated in the ditch on that side of the road with great rapid-
ity, while on the opposite side, it rushed by with all the tumble
and roar of a river. Shortly after this first demonstration, another
might have been discovered at the junction of the cross roads;—
a black woolly looking object, thrust up from the entrance of the
drain; close observation would have shown it to be constantly in-
creasing in size, until a human form rose from the ditch, and the
pent up waters flowed with gurgling happy roar through their
wonted channel.

The figure moved with the utmost caution, startled by
every unusual sound, until a feeble, faint moan struck upon its
ears from the direction of the bank before named. Frequent repe-
tition banished all hesitancy, and the figure moved noiselessly
toward the spot, and was soon engaged in moving Joe from a
perfect shower bath—the water from the field above having
passed over him from the commencement of the storm.

Sam, for it was our intelligent contraband, who emerged
from the drain—having sought its security at the commencement of the skirmish—was soon in close consultation with Joe.
The cool reviving rain had probably saved the life of the latter,
though he was entirely prostrate from his wound. After shield-
ing him with some brush, and wrapping his own coat about the
racked and bleeding form, Sam started on his mission. His master was about one mile from the crossroads on the left, and the
rebel cavalry picket was about one fourth of a mile this side of it.
Perfectly familiar with the country, he came in behind the picket
post close enough to see that the guard was omitted; crawling
stealthily toward the out-buildings, he saw the glare of a fire
streaming from the corn crib. Approaching it from the rear, he
discovered through the logs of the building, a number of men
huddled together on some straw, and a guard standing at the
door; close to the door, on the inside of the building, two other
forms clad in rebel uniform, were sleeping soundly, after the excitement of the day. It took but a short time to solve this problem. The officer in command of the rebels had turned the pickets
into a guard, moving them back to these out-buildings, so as to
rest as many of his men as possible, thinking that his afternoon's
success, and the storm, would be all the protection that was

needed for the night. Here was a grand opportunity for strategy; crawling to the stables he found the horses of the rebel guard all harnessed. His purpose was to have obtained a horse to carry Joe toward his own line; but the close proximity of the out-buildings prevented this, feeling satisfied with his reconnoissance, he returned to report. After mature deliberation, he left Joe again, going this time over the road toward our line. Joe thought our picket line could not be more than a mile and one half from the cross roads. Sam traveled through the Virginia mud at a fearful rate, until the peculiar rattle of a rifle, and a command to halt, sent its thrilling tremor all over him.

He had not traversed half the distance indicated by Joe, when he reached our line. A short conference with Captain— soon created a stir; ten picked men followed Sam, while a mounted orderly of the cavalry corps went post haste toward town for an ambulance. One hour and a half after this, at about two and one half A.M., our expedition returned, with all who had been captured the evening before, and three prisoners with their horses and equipments, Joe having been carried upon a stretcher made with two sticks and a blanket. The ambulance bore the sufferers to the division hospital, where they were soon in the midst of untold comforts. Joe saw upon the pillow case the letters, "U.S.S.C.," and could not avoid wondering and philosophizing about their meaning. "U.S." he knew stood for "Uncle Sam," had the other "S.C." got turned around? Did it not stand for "Confederate States"? Musing thus about the two, he fell into a troubled sleep.

"DIALOGUES": POLITICS AS THEATER

When the news of Abraham Lincoln's assassination reached Henry Wadsworth Longfellow's home in Cambridge, Massachusetts, his children were shocked. Their neighbor and classmate, Henrieta Dana, recalled years later that "we children were stunned with amazement and vague terror . . . that such a thing could ever happen in our civilized age, in our own free country, to our own good and dear President."[*] The children soon found a way to ease their pain by re-creating the tragedy, from Lincoln's entrance into the presidential box at Ford's Theater (the east veranda of Craigie House), to Booth's leap onto the stage below (the croquet lawn), and even the shooting of the assassin in the burning barn.

---

[*]Henrieta Channing Skinner, *An Echo From Parnassus* (New York: Sears, 1928), 175.

Henrieta and her friends were processing their grief, of course, but they were also taking part in a favorite midcentury pastime: amateur theatricals, which could be performed at school or at home and with or without costumes or audiences. For instance, the 1863 diary of a young New Yorker, Louis Gratacap, recorded spending numerous afternoons and evenings with friends, staging impromptu plays and burlesques for their own and their families' amusement. For those readers who preferred formal scripts, *The Student and Schoolmate* offered a new playlet—called a "dialogue"—almost every month, many relating to the war. Presented in two parts, "The Comedy of Secession" was a thinly veiled allegory of the secession crisis and the first year of the war, in which an unruly gang of girls— the Misses "Louisa Anna," "Caroline," "Flora Dee," and others—try to break up "Madam Columbia's" girls' school, the "Union Seminary." Some references may seem a little obscure to late-twentieth-century readers. For instance, in Act II the girls representing Massachusetts and Rhode Island struggle with Southern girls to keep Miss Mary Land in the Union Seminary, a reference to the troops from New England who helped hold Baltimore and Maryland for the Union in the spring of 1861. Miss K. Tucky (Kentucky) also displays serious reservations about secession, and her Northern friends call on her traditional moderation and willingness to compromise in convincing her to remain in school. Even Great Britain is represented. As "a neutral old lady," she tries to keep both sides happy. But avid subscribers to wartime children's magazines would have easily recognized the politicians and generals mentioned, appreciated the numerous puns, and understood the historical allusions, diplomatic references, and constitutional arguments that had long dominated headlines, pulpits, and parlors.

"The Comedy of Secession"
The Student and Schoolmate 11 (August and September 1862), 279–83, 314–19

MADAM COLUMBIA, *Principal of the Union Seminary.*

MADAM BRITANNIA, *a neutral old Lady, fond of giving advice.*

MADAM LA RUSSE, *a conservative old Lady.*

LA BELLE FRANCE, *fascinating, but cautious.*

GODDESS OF LIBERTY, *a popular belle.*

PUPILS OF THE UNION SEMINARY.

MISS CAROLINE, MISS GEORGIANA, MISS FLORA DEE, MISS LOUISA ANNA, MISS ALIE BALMY, MISS VIRGINIA, MISS MARY LAND, MISS K. TUCKY, MISS SUE WYRE, MISS TENNIE C., MISS MAINE, MISS N. HAMPSHIRE, MISS VERMONT, MISS MASSACHUSETTS, LITTLE RHODY, MISS CONNECTICUT, MISS N. YORK, MISS PENN, MISS OHIO, MISS INDIANA, MISS ILLINOIS, et al.

ACT I

Madam Columbia.: This is disgraceful! For eighty-six years this has been one of the most prosperous and quiet Seminaries in the world. Now we are all in confusion. Half a dozen of the young ladies have become exceedingly rebellious, and threaten to leave—secede, they call it—without reason or justice, and contrary to the wishes of their fathers and mothers. Half a dozen more of them are sulky and impertinent, and I don't know whether they will stand by the rules of the school or join the malcontents. They give me a world of trouble, but I intend to make them behave themselves.

(Enter Caroline, singing "Dixie.")

Caroline.: Well, madam, I have come to say good-by—to bid you a solemn farewell.

Mad. C.: Indeed! And pray where are you going?

Car.: I am going to leave the Union Seminary; I suppose it is none of your business how or where I am going.

Mad. C.: I think it is, Miss Caroline, and I think you will find before you proceed much farther, that the old Union Seminary has the will and the power to enforce obedience.

Car.: I don't care a straw for the Union Seminary! Let me add that I dislike the name and place altogether.

Mad. C.: Caroline, I am ashamed of you, and you ought to be ashamed of yourself. You have disgraced your ancestors.

Car.:   Indeed, madam, this is very strong language.

Mad. C.:   What would your highly respectable progenitors, the Sumters, the Marions, the Pinkneys, say, if they could step out of their honored graves, and behold the infamy of their darling child?

Car.:   Infamy, madam?

Mad. C.:   Certainly, Caroline; we can call it by no milder name than infamy. Haven't you trampled upon my flower beds, broken into my storehouses, and even robbed my chicken coops?

Car.:   Madam, these things belonged to me as much as to you.

Mad. C.:   They were the property of the Union Seminary—an Institution founded for the education and progress of future generations as well as the present. Here come your companions in infamy.

(Enter Flora Dee, Louisa Anna, Alie Balmy, and Georgiana.)

Car.:   You are insulting, Madam Columbia. You treat me and my companions like children—as though we had no rights, and were of no account whatever.

Mad. C.:   As pupils in the Union Seminary, with someone to take care of you, no doubt you are very respectable persons; but as wandering stars, as vagrants and poachers on the manor of your Uncle Sam, you will become a nuisance to yourself and everybody else.

Geor.:   I think we are abundantly able to take care of ourselves.

Mad. C.:   You have broken into your Uncle's storehouses, stolen his gold and his hardware, Georgiana. This is not the way to get along.

Geor.:   O, we will pay for all we have taken.

Mad. C.:   Pay for it! Can the chicken thief compound his felony by paying for the fowls he stole?

Flora.:   We have been foully wronged! The chickens belonged to us by right.

Mad. C.:   You impudent minx! How dare you make such an assertion! You are little better than a pauper, Flora Dee. Who paid for the very ground you stand upon, but Uncle

Sam? Who has poured out money like water to protect and defend you? Who bought off and drove off the insatiate savage when he prowled at midnight round the couch on which you slept? For shame, Flora Dee! to treat your friends with such black ingratitude.

Lou.:   Madam, you take advantage of Flora's good nature to impose upon her.

Mad. C.:   No doubt she is a very good natured thief, a lovely and amiable rebel! I do not wonder that you sympathize with her, for birds of a feather flock together. All I have said of her, and more, is true of you.

Lou.:   Will you be kind enough to remember that I have done more for this Seminary than any other individual.

Mad. C.:   You did very well while you behaved yourself like a lady. Let me ask you to remember that this Institution has done more for you than for any half dozen of its pupils.

Alie.:   Now, I should like to ask what fault you have to find with any of us. We are dissatisfied, and intend to leave—in short to secede. What objection can you reasonably offer to such a course?

Mad. C.:   Your fathers placed you in the Union Seminary, with the understanding that you were to remain here. They placed you in charge of Uncle Sam, the Chairman of the Trustees of this Institution. The old gentleman has taken excellent care of you, watched over your interests and your progress with untiring zeal. He has humored, petted, indulged you, even beyond what a wise and prudent guardian should do.

Alie.:   He is a grim, obsolete old fogy!

Lou.:   A tyrant and an oppressor!

Car.:   An abominable old wretch!

Geor.:   A fossilized humbug!

Flora.:   The conglomerated effervescence of superannuated stupidity!

Mad. C.:   This abuse I might well expect from you after such an exhibition of base ingratitude.

Lou.: Really, madam, I can't see that you have the slightest cause to complain. We merely intend to establish another Institution, to be called the Confederate Seminary.

Mad. C: And, pray, where do you intend to locate it?

Lou.: O, just south of here.

Mad. C.: Yes; and upon lands belonging to the trustees of this Seminary. Do you really think that Uncle Sam will permit you to establish a rival institution upon his grounds?

Geor.: I don't see that he can help himself. We have prepared our plans, and intend to put them in execution immediately.

Flora.: We shall open the new establishment at once, and have Jeff. Davis for Principal.

Lou.: And Beauregard* for dancing master.

Alie.: And Cobb† for treasurer.

Car.: "Still so gently o'er me stealing"—and Floyd†† for chief Purveyor.

Geor.: And Prof. Maury§ for entomologist. He knows all about the bug.

Car.: What bug?

Geor.: Humbug!

---

*Gen. Pierre G. T. Beauregard, who directed the bombardment of Fort Sumter, was field commander of the victorious rebels at the first Battle of Bull Run and in 1862 commanded Confederate troops in Mississippi.

---

†Howell Cobb, former speaker of the U.S. House of Representatives, governor of Georgia, and secretary of the treasury, who, after President Abraham Lincoln's election, urged Georgians to secede and who later became a Confederate general.

---

††John Floyd, a Virginia politician, was secretary of war during the four years preceding the secession of the South. He was believed by Northerners to have transferred munitions and supplies—in his capacity as head of the War Department—to Southern forts and facilities just before the secession crisis. The property then fell into the hands of Confederates when they captured the forts, thereby supplying some Southern military units.

---

§Matthew Fontaine Maury won fame as a pioneering meteorologist and oceanographer for the U.S. Navy in the 1840s and 1850s; he became a Confederate naval officer when the war began.

Flora.: And Wigfall* for Chaplain.

Lou.: And Wise†—let me see—what shall we do with Wise?

Alie.: We will invent an office for him. We will make him Bragmaster-General.

Mad. C.: All this is very fine. The treacherous rascals whom you mention have left my service; and I shall no longer permit them to prowl about my manor. As for you, young ladies, if you do not at once return to your duty, and obey the rules of this Institution, I shall direct Mr. Lincoln to bring you to a realizing sense of your obligations to this establishment.

Car.: But, madam, we have seceded. We have nothing more to do with you, or you with us.

Mad. C.: Let me assure you that you are making a mistake—a tremendous blunder. There is no such word as Secession in the vocabulary of the Union Seminary. Your infamous plot shall be foiled, and you shall be punished for your folly and wickedness. *(Exit.)*

Geor.: The old lady is as spunky as a cat that has lost her kittens.

Flora.: Never mind her; she is of no account.

Lou.: But it will be well to proceed carefully, for you know Uncle Sam is a stout and rugged old fellow.

Alie.: Nonsense! He would be as powerless as a spring chicken in a northeast gale.

Car.: Certainly he will. Everybody will sympathize with us. Besides we have strong friends on the other side of the ocean. That stiff old lady, Madam Britannia, and sweet, smiling La Belle France will espouse our cause, and patronize the new Seminary to the utmost of their ability.

Geor.: But there are only a half dozen, or so, of us. What will the rest of the pupils in the institution do?

Flora.: Do? They will go with us, of course—at least, a majority of them will.

———

*Louis T. Wigfall, the fire-eating Confederate and U.S. senator from Texas.

———

†Henry Wise, a Virginia congressman and governor, became an unsuccessful Confederate general. He was an inveterate optimist who was an enthusiastic and vocal supporter of slavery and states' rights.

Geor.:   Perhaps not.

Lou.:   We mustn't get into a scrape that we can't get out of. There are those six New England Yankee girls—I am sure they will stand by Uncle Sam.

Alie.:   I hope they will; I am sure we don't want them.

Car.:   No; we will leave them out in the cold. Nearly all the rest of the ladies will join us.

Flora.:   Let me see: we may certainly depend upon Mademoiselles Virginia, Mary Land, Miss K. Tuckie, and Miss Sue Wrye and Miss Tennie.

Geor.:   To be sure. They will go with us. They may need a little coaxing.

Alie.:   But we must do something besides talk.—Ah, there comes a young lady who has always been exceedingly popular in this establishment. We must persuade her to go with us—I mean the lady whose portrait is on the coin—generally called the Goddess of Liberty.

Car.:   She is an arrant humbug!

Geor.:   We don't want her!

Flora.:   Certainly not; she doesn't know the differences between a tinker and a nabob; between a magnate and a mudsill.

Lou.:   Hush! Hush! Are you mad? Don't you see that we must conciliate this popular demoiselle? She is very pretty, and the masses worship her. We must use her to win over our doubtful sisters.

Alie.:   Well, Caroline, we will leave her with you, while the rest of us attend to other matters.

(Exit all but Caroline.)

Act II:

Car.:   Goddess of Liberty! It's a very pretty name, and I suppose we must keep on the right side of her.

(Enter Goddess of Liberty.)

Car.:   I can hardly stoop to conciliate this fascinating belle, but I suppose I must, and I will try. Mademoiselle, I am your very obedient, humble servant. *(Bows low.)*

Lib.:   No, you are not.

Car.:   I assure you of my entire devotion.

Lib.:   You are a hypocrite.

Car.:   Nay, you don't understand me. We are going to establish a new institution to be called the Confederate Seminary, just south of here, and we very much desire your presence and your influence.

Lib.:   Do you, indeed? You are very gracious, and condescending to honor me with your patronage.

Car.:   You do not comprehend. We wish to have you with us as one of the family.

Lib.:   In other words, you wish me to become a cat's paw to enable you to delude weak and unsuspecting people into the support of your new establishment. May I inquire why you propose to leave the Union Seminary?

Car.:   Because our rights have been trampled upon.

Lib.:   Nonsense! You mean if you cannot be the greatest toad in the puddle, you will set the river on fire, if you can.

Car.:   You misjudge me.

Lib.:   You know me well, Caroline; you know that I never trifle with my friends. You are a hypocrite! Uncle Sam has done everything he can to make the Union Seminary a pleasant and profitable place for you. He has supported and defended you, and given you every privilege you could possibly desire.

Car.:   You are mistaken. What do you think of that rail-splitting clodhopper, who has just been made Steward over us?

Lib.:   He is one of my friends—an honest and a true man. He will respect all your rights.

Car.:   But we will not remain under his administration.

Lib.:   Won't you, indeed? Perhaps the Steward will compel you to remain.

Car.:   Ha, ha, ha! That is very good! I should like to see him do it.

Lib.:   Probably you will have that pleasure before long. You forget that nearly all the members of the Institution will stand by their Alma Mater—the glorious old Union—

Miss Caroline, some eighty odd years ago, some of my friends—your ancestors were among them—adopted a certain device, which is commonly called the Star Spangled Banner. Here it is. *(Displays the flag.)* When the old Union is in danger, it is only necessary to point to *this*, and all except your miserable faction, will rush to its support.

Car.: I think not. Here are several who will do nothing of the kind.

*(Enter Virginia, Mary Land, Miss K. Tuckie,
Miss Tennie C, and Miss Sue Wrye.)*

Car.: Of course you will go with us into the Confederate Seminary, Virginia?

Vir.: Well, I don't know. I have a great many doubts.

Lib.: And well she may have. Shame, for even having a doubt. Virginia, can you be false to the memory of Washington, your truest and best friend, one of the revered founders of the old Union?

Vir.: Well, the truth is, my friends are all going, and I can't very well help it.

Mary.: If Virginia goes, I suppose I must go too.

Lib.: Shame, Mary Land!

(Enter Mass. and Little Rhody.)

Mary.: I must go.

Mass.: No, you shall not!

Little R.: Not if I can help it!

Car.: But you can't help it. *(Seizes her by the arm, and is assisted by Virginia.)*

Mass.: We will try, at any rate. *(Takes Mary by the other arm.)*

Little R.: Don't let her go. *(Assists Mass. They pull in opposite directions.)*

Mary.: O dear! Let go of me! You will pull me all to pieces! You will kill me! *(Caroline and Virginia release her.)*

Car.: But you will come with us, Miss Sue Wrye?

Sue.:   Well, I want to go, and I don't want to go.

    (*Enter Indiana, Illinois, and Iowa.*)

Vir.:   O, come! Come over! Your friends are all with us.

Ind.:   No, they are not, and you can't go. No Price can buy you. (*The struggle is repeated, and Indiana triumphs.*)

Vir.:   You will certainly join us, Miss K. Tuckie.

K.T.:   Yes, I think I will. (*Walks over.*)

Car.:   Bravo! Kate. I honor, respect, and love you!

Vir.:   Just what we might have expected of Kate—noble, generous, and true hearted.

K.T.:   On second thought, I guess I won't go over. (*Walks back.*)

Lib.:   Just what I might have expected of Kate—noble, generous, and true hearted. Thy friends, Kate, thy Clay, thy Crittenden, all thy noble ones, were my friends. They were always true to this. (*Pointing to the flag.*)

K.T.:   So am I. Breckinridge may go to grass!*

Vir.:   Ah, Miss Tennie, there can be no doubt about you.

Ten.:   I always liked the old Union, but I suppose it is of no use for me to stop here any longer. (*Crosses over.*)

Lib.:   For shame, Tennie!

    Amid the din of coming battle,
    Old Jackson's bones will surely rattle!

---

*The home state of "The Great Compromiser," Henry Clay, and of John J. Crittenden, who offered a last-ditch compromise in the U.S. Senate to prevent war in late 1860, Kentucky was perhaps the most famously divided state in the country. Although it never seceded from the Union, it tried to remain neutral during the first few months of the war. However, both Union and Confederate armies soon invaded, and the battle for this crucial state lasted nearly two years. About one-fourth of the 100,000 Kentuckians who fought in the war served the Confederacy, including John C. Breckinridge, who as vice president of the United States in 1860 ran as the presidential candidate of the Southern Democrats, whose platform threatened that the South would secede if Lincoln was elected president. In the fall of 1861, he left the Senate to serve as a Confederate general.

How dare you, while thus sinking down low,
Confront the curse of Parson Brownlow?*

(Exeunt all but Lib. and Car.)

Car.:   Perhaps, my sweet friend, you will yet conclude to go with us.

Lib.:   Never! Where this stays *(Points up to the flag.)* I shall stay! When this goes down, I shall go down with it! *(Exit.)*

Car.:   Don't be rash. Ah, here come some of our foreign friends.

(Enter Mad. Britannia.)

Madam Britannia, I am delighted to see you. Of course you intend to sustain the new movement?

Mad. B.:   My sympathies are with you, but you see there is a little difficulty in the way. I have just been talking over the matter with Madam Columbia, and for decency's sake, I promised to be neutral.

(Enter Georgiana.)

Car.:   Neutral.

Geor.:   Why, that is worse than nothing.

Mad. B.:   Why no, my child; my sympathies are with you, and I can help you a great deal. But we must be very cautious. You see I have certain business relations with Madam Columbia, which might be disturbed by an open rupture.

Geor.:   And you have certain business relations with us which may be disturbed if you don't go with us.

Car.:   No shuffling, old lady.

Mad. B.:   Hush! I will help you to the utmost of my ability. Hush—sh! Here comes Madam Columbia, and we must be very careful.

---

*Andrew Jackson, a loyal Southerner and Tennesseean, had nevertheless pushed the Union to the brink of civil war during the Nullification Controversy of 1831 when he threatened to use the army to force South Carolina to back away from its nullification of a federal tariff. The Rev. William Brownlow was a Tennessee Unionist who published a book about the persecution of Southern Unionists during the war and afterward served as governor of Tennessee.

(Enter Madam Columbia.)

(To Mad. C.:) Madam, I am glad to meet you now, as I always am. I sincerely regret that you are involved in this trouble. *(To Geor.:)* Certainly, I'll help you. *(To Mad. C.:)* But you have my sympathies, Madam Columbia. *(To Geor.:)* My heart is with you in this new movement, and as soon as I can decently do so, I will acknowledge the new Seminary. *(To Mad. C.:)* And I trust, Madam Columbia, that you will be able to put down this infamous rebellion. *(To Geor.:)* And if you want provisions, cutlery, hardware, I will send them to you; but we must be very cautious. *(To Mad. C.:)* Yes, Madam Columbia, I hope you will be able to put down this infamous rebellion. *(To Geor.:)* You may depend upon me for all the assistance in my power, but for the present, I must remain neutral.

Mad. C.:   You seem to manifest your neutrality in the most extraordinary manner. You have been sending every comfort to the insurgents.

Mad. B.:   Madam, you are disposed to find fault, and to be quarrelsome. Madam, I protest against your course. Why do you wish to oppress these poor children, flesh of your flesh, and bone of your bone? Let them go, if they wish. Why will you attempt to subjugate them?

Mad. C.:   Because they are rebels and traitors. Why do you put down a rebellion in the Indian, Canadian, or Irish branches of your establishment? I think madam, that you had better mind your own business.

Mad. B.:   This isn't the first time you have insulted me, madam. I demand satisfaction! If you don't apologize, I will pull the house down over your head! I will break down the doors of the apartments, which you have fastened upon these young ladies, and let them out, and let in all the world. *(To Geor.)* What do you think of that?

Geor.:   Very good. Pray, quarrel with the old lady if you can.

Mad. B.:   *(To Mad. C.)* I will pull the house down over your head; and my friend La Belle France will assist me.

(Enter La Belle France.)

La B.:   Pardonnez-moi, madame. Shall I put my fingaire in ze fire? No! I will mind my own beeseness—s'il vous plait.

Ze traitaire, ze rebelleong—vat zis you call him?—trouble me vaire much. But shall I put my fingaire in ze fire? No, Madame. J'en suis tres fachee.

(Enter La Russe.)

La Russe: Madam Columbia, you have my sympathies. When I have a rebellion in my establishment, I always put it down, and I hope you will do the same. Do your duty to yourself and the world. I will sustain you for one.

Mad. B.: *(To Geor.)* Don't be alarmed; your cause is safe. I will get up a quarrel with the old lady. You are doing very well.

(Enter Louisa Anna.)

Lou.: Everything is going against us! They have got Miss Tennie back, and Sue and Mary and Kate are actually making faces at us.

(Enter Mass.)

Mass.: I have the pleasure of informing you, Miss Lou, that "Picayune Butler's come to town." He is stopping at the St. Charles, and has already proved that he can keep a hotel.*

Lou.: I was never so vexed in my life!

Mad. C.: Madam Britannia, you hear the news. My Steward is doing the work which I gave him to do.

Mad. B.: *(Obsequiously.)* Madam Columbia, I am your most obedient, humble servant. You know I always sympathized with you, and always hoped you would be able to put down this rebellion.

(Enter Maine.)

---

*Gen. Benjamin Butler, a politician turned general, who commanded Massachusetts troops when they were attacked by Baltimore civilians on their way to Washington, earned the hatred of Southerners with his tough administration of occupied New Orleans, and he first applied the status of "contraband of war" to slaves coming into Union lines. Butler was a better politician than a soldier and remained popular among many Northerners.

Maine: Madam, we have caught half a dozen of the naughty girls; and we have got a whole nest of them penned up in Miss Virginia's front parlor. McClellan* will unearth them very soon.

Lou.:   Things are against us—fiddle, faddle!
I think we might as well skedaddle.

(Exeunt all but loyal ladies.)

Mad. C.:   I am satisfied with the course of events, and I hope my children will all learn a lesson from what has transpired that will last them to the end of time. But it is time for school to begin. *(Rings the bell, and Liberty and the loyal ladies enter.)* Ah, Miss Tennie, I am glad to see you back again. I hope the whipping you have had has cured you of any desire to flirt with that abominable Jeff. Davis, Wigfall, and Toombs.[†]

K.T.:   Poor Jeff.! He has been jilted.

Mad. C.:   Don't you like him, Miss Tennie?

Miss T.:   Kinder! *(Bites her thumb.)*

Little R.:   As for Wigfall—it will be more than a wig fall; head and all will fall with the wig.

Maine: And Toombs—"Hark from the Toombs, a doleful sound!"

Mass.:   I beg your pardon, Madam, but can you tell me why this rebellion is like a boot?

Mad. C.:   I cannot.

Mass.:   Because we put our Foote into it.[††]

Little R.:   Very true; but why is General Floyd like a butcher?

---

*Gen. George B. McClellan, lionized by his troops and by large segments of the public, was the commanding general of the Union Army from the fall of 1861 through the summer of 1862. His caution cost him a major victory in the 1862 Peninsular Campaign.

[†]Robert Toombs, a Georgia congressman and senator, resigned from the Senate in early 1861 to organize the secession movement. Failing to become president of the Confederacy, he served briefly as Confederate secretary of state and as a general until 1863.

[††]Capt. Andrew Hull Foote was the well-known commander of the U.S. Navy forces on the Upper Mississippi that helped capture Forts Henry and Donelson in the spring of 1862. Wounded in the Fort Donelson engagement, he was relieved of duty and promoted to rear admiral.

Maine: Like a tallow candle, you mean—because he runs away.

Little R.:   No; because he steels his knife before he uses it.

Mad. C.:   Fie! Fie! children. Punning is a vicious habit. Now let us sing our morning song, and attend to our duties.

          (They sing the Star Spangled Banner.)

PUBLIC PATRIOTISM

Civil War-era schoolchildren commonly had to devote part of a class day every week or two to delivering "declamation" pieces, and during the crisis students of all ages regularly recited verse or essays on war themes. On "speaking day," Gerald Norcross and his Boston classmates delivered compositions such as "War Sometimes a Duty" and "Who Says We Have Failed?" in addition to well-known poems such as the stirring "Barbara Frietchie" and "Sheridan's Ride," or the tear-jerker "Home News

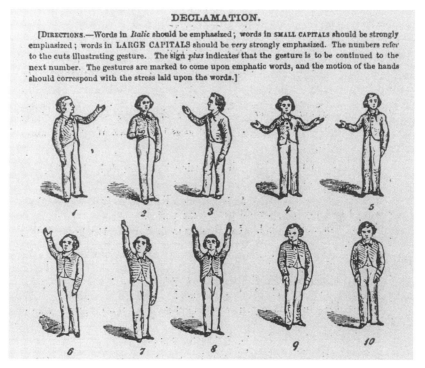

DECLAMATION.

[DIRECTIONS.—Words in *Italic* should be emphasized; words in SMALL CAPITALS should be strongly emphasized; words in LARGE CAPITALS should be *very* strongly emphasized. The numbers refer to the cuts illustrating gesture. The sign *plus* indicates that the gesture is to be continued to the next number. The gestures are marked to come upon emphatic words, and the motion of the hands should correspond with the stress laid upon the words.]

A diagram of appropriate gestures to make while reciting the declamation pieces published every month in The Student and Schoolmate.

in Battle-Time." Although they were no doubt intended to bolster the patriotism of the performers and their audience, it did not always work out that way, at least according to a rather smug young Bostonian named Charles Stratton. On a June day in 1862, he and the other boys at the Boston Public Latin School had to take part in a declamatory exercise. By the time the last speaker closed with "Glory, Glory, Hallelujah," Charles wrote in his diary that the "old worn-out pieces" recited half-heartedly by the young men had reduced the entire class to laughter.*

Such disrespect would have shocked Oliver Optic, who included a deadly serious, uplifting declamation in every issue of his magazine. Obviously intending that readers memorize and perform these pieces, Optic included a chart with ten numbered gestures. Whenever the speaker came to a number in the text, he was to take the pose corresponding to that number on the chart. The offerings ranged from poems to excerpts, from speeches to satiric verses. Some are still famous; others are more obscure, although their authors are not. "We Are Coming, Father Abraham, Three Hundred Thousand More" is a patriotic song announcing the nation's support for President Lincoln's 1862 call for troops, while the more forgettable "Battle Autumn of 1862" is noted mainly because it was written by John Greenleaf Whittier. A small portion of Edward Everett's mammoth oration at Gettysburg also appeared. It included a haunting reference to the possibility that farmers would be turning up the "fearful missiles of modern artillery" in their fields for years afterward. Probably unknown to Everett, by the fall of 1863 at least two local boys had already been killed by shells that had exploded when they tried to salvage the powder inside.

"Three Hundred Thousand More"
The Student and Schoolmate 11 (September 1862), 312–13

We are[2] coming, Father Abraham, three hundred thousand more,
From[3] Mississippi's winding stream and from[1] New England's shore;
We leave our plows and workshops, our wives and children dear,
With hearts too full for utterance, with but a silent tear;
We dare not look[5] behind us, but steadfastly[2] before—
We are coming, Father Abraham—*three hundred thousand more!*

---

*Charles Stratton, "Extracts from the Diary of a Member of the Graduating Class of the Boston Public Latin School," pp. 14–15, Department of Rare Books and Manuscripts, Boston Public Library, Boston, Mass.

If you look across the hilltops that meet the *northern* sky,
Long moving *lines* of rising dust your vision may descry;
And now the wind, an instant, tears the cloudy veil aside,
And floats[8] *aloft* our spangled *flag* in *glory* and in *pride*;
And[3] *bayonets* in the sunlight gleam—and bands brave *music* pour—
We are[4] *coming*, Father Abraham—*three hundred thousand* more!

If you look up all our *valleys*, where the growing *harvests* shine,
You may see our sturdy *farmers* fast forming into line;
And *children* from their mother's knees are pulling at the weeds,
And learning how to *reap* and *sow*, against their country's needs;
And a farewell group stands[5] weeping at every cottage door—
We are[4] *coming*, Father Abraham—*three hundred thousand more!*

You have called us, and we're[2] coming, by *Richmond's* bloody tide
To lay us down for[4] *Freedom's* sake, our *brother's* bones beside;
Or from foul[6] *treason's* savage grasp to *wrench* the murderous blade,
And in the face of *foreign* foes its fragments to parade.
Six hundred thousand loyal men and *true* have gone before—
We are[4] coming, Father Abraham—*three hundred thousand*[4] more!

—*N.Y. Evening Post.*

"The Battle Autumn of 1862"
John Greenleaf Whittier
The Student and Schoolmate 11 (November 1862), 388–89

The flags of[5] *war* like storm-birds fly,
The charging *trumpets* blow;
Yet rolls no[7] *thunder* in the sky,
No[9] *earthquake* strives below.

And *calm* and *patient*, *Nature* keeps
Her ancient promise well,
Though o'er her *bloom*[5] and[3] *greenness* sweeps
The *battle's* breath of hell.

And still she walks in golden hours
Through *harvest-happy* farms,
And still she wears her[4] fruits and[4] flowers
Like jewels on her arms.

What mean the[2] *gladness of the plain*,
This[2] *joy* of eve and morn,
The[2] *mirth* that shakes the beard of grain
And yellow locks of corn?

Ah! eyes may well be full of *tears*,
    and hearts with[5] *hate* are hot;
But even-paced come round the years
    And *Nature* changes not.

She meets with[4] *smiles* our bitter grief,
    With[5] *songs* our groans of pain;
She mocks with tint of *flower* and *leaf*
    The[3] *war-field's* crimson stain.

Still, in the *cannon's* pause, we hear
    Her sweet thanksgiving *psalm*;
Too near to God for[5] *doubt* or[5] *fear*,
    She shares the eternal *calm*.

She knows the[9] *seed* lies safe below
    The fires that blast and burn;
For all the tears of blood we *sow*
    She waits the rich *return*.

She sees with clearer eyes than ours
    The[4] *good* of[4] *suffering* born,—
The hearts that *blossom* like her flowers
    And *ripen* like her corn.

Oh, give to us, in times like these,
    The *vision* of *her* eyes;
And make her[3] *fields* and fruited *trees*
    Our golden *prophecies;*

Oh, give to us her finer *ear!*
    Above this stormy din,
We, too, would hear the bells of cheer
    Ring[4] *peace* and[4] *freedom* in!

"Extract from the Oration of Edward Everett, at Gettysburg"

The Student and Schoolmate 13 (March 1864), 88–89

And now, friends, fellow-citizens of Gettysburg and Pennsylvania, and you from remoter States, let me again invoke your[4] *benediction*, as we part, on these honored[10] *graves*. You feel, though the occasion is mournful, that it is *good* to be here. You feel that it was greatly *auspicious* for the cause of the country, that the men of the[1] *East* and the[3] *West*, the men of nineteen sister States, stood side by side on the perilous ridges of the battle. You now feel it a new bond of[4] *Union*, that they shall lie[9] *side* by *side* till a clarion *louder* than that which marshaled them to the *combat* shall awake their slumbers. God bless the[8] *Union*. It is *dearer* to us for the *blood* of those brave men shed in its defence. The[3] *spots* on which they stood and fell; these *pleasant* heights; the fertile[3] *plain* beneath them; the thriving *village* whose streets so lately rang with the strange din of war; the *fields* beyond the ridge, where the noble[6] *Reynolds** held the advancing foes at bay, and, while he gave up his own life, *assured* by his forethought and self-sacrifice the[4] *triumph* of the two succeeding days; the little[3] *streams* which wind through the hills, on whose banks, in after times, the wondering ploughman will turn up, with the rude weapons of savage warfare, *the fearful missiles of modern artillery; the Seminary ridge; the peach-orchard, Cemetery, Culp,* and *Wolf* Hill, *Round Top, little* Round Top, humble[5] *names,* henceforward dear and famous; no lapse of[1] *time,* no distance of[3] *space,* shall cause[4] *you* to be forgotten. "The whole[10] *earth,*" said Pericles, as he stood over the remains of his fellow citizens, who had fallen in the first year of the Peloponnesian War, "the whole[10] *earth* is the *sepulchre* of illustrious *men.*" All[4] *time,* he might have added, is the[4] *millennium* of their glory. Surely I would do no injustice to the other noble achievements of the war, which have reflected such *honor* on *both* arms of the service, and have entitled the[4] *armies* and the[4] *navy* of the United States—their *officers* and *men*—to the warmest *thanks* and the richest *rewards* which a grateful people can pay. But *they,* I am sure, will *join* us in saying, as we bid farewell to the *dust* of these[9] *martyr-heroes,* that[4] *wheresoever* throughout the civilized *world* the accounts of this great warfare are read, and down to the *latest* period of recorded time, in the glorious annals of our common country, there will be no[6] *brighter* page than that which relates to[4] THE BATTLE OF GETTYSBURG.

ACTING ON THEIR CONVICTIONS

Optic clearly believed that his editorializing and disseminating and inspiring would bear patriotic fruit. In a dialogue published in May 1863, a few months after the Confederates were finally driven out of Kentucky for the last time, he showed a company of Unionist boys acting on their patriotism by standing up to the prickly Confederate Gen. Braxton Bragg, whose men keep knocking down the boys' play forts. Kentucky was perhaps the most famously divided state in the Union; rejecting

---

*Maj. Gen. John F. Reynolds, commander of I Corps in the Army of the Potomac, was killed leading his men onto the battlefield at Gettysburg on July 1, 1863.

extremists in both the North and the South, the state tried to remain neutral when the war began. Ninety thousand Kentuckians served in the Union army, but Southern sympathies were strong enough to inspire the formation of a "Confederate" government for Kentucky, and thousands of men also enlisted in the Confederate army. Few Northern children had the chance to express their loyalty as dramatically as the "Union Boys in Kentucky," yet it is not hard to imagine the tens of thousands of boys who had formed their own companies (see Chapter Three) dreaming of winning just such a confrontation with real-live Rebels with the same combination of style and pluck.

"Union Boys in Kentucky"
The Student and Schoolmate 12 (May 1863), 151–56

CHARACTERS—GENERAL BRAGG; SENTINEL; JAMES KENNEDY; LESLIE; STEPHEN; EUGENE; JOSEPH; CHARLES; ARTHUR; EDWIN; COUSIN PETER; JOHNNIE; GEORGIE; WALTER.

SCENE I.—*A play-ground—Crowd of Boys.*

(*Enter James.*) Here it is again, boys; our forts are all destroyed, after our hard day's work yesterday. This makes the third time. No more fun for us as long as this war lasts.

Leslie: Well, the rebel soldiers are *scoundrels,*—that is what they are!

Stephen: I should like to know if there is anything which they haven't done to torment us?

Eugene: For my part, I wish I didn't live in Kentucky. I'd just like to turn into a bold Robin Hood, and get over the river, and live in the Ohio woods until peace is declared. What do you say, boys?

Joseph: I wish we were not boys. If I were big enough to carry a sword and a gun, I would drive them out of the land faster than neighbor Dobson's dog ever went out of his father's store.

James: And what if we are boys? I for one have no mind to bear this treatment any longer.

All: Good, James; right! right! (*Enter Charles.*)

Charles: Such persecutions! If we boys don't get insults enough from the rebels, then I would like to know who does. I am sick of the sight of a soldier, and the name of one, too.

All: What now?

Charles: Why, our two sail-boats are all cut to pieces, and the fence round our new play-ground is taken for fire-wood. I feel mad enough to drink the Ohio river up.

Joseph: Pray, don't do that!

Edwin: There is no end to their robberies.

(Enter Peter, out of breath.)

Eugene: What is the matter, Peter?

Peter: Matter enough I should think. Those pesky soldiers have taken down our tent and lugged it off with them, and the flag on top of it, they have cut up so fine you can't find a whole star. I found it in the duck-pond.

James: Well, I won't bear it any longer. Let us assert our rights, and get up a rebellion! If I could have my way, I would drive every soldier out of the city.

Leslie: That would be a glorious thing, if we could do it.

Arthur: We can do it. Didn't you ever hear how Napoleon with only a handful of men used to capture cities, and even great nations?

Charles: But we have not even a handful of men.

Arthur: True; but we have boys enough and they will do just as well.

Edwin: They won't dare shoot guns and pistols at us.

Eugene: I am sure, I wish it could be done.

Charles: *(with much spirit.)* Let us rebel, then!

Arthur: Who will join in the rebellion?

James: I will, with all my heart, I am ready.

Charles: Then you shall be our Napoleon, our generalissimo.

All: He shall! He shall!

James: Well, then boys, who is ready to strike a blow for freedom?

All:	I will! I will!
Joseph:	"O, Liberty! thine hour is come."

(*Enter Johnny.*)

Johnny:	Make way for liberty!
Arnie:	Freedom forever!

(*Georgie running in.*)

Georgie:	I am with you, too. Hooray!
Peter:	I have got patriotism enough for you!
Charles:	Then let us rouse the city, and assert our rights at once.
Stephen:	I don't believe we can drive the soldiers out of the city.
Eugene:	You take counsel of your fears rather than your hopes, Lieut. Woodbury.
James:	"Who would be free, themselves must strike the blow!"
Charles:	"Strike, till the last armed foe expires!"
Eugene:	"Strike, for your altars and your fires,"—and shout, "Long live America!"
Leslie:	Peace, boys! Order, order! Now Gen. Kennedy, how are we going to assert our rights?
James:	I will tell you. We must first organize a company, then form a line of march, and with drum and fife and colors, wait upon Gen. Bragg at his tent, and tell him we will not be insulted by his soldiers or any other rebel soldiers.
All:	Hurra! Hurra! Hurra!
James:	We will now proceed to the play-ground, and train awhile; for a great deal, you know, depends upon our appearance.
All:	Hurra! Hurra! Hurra!

(*Exeunt,—A short pause and then without.*)

Hurra! Hurra!

SCENE II.—*Play-ground; boys dressed in uniform; ten minutes allowed for training and marching with fife and drum under Gen. Kennedy's orders.*

James: Well, boys, I think my company is presentable; we will now proceed to the general's headquarters. Forward, march! [*March off the stage.*]

SCENE III.—*Gen. Bragg's headquarters; A sentinel pacing to and fro with a musket over his shoulder—noise of drum and fife at a distance.*

Sentinel: What in the name of wonder can that be? Are they up in arms again in this rascally town? A troop of boys as I live! Stars and stripes, too! O, the land is full of rebellion. It is full of it, and running over.

(The boys halt in front of the tent, and James approaches the sentinel, with the standard in hand.)

James: Is Gen. Bragg at home?

Sent.: Who are you?

James: We are Kentucky boys, sir.

Sent.: And what do you want here?

James: We come for our rights; and we wish to speak to the Confederate general.

Sent.: The Confederate general has better business than listening to a parcel of good-for-nothing boys like you. I shall do none of your messages.

James: As you please, sir; but here we wait until we see Gen. Bragg: We will see him; and he shall do us justice.

All: Hurra! Hurra! Hurra!

Sent.: That you little rascals would be to hang you, and your cowardly countrymen. Such a fuss, and by a parcel of boys, too!

All: Cowards, do you call us! Say it again, if you dare!

(General Bragg and one of his Aides step out.)

Gen. Bragg: What is the matter here? Why this disturbance?

James: Gen. Bragg, we come to complain of the insults and outrages of your soldiers. They ruin our forts, destroy our playgrounds, and do everything else that is mean. We have spoken more than once to no purpose, and now we have come to say, that we cannot, and we will not endure it any longer.

Gen. Bragg: (*Aside*.) Good Heavens! liberty is in the very air, and the boys breathe it. (*To the boys*.) Go, my brave lads; you have the word of Gen. Bragg that your sports shall not be disturbed again without punishment to the offender. Does that satisfy you?

James: Yes, Gen. Bragg; and in the name of my company, I present you thanks.

Gen. Bragg: No thanks; you are brave boys; I see plainly you are Confederate boys.

All: No, sir; Union boys—Union boys—Union boys, sir. Hurra! Hurra!

(The drum strikes up and the little band march off with flying colors.)

SCENE IV.—*Boys assembled on the Play-ground.*

(Enter Leslie, waving his cap.) Three cheers for company A!

(Enter Eugene.)

Eugene: My congratulations to the soldiers of said company in general, and to you, Gen. Kennedy, in particular.

Edwin: Didn't we have a nice time though, boys?

Johnnie: Our success was complete; our triumph is sure.

Joseph: Our rebellion is to some purpose.

Walter: Who would have thought of that big general being so polite to us, boys?

(Enter Charles and Arthur singing.)—

"Yankee-doodle came to town
Riding on a pony,
Stuck a feather in his cap,
And called it Macaroni."

Charles: Boys, I think we may venture on new exploits to-day.

Arthur: I, for one, feel as if I had risen in importance; no more Latin grammars for me, so long as such a field of action lies before me.

Arnie: What are you reading for? How stupid you are! Why don't you wake up to a realizing sense of this great occasion? You haven't a bit of patriotic blood in your veins!

Leslie:	*(Jumping up.)* Haven't I though? Didn't my grandfather's uncle's brother's first cousin fight in the battle of Bunker Hill, and kill the Duke of Wellington, after he had defeated the Russians in the battle of Cerro Gordo?
Arnie:	You must be crazy.
Johnnie:	Our victory must have unsettled his mind.

(Enter Peter.)

Peter:	*(Capers about the stage and sings.)* Teu-ral-leu-ral-leu.
Charles:	What ails you, Peter? What in the world is the matter with you? Have the rebels surrendered?
Peter:	Not quite, but I don't think I shall leave for New Hampshire until they do, though; the news this morning makes a fellow feel happy; for I hear that the rebels think this place is getting too hot to hold them, and they are getting ready for a move. They mean to be off directly, I am pretty sartain.
Walter:	Hurra! That is good news.
Johnnie:	It is all owing to our courageous attack on the general.
Edwin:	Let us run up a new flag-staff immediately.
Georgie:	*(Swinging his cap.)* I am ready for anything.
Stephen:	There is nothing like bravery.
Eugene:	"Where there is a will, there's a way."
Arthur:	Boys, we have asserted our rights, let us maintain them.
Charles:	Boys, depend upon it, we are destined to go forth "conquering and to conquer"; depend upon it.
George:	Depend upon it!
Charles:	Liberty will soon be restored to the Union.
All:	Go on! Go on! A speech from Col. Tufts.

(Eugene runs for a box, which Charles mounts.)

Charles:	A great triumph has been achieved; victory has perched upon our banners. Ladies and gentlemen, "we have met the enemy and they are ours"; and I now announce to you, that our rebellion has been entirely successful. The soldiers have been driven from the city, and the star of

Young America is in the ascendant. We have purchased our Independence, and slavery, and tyranny, and *oppression* are abolished; and, once more I say to you, that Young America is FREE.

Eugene: Hush! Here comes our commander-in-chief,—the brave Major-General Kennedy.

Charles: (*Bowing.*) Honor to the brave Gen. Kennedy! You are welcome.

All: (*Taking off their caps.*) You are welcome.

James: Company A; fall into ranks!

SCENE V.—*Four or five officers stand facing the line of soldiers.*

Officers (lifting their swords)—
Arm, arm for the battle—invasion has come—
His shadow has darkened our soil.

Soldiers—
We are ready—all ready—our swords shall strike home
Ere the rebel has gathered his spoil.

Officers—
Arm—arm for the battle—'tis liberty calls,
The rebels are leagued as her foe.

Soldiers—
We are ready—all ready—our hearts are her walls
Which traitors shall never o'erthrow.

Officers—
Arm—arm for the battle, our children and wives
Are sinking with terror oppressed.

Soldiers—
We are ready—all ready, and pledged are our lives,
That these dear ones in safety shall rest.

Officers—
Arm—arm for the battle—and cowards may fly
The foe like a torrent sweeps on.

Officers and soldiers (officers wheel to the audience)—All—
We are ready—all ready—we'll shout ere we die
Hurrah! for the victory is won.

3

Playgrounds into Paradegrounds

Civil War Children at Play

Children—in fiction and in real life—yearned to take up the cause of the Union or of the Confederacy. One way they could do this was through their play. Commercially produced games took children on a farcical visit to a Union Army camp, asked them to answer trivia questions about battles and generals, and let them pretend to be maritime heroes in a maze called Running the Blockade. Other war-related toys included a mechanical Walking Zouave doll and jigsaw puzzles depicting war scenes.

The most popular pastime was playing soldier. Boys, and a few girls, mustered their own military companies. "Each school had its play-ground transformed into a parade-ground," said an early historian of the Civil War in Illinois, "while small drums, miniature cannon and harmless small arms were the playthings of the nursery."* Julia Dent Grant—the wife of Gen. Ulysses S. Grant—recalled boys "playing at war, wearing military caps, beating small drums, guarding the crossing, and demanding counter-signs."† Boys may have dominated the military operations conducted on the nation's playgrounds, but girls wanted to get into the action, too. After one little girl in Yonkers, New York, failed to convince her older brother to take her along when his regiment marched off to the war, she somehow got hold of a soldier's

---

*T. M. Eddy, *The Patriotism of Illinois: A Record of the Civil and Military History of the State in the War for the Union, Vol. 1* (Chicago: Clark and Co., 1865), 75.

---

†John Y. Simon, ed., *The Personal Memoirs of Julia Dent Grant* (New York: G. P. Putnam and Sons, 1975), 89.

cap, canteen, and drum, which she practiced beating as she marched "up and down the path in front of our house," until, as she wrote many years later, "every head in the street must have ached." She even journeyed all the way to her brother's camp to volunteer her services to the U.S. Army. When the colonel of the regiment declined her offer to enlist, she doggedly returned home, "made a tent of my sheets, and with a broom for a musket, drilled myself till I was so tired that I fell asleep."*

Although military events naturally captured their imagination, children also acted out less bloody facets of the war. The Rogers children of Tama County, Iowa, for instance, accompanied their father to war meetings and then re-created the speeches and patriotic songs for their mother when they returned home. A boy in Boston constructed a child-size version of a panorama by coloring illustrations from *Harper's Weekly*, pasting them together, and narrating the events they portrayed to his audience of young neighbors and relatives. A budding theatrical manager directed friends and siblings in epic tragedies set on Southern plantations and battlefields.

The singular experiences of Southern children shaped the ways they played at war. Nannie Belle Maury mimicked the women that she had seen in various wartime situations. One day, as she was "playing ladies" with a little friend, her mother overheard her declare, "Upon my word an' honour, Sir, there are no letters and papers in this trunk at all"—the exact words of the protest she had heard Mrs. Maury utter to a Yankee guard as the family escaped from Fredericksburg some weeks before. The ways that the war infiltrated their children's every waking moment worried at least one mother. "Almost their entire set of plays have reference to a state of war," she related. Her five-year-old son staged marches and battles with paper soldiers, took prisoners, built hospitals with blocks and corncobs, made ambulances with chairs, and administered pills to his rag dolls. "He gets sticks and hobbles about," recorded his mother in her diary, "saying that he lost a leg at the Second battle of Manassas." In a scene straight out of a romance novel, her children and their little friends interrupted one of their doll parties when imaginary Yankees suddenly appeared and the paper soldiers had to scramble to meet the foe.†

---

*Jeannette Leonard Gilder, *Autobiography of a Tomboy* (New York: Doubleday, 1904), 202–10.

---

†Alice Maury Parmelee, ed., *The Confederate Diary of Betty Herndon Maury, 1861–1863* (Washington: Privately Printed, 1938), 89; Elizabeth Preston Allan, ed., *The Life and Letters of Margaret Junkin Preston* (Boston: Houghton Mifflin, 1903), 158–59, 179.

Playing at war was one way that Civil War children processed the frightening conflict swirling around them. It let them feel a part of the war their brothers and fathers were fighting. And, like all forms of play, it provided a safe place to act out their fears and fantasies. Every parent knows that children will uncannily detect stress and perceive events affecting their families; Civil War children were no different.

BOY SOLDIERS

Boys of all ages learned the names of the great and not-so-great generals of the Civil War as well as the battles they won and lost. In the fictional as well as the real-life version of the children's war, they applied the knowledge they gained from fathers' letters home or newspapers by organizing their own boys' companies. Some even based their drills on *Hardee's Tactics*, the leading U.S. Army training manual (written in the 1850s by William Hardee, an officer who later became a Confederate general), which was available in many bookstores during the war. Like the men's companies they mimicked, the boys chose names for their units. Some, as in the story "The Yankee Zouaves," were attracted to the colorful uniforms that many of the original Union regiments wore as they marched off to war. French Zouaves had won acclaim for their fighting in the Crimea a few years earlier, and for their baggy red pants, tight blue jackets, and natty tasseled fezzes. Their fame inspired amateur militia companies—such as Elmer Ellsworth's Chicago U.S. Zouave Cadets—to adopt the flashy style of the French fighters.

In the decade before the war, writing for boys and girls had begun to separate into two separate and exclusive genres. Accordingly, children's wartime fiction failed to portray girls as anything but interested spectators of the boys' companies. They giggle on the sidelines or are captured or chased away; at best, they can be "daughters of the regiment," purely honorary positions— mascots, really—also adapted from European models. Although it was probably true that more boys than girls took up "arms" against imaginary enemies, many girls did express their patriotism in the age-old tradition of mimicking the drama of military training and battle. One young Louisianan was so adept at the manual of arms that she and her brothers would heckle the raw recruits fumbling through their maneuvers in a field near their home.

The "enlistment" of fictional children marked a striking contrast to the pacifistic notions of prewar writing for children, in which violence was abhorred and where good rarely came of a martial bearing or angry outburst. In fact, along with temperance, pacifism was one of the pet reform movements of writers for children throughout the antebellum years. Yet during the war, authors clearly acknowledged the righteousness of a war fought to save the Union and, later, to end slavery. This dramatic shift toward accepting conflict was reflected in admiring biographies of generals, in the military jargon that appeared in games and stories, and in the frequency with which youngsters of all ages were depicted as eager recruits in boys' companies.

"The Children's Attic"
N. L. E.
The Little Pilgrim 10 (July 1863), 93–94

It certainly looked very much like a rainy day: the clouds were gray and leaden, and already a few drops were falling into the brook and making little circles all over it.

Johnnie stood at the window and watched it all with rather a sorry face, for mamma said if it rained the boys must not go to school, and there were those new, thick shoes, with shiny tops and slippery soles that he wanted so much to wear today. He would not believe that the circles in the water were made by rain drops—they were "lucky bugs," he said, so he went out and stood on the piazza, but one drop came down plump on his nose as he looked up at the sky, and another, and yet another, till a whole shower of them came dashing into his eyes and on his hands to make him believe his mother. It certainly was a rainy day; "going to be a hard storm, too," papa said, as he came up from the post office, reading the morning paper; so Johnnie came into the house, quite pleasantly, and said, "Well, mamma, I suppose we shall have to play in the attic today."

Happy for Johnnie that he could say "we"; that he was not obliged to play alone that stormy day; so far from that, the Brooks' children were for all the world like a flight of stairs, of which Master Johnnie was the top stair. The next step down came Alfred, a rogue of a boy, always ready for a laugh and a frolic, but whose feet went rather laggingly to school, even though they had new shoes on them.

Next in order came solemn, four-year-old Benjamin, with hard, round cheeks, and chubby legs. Julie, her brothers' pet, is two years old, and baby Alice still stares with unmeaning eyes at the top of her cradle.

"Come, boys," said Johnnie, "let's go to the attic," so away clattered the six little feet, up to their own special domain, and there let us follow them.

Was there ever a nicer place for little boys to spend a rainy day in? All the cosier because the rain came down now hard and fast, making a great noise on the roof above them, and making it seem so good to have a home of their own to spend stormy days in.

Now do not suppose that this attic is a finished chamber, with plastered walls and painted floor. Not at all. It is a large, old-fashioned, open garret, where the boys can drive nails all day long in the naked boards and beams, and have things pretty much their own way. The walls are partly covered with pictures, that they have cut out of newspapers and pasted up themselves. A rocking horse, all saddled and bridled, stands in one corner; a nice little swing hangs from the beams overhead; a low shelf on one side answers for a carpenter's bench, and is covered with carpenter's tools—got up in miniature. A table, just high enough for the children, and made on purpose for them, is there too, and around it are three little chairs; while playthings of all kinds are lying about the floor.

"Let us play school," said Johnnie, "and I'll be the teacher."

"Ho! school!" said Alfred, "'tis bad enough to go to school really, without playing it at home! No, we'll play soldiers, and I'll be first lieutenant." Alfred's ambition was quite equal to the post of captain, but Johnnie always claimed that as his birthright.

It was nothing new for the boys to play soldiers. On one side of the garret was a queer looking tent, which they had set up for themselves, made of a worn-out carpet; this they called "Camp Brooks." An odd-looking tent it was; so low, that not even chubby little Benjamin could stand upright in it, but perhaps no foot-sore, battle-worn soldier ever enjoyed the rest of a tent more than they did this, as they crept in at one end and sat under its shadow on the hard garret floor.

Happy little soldiers, to know nothing of war but its mimicry—nothing of camp life but their own "Camp Brooks!" Their mother had made them paper caps, with tassels of red, white and blue, and putting these on, they marched off sturdily round the attic, Captain Johnnie ahead, the gallant lieutenant following, and the only private trying hard to make his short legs keep step with his brothers'.

"Halt!" shouted the captain. "Form in line!" and the line was formed as straight and long as the one small boy composing it could do it. "Forward on the double quick!" and away they ran, till poor Benny, catching his toe in a crack, came ingloriously to the ground.

"He must be carried to the hospital," said Ally, but just as his officers were tugging him off to the tent, mamma appeared at the door with little Julie, who came pattering in, shouting—

"Hurrah for stripes and blues! Julie will be sojer with Johnnie."

"Oh no, Julie, you'll spoil all our fun! Girls can't be soldiers, can they mamma?"

"Not often," said mamma, "though there was a girl once who led a great army to battle and to victory; but you can call Julie the daughter of the regiment, or as you have a wounded man here for the hospital, you will want her for a nurse."

"Mamma," said Alfred, "I wish we had some rations."

"Oh ho!" laughed mamma, "you want to put me at the head of the commissary department, do you? Well, I must make a raid on the pantry then"; so going downstairs she sent up Bridget with a nice tray, holding four little white mugs, a pitcher of milk, and a plate of hot, light gingerbread. Did ever soldiers fare better—and would it not be for the comfort of soldiers of a larger growth, if the mothers and the Bridgets could go with the army?

"Bless the childers!" said the good-hearted Bridget, "I'll bet they are having a good time."

"Oh, Bridget," said Benny, his round eyes full of reproof, "you must not say bet—'tis very wicked; but perhaps," he added by way of apology, "you did not have a mamma to tell you it was wicked."

"O hone, what a boy!" said Bridget, setting down the tray, and going off with a laugh playing about her mouth for the boy, and a tear in her eye for the old mother lying dead under the green grass of "swate Ireland."

And so, while the rain came dashing against the windows, and pattering on the roof, making some poor homes desolate and cold, chilling through the real soldiers as they lay wounded and dying on the wet ground after a dreadful battle—these little make-believe soldiers, with their paper caps and wooden guns, laughed and played through the rainy day in the children's attic.

"The Yankee Zouaves"
The Little Pilgrim 9 (October 1862), 133–34

On a beautiful Saturday afternoon in the latter part of May, a group of boys were standing under the apple trees of an old-

fashioned garden, busily discussing some subject, which seemed
to be of more than usual importance.

It was a fine large garden in which they stood, well
stocked with apple and pear trees, carefully trained grape vines,
and flourishing rows of currant and raspberry bushes. The bor-
ders were brilliant with the bloom of the peonies, and of the
house plants, which had been brought from the sunny windows,
where they had been placed during the winter, to adorn the garden beds.

Under the thick shade of the apple trees nothing would
grow, and here the boys were allowed to meet to settle the affairs of a new Zouave company, which they were about to organize. The officers, ten in all (the company numbered twenty),
had been appointed, but there were still the questions of the
name and the uniform to be decided.

A formal meeting was to be held, but they were waiting
for the lieutenant, who had not yet appeared. As it grew late,
however, and the missing officer still delayed his coming, they
determined to proceed to business without him.

"Silence!" shouted the captain at the top of his voice.

Will Boyton was the captain, and he brandished a sword
which his grandfather had worn at militia drills.

The orderly, hearing the voice of his captain, came slid-
ing down the trunk of the apple tree which he was climbing, and
finding that silence did not immediately ensue, shouted "'Bey
your s'perior officers."

The two commands drew the attention of the boys and
produced comparative silence; so the captain commenced—
"Now fellows, first we'll choose a name. What do you say to the
Anderson Zouaves?"

There was a confused shout of "Yes, No, don't like it, it's
too old"; and then the voice of the orderly made itself heard,
"Put it to vote! Put it to vote!"

It was put to vote accordingly, and the noes exceeded
the ayes. But there were many other names to choose from, and
each boy was ready with his proposal. One favored Ellsworth,
another Lincoln, some patronized Butler or Sprague (for these
were Rhode Island boys) but they could not agree upon any.*
They were all too common. The boys wanted something new
and striking. The Juvenile Zouaves was suggested by the tallest

---

*Gen. Benjamin Butler, a Massachusetts politician whose fame far outweighed his mili-
tary competence, and William Sprague, the erratic governor, senator, and sometime soldier from Rhode Island.

boy in the company. He was one of those thin boys who grow suddenly very tall, without growing broad and strong in proportion. But the orderly, who though short in stature, was mighty in spirit, objected in strong terms to the adjective.

"Our uniform is going to be red, white and blue," said one little fellow, "we might be called the Banner Zouaves."

"No, that isn't going to be our uniform. It isn't going to have any white in it," said the captain. This led to a great deal of lively talking about the uniform, and the name was quite forgotten for a time. But in the midst of the discussion a whistle was heard, and the boys looking up, saw the lieutenant approaching.

"Ho, you're a pretty fellow! What have you been about this whole time?" Such were the greetings that welcomed the delinquent officer.

"Couldn't help it. Had to stay in," answered the lieutenant.

The fact was that the second in command, having been very much engaged all the week in getting up his uniform, and in other soldier-like employments, had rather neglected his school duties, and as he had not got the required number of marks, had been obliged to stay in school half the afternoon.

"Well, what have you been about?" inquired the lieutenant, after his explanations were over.

"Oh! we've been choosing a name," answered the orderly, "and I've just thought of a splendid one. Fellars, let's be called the Yankee Zouaves."

"The Yankee Zouaves! Capital! Just the thing." There had been the Chicago Zouaves, and New York Zouaves, but they were the first Yankee Zouaves. They were all unanimous, so the question of the name was settled.

And now about the uniform. The lieutenant knew all about that. They must have red flannel caps, and trousers made very full, and blue jackets. That was the regular Zouave uniform, he had found out.

"But that'll be too expensive," the captain remonstrated. "Why, flannel costs seventy-five cents a yard; my mother said so, and then we'll have to have them made."

"No we won't," said the lieutenant, "we can have them made at home; and besides I found a store where they said they'd sell me flannel for twenty-five cents a yard."

"Well, I guess that won't break us," said the captain. "Come, let's drill."

"Yes, let's drill," echoed the whole company. So after many commands from the captain, and entreaties to "behave" themselves from the lieutenant, and many admonitions to "'bey their s'perior officers" from the orderly, the company formed and the drill commenced.

"Dress!" shouted the captain, and with much exertion on the part of all the officers, the lines were straightened. A very creditable drill was kept up for some time. Occasionally a dispute would arise between the officers concerning the movements. The officers had been chosen because they belonged to a military school, and were supposed to know all about drilling. Then the orderly would bring out his volume of Hardee's *Tactics*, which he had brought with him, and all the officers felt themselves obliged to submit to such authority. So there was no quarreling.

At last, when the captain found that his men were getting restless, he gave the order, "Forward, march!" The drummer, who had found it very difficult to keep still so long, now commenced in good earnest. The fife struck up Yankee Doodle, and the whole company marched gayly down the garden path. Just at this time, some members of a rival company were discovered looking over the fence. At this the boys raised a great shout and rushed to the encounter. It was very fortunate that the most direct road to the enemy was down the path and out the gate, for if there had been a shorter cut, I fear the garden would have suffered. But in spite of their haste, when they reached the street the enemy had disappeared. Finding that they were inferior in numbers, they had taken to stratagem, and were now stationed round the next corner, each armed with a stone or a lump of dirt, awaiting the approach of their enemy.

When Captain Boyton found that the foe had fled, he began to remember that his mother had charged him to keep his company in order whilst they were on her premises. So he led back his rather rebellious troop into the garden, and shut the gate. But all the boys kept a sharp look out during the rest of the afternoon, and the orderly contrived to have a stone always within reach of his hand.

It would take a long time to describe all the marching and countermarching, and wheeling and double-quicking that were performed that afternoon by the Yankee Zouaves. It was not until the tea-bell was heard ringing in the house, that the lieutenant declared it was "grub time," and they all agreed that it was time to stop. So the captain shouted, "Halt."

"Fellers," said the orderly, "the Yankee Zouaves will meet next Monday, after tea, in this place. The company may disband. Break ranks and be off with you!"

"Little Prudy's Captain Horace"
Sophie May
The Student and Schoolmate 14 (October 1864), 113–15

The boys all said there was nothing "mean" about Horace. He would neither abuse a smaller child, nor see one abused. If he thought a boy was doing wrong, he was not afraid to tell him so; and you may be sure he was all the more respected for his moral courage.

Horace talked to his schoolmates a great deal about his father, Captain Clifford, who was going to be a great general some day. "When I was home," said he, "I studied pa's book of tictacs [tactics], and I used to drill the boys."

There was a loud cry of "Why can't you drill us? Come, let's us have a company, and you be cap'n!"

Horace gladly consented, and the next Saturday afternoon a meeting was appointed at the "Glen." When the time came, the boys were all as joyful as so many squirrels suddenly let out of a cage.

"Now look here, boys," said Horace, brushing back his shingled hair, and walking about the grove with the air of a lord; "First place, if I'm going to be captain, you must mind; will you? say!"

Horace was not much of a public speaker; he threw words together as it happened; but there was so much meaning in the twistings of his face, the jerkings of his head, and the twirlings of his thumbs, that if you were looking at him you must know what he meant.

"Ay ay!" piped the little boys in chorus.

"Then I'll muster you in," said Horace, grandly. "Has everybody brought their guns? I mean sticks, you know!"

"Ay, ay!"

"I want to be corporal," said Peter Grant.

"I'll be major," cried Willy Snow.

"There, you've spoke!" shouted the captain. "I wish there was a tub or bar'l to stand you on when you talk."

After some time an empty flour barrel was brought, and placed upright under a tree, to serve as a dunce-block.

"Now we'll begin 'new," said the captain. "Those that want to be mustered, rise up their hands; but don't you snap your fingers."

The caution came too late for some of the boys; but Horace forgave the seeming disrespect, knowing that no harm was intended.

"Now, boys, what are you fighting about?—Say, 'for our country'!"

Boy companies collide in a scene from "Little Prudy's Captain Horace."
From The Student and Schoolmate.

"For our country!" shouted the soldiers, some in chorus, and some in solo.

"And our flag," repeated the boys, looking at the little banner of stars and stripes, which was fastened to the stump of a tree, and faintly fluttered in the breeze.

"Long may it wave!" cried Horace, growing enthusiastic, and pointing backward to the flag with a sweep of his thumb.

"There ain't a 'Secesh' in this company; there ain't a man but wants our battle to beat! If there is, we'll muster him out double-quick."

A few caps were flourished in the air, and every mouth was set firmly together, as if it would shout scorn of secession if it dared speak. It was a loyal company; there was no doubt of that. Indeed, the captain was so bitter against the South, that he had asked his aunt Madge if it was right to let southernwood* grow in the garden.

---

*Southernwood is a European shrub sometimes used for making beer.

"Now," said Horace, "Forward! March! 'Ploy column!—No, form a line first! 'Tention!"

A curved, uncertain line, not unlike the letter S, gradually straightened itself, and the boys looked down to their feet as if they expected to see a chalk-mark on the grass.

"Now, when I say 'Right!' you must look at the buttons on my jacket—or on yours, I've forgot which; on yours, I reckon. Right! Right at 'em! Right at the buttons!"

Obedient to orders, every boy's head dropped in a moment.

"Stop!" said Horace, knitting his brows; "that's enough!" There seemed to be something wrong, he could not tell what.

"Now you may 'bout face; that means whirl round. Now march! one, two, quick time, double-quick!"

"They're stepping on my toes," said bare-footed Peter Grant.

"Hush right up, private, or I'll stand you on the bar'l."*

"I wish't you would," groaned little Peter; "it hurts."

"Well, then, I shant," said the captain, decidedly; "for 'twouldn't be any punishing—Can't some of you whistle?"

Willy Snow struck up Yankee Doodle, which soon charmed the wayward feet of the little volunteers, and set them to marching in good time. Afterward their captain gave instructions in "groundin' arms, stackin' arms, firin', and countin' a march," by which he meant "countermarching." He had really read a good many pages in Infantry Tactics, and had treasured up the military phrases with some care, though he had but a confused idea of their meaning. "Holler-square!" said he, when he could think of nothing else to say. Of course he meant a "hollow square."

"Shall we holler all together?" cried a voice from the midst of the ranks.

The owner of the voice would have been "stood on a barrel," if Horace had been less busy thinking.

"I've forgot how they holler, as true as you live; but I reckon it's all together, and open your mouths wide."

At this, the young volunteers, nothing loath, gave a long, deafening shout, which the woods caught up and echoed.

Horace scratched his head. He had seen his father drill his men, but he could not remember that he had ever seen them scream.

---

*One of the many public punishments for a Civil War-era soldier was to be exhibited on a barrel in plain view of his comrades for hours at a time.

A pitched battle came off next, which would have been a very peaceful one if all the boys had not wanted to be Northerners. But the feeling was greatly changed when Horace joined the Southern ranks, saying "he didn't care how much he played Secesh, when everybody knew he was a good Union man, and his father was going to be a general." After this there was no trouble about raising volunteers on the rebel side.

The whole affair ended very pleasantly, only there was some slashing right and left with a few bits of broken glass, which were used as swords; and several mothers had wounds to dress that night.

"The Fort and How It Was Taken"
Christie Pearl
The Student and Schoolmate 11 (August 1862), 273–74

"Halt!" screamed the commander of the company, a bright looking blue eyed boy, with a wooden sword and drum, and the six boys who formed his company stopped and kicked up their heels, and pranced about like so many horses. They had paper hats trimmed with colored streamers of various materials, and broomsticks for guns, and one boy had tied around his neck his mother's best coffee pot, and was drumming on it with right good will. By the way, he had a good shaking the next morning.

"Hurrah for the broomstick regiment!" shouted a bevy of school girls who were coming around the corner.

"Charge broomsticks!" shouted the captain, and the company charged upon the girls who scattered in all directions, except one bold, black-eyed girl, who defiantly placed herself against a wall, saying, "Come one, come all, this rock shall fly from its firm base as soon as I! Come on, boys, I ain't afraid of you!"

"A fort! a fort to take!" shouted the boys.

"Fire!" said the captain, and the broomsticks were brought on a level with the boys' shoulders, and unearthly sounds issued from their mouths, representing the "bang!" of the guns, but the girl put her hands to her ears, and stood firm.

"Charge broomsticks!" shouted the captain mischievously. They charged, and one boy snatched her hat from her head and carried it aloft on his bayonet, but she still stood laughing. "We will detain her prisoner until she surrenders," said the captain after calling a council of war, and the broomsticks were placed horizontally in the hands of the boys, as they formed a circle around her.

"You are our prisoner, surrender!" shouted the captain, but she shot a few flashes of fire from her eyes, and exclaimed, "You are very gentlemanly, Tom Harris, to treat a lady so rudely—not that I couldn't put the whole rabble of you to flight if I chose!" They looked rather frightened at this speech, and the coffee pot boy whispered to his neighbor, "Hadn't we better retreat?"

"Silence! It's of no use, Miss Kate Kerrigan, you are my prisoner, and you may as well surrender gracefully," said the commander.

"Your terms?" she asked.

"Upon your own conditions."

"That you drill before me fifteen minutes, give me back my hat, and behave like perfect gentlemen for the next fortnight!"

The drill was gone through with, and Kate mischievously enjoyed the weariness of the boys. "Halt! attention! Let's adopt Miss Kate as the daughter of the regiment!"

"Agreed! Three cheers for Kate!" was the response, and while the boys were cheering lustily, Kate watched her opportunity, and ran away down the street.

NURTURING WARRIORS

If boys naturally dominated the military side of children's play, girls naturally took behind-the-lines roles as nurses. "Nelly's Hospital" by Louisa May Alcott is the most elaborate description of a little girl's attempt to share in the great effort to save the Union. Inspired by her brother's long convalescence, Nelly organizes her own hospital for the wounded fauna she finds in her neighborhood. Alcott's story includes several elements common to children's literature of the period. Although Nelly is the central character, she is relegated to the role of nurse. The "surgeon" is a boy, of course, but in this collision of class and gender, gender wins: the boy in question is Tony, the gardener's son. As Tony and Nelly prepare their hospital and begin treating "patients," Nelly learns generosity of spirit in caring for a gray "rebel" snake and reaps the rewards of charity in freeing a black fly—her "contraband"—from a spider web representing the bonds of slavery. In a bit of literary foreshadowing, Nelly becomes a worker for the Sanitary Commission—for which Mrs. March in Alcott's *Little Women* would later toil.

"Nelly's Hospital"
Louisa May Alcott
Our Young Folks 1 (April 1865), 267–77

Nelly sat beside her mother picking lint; but while her fingers flew, her eyes often looked wistfully out into the meadow, golden with buttercups, and bright with sunshine. Presently, she said, rather bashfully, but very earnestly, "Mamma, I want to tell you a little plan I've made, if you'll please not laugh."

"I think I can safely promise that, my dear," said her mother, putting down her work that she might listen quite respectfully.

Nelly looked pleased, and went on confidingly. "Since brother Will came home with his lame foot, and I've helped you tend him, I've heard a great deal about hospitals, and liked it very much. To-day I said I wanted to go and be a nurse, like Auntie Mercy; but Will laughed and told me I'd better begin by nursing sick birds and butterflies and pussies before I tried to take care of men. I did not like to be made fun of, but I've been thinking that it would be very pleasant to have a hospital all my own, and be a nurse in it, because, if I took pains, so many pretty creatures might be made well, perhaps. Could I, mamma?"

Her mother wanted to smile at the idea, but did not, for Nelly looked up with her heart and eyes so full of tender compassion, both for the unknown men for whom her little hands had done their best, and for the smaller sufferers near home, that she stroked the shining head, and answered readily: "Yes Nelly, it will be a proper charity for such a young Samaritan, and you may learn much if you are in earnest. You must study how to feed and nurse your little patients, else your pity will do no good, and your hospital become a prison. I will help you, and Tony shall be your surgeon."

"O mamma, how good you always are to me! Indeed, I am in truly earnest; I will learn, I will be kind, and may I go now and begin?"

"You may, but tell me first where will you have your hospital?"

"In my room, mamma; it is so snug and sunny and I never should forget it there," said Nelly.

"You must not forget it anywhere. I think that plan will not do. How would you like to find caterpillars walking in your bed, to hear sick pussies mewing in the night, to have beetles clinging to your clothes, or see mice, bugs, and birds tumbling down stairs whenever the door was open?" said her mother.

Nelly laughed at that thought a minute, then clapped her hands and cried: "Let us have the old summer house! My doves only use the upper part, and it would be so like Frank in the story book. Please say yes, again, mamma."

Her mother did say yes, and snatching up her hat, Nelly ran to find Tony, the gardener's son, a pleasant lad of twelve, who was Nelly's favorite playmate. Tony pronounced the plan a "jolly" one, and, leaving his work, followed his young mistress to the summer house, for she could not wait one minute.

"What must we do first?" she asked, as they stood looking in at the dim, dusty room, full of garden tools, bags of seed, old flower-pots, and watering cans.

"Clear out the rubbish, miss," answered Tony.

"Here it goes then," and Nelly began bundling everything out in such haste that she broke two flower-pots, scattered all the squash seeds, and brought a pile of rakes and hoes clattering down about her ears.

"Just wait a bit, and let me take the lead, miss. You hand me things, I'll pile 'em in the barrow and wheel them off to the barn; then it will save time, and be finished up tidy."

Nelly did as he advised, and very soon nothing but dust remained.

"What next?" she asked, not knowing in the least.

"I'll sweep up while you see if Polly can come and scrub the room out. It ought to be done before you stay here, let alone the patients."

"So it had," said Nelly, looking very wise all of a sudden. "Will says the wards—that means the rooms, Tony—are scrubbed every day or two, and kept very clean, and well venti-something—I can't say it; but it means having a plenty of air come in. I can clean windows while Polly mops, and then we shall soon be done."

Away she ran, feeling very busy and important. Polly came, and very soon the room looked like another place. The four latticed windows were set wide open, so the sunshine came dancing through the vines that grew outside, and curious roses peeped in to see what frolic was afoot. Then walls shone white again, for not a spider dared to stay; the wide seat which encircled the room was dustless now,—the floor as nice as willing hands could make it; and the south wind blew away all the musty odors with its fragrant breath.

"How fine it looks!" cried Nelly, dancing on the doorstep, lest a foot print should mar the still damp floor.

"I'd almost like to fall sick for the sake of staying here," said Tony, admiringly. "Now, what sort of beds are you going to have, miss?"

"I suppose it won't do to put butterflies and toads and worms into beds like the real soldiers where Will was?" answered Nelly, looking anxious.

Tony could hardly help shouting at the idea; but, rather than trouble his little mistress, he said very soberly: "I'm afraid they wouldn't lay easy, not being used to it. Tucking up a butterfly would about kill him; the worms would be apt to get lost among the bed-clothes; and the toads would tumble out the first thing."

"I shall have to ask mamma about it. What will you do while I'm gone?" said Nelly, unwilling that a moment should be lost.

"I'll make frames for netting to the window, else the doves will come in and eat up the sick people."

"I think they will know it is a hospital, and be too kind to hurt or frighten their neighbors," began Nelly; but as she spoke, a plump white dove walked in, looked about with its red-ringed eyes and quietly pecked up a tiny bug that had just ventured out from the crack where it had taken refuge when the deluge came.

"Yes, we must have the netting. I'll ask mamma for some lace," said Nelly, when she saw that; and, taking her pet dove on her shoulder, told it about her hospital as she went toward the house; for, loving creatures as she did, it grieved her to have any harm befall even the least or plainest of them. She had a sweet child-fancy that her playmates understood her language as she did theirs, and that birds, flowers, animals and insects felt for her the same affection which she felt for them. Love always makes friends, and nothing seemed to fear the gentle child; but welcomed her like a little sun who shone alike on all, and never suffered an eclipse.

She was gone some time, and when she came back her mind was full of new plans, one hand full of rushes, the other of boots, while over her head floated the lace, and bright green ribbon hung across her arm.

"Mamma says that the best beds will be little baskets, boxes, cages and any sort of thing that suit the patient; for each will need different care and food and medicine. I have not baskets enough, so, as I cannot have pretty white beds, I am going

to braid pretty green nests for my patients, and while I do it,
mamma thought you'd read to me the pages she has marked, so
that we may begin right."

"Yes, miss; I like that. But what is the ribbon for?" asked
Tony.

"O, that's for you. Will says that, if you are to be an
army surgeon, you must have a green band on your arm; so I got
this to tie on when we play hospital."

Tony let her decorate the sleeve of his gray jacket, and
when the nettings were done, the welcome books were opened
and enjoyed. It was a happy time, sitting in the sunshine, with
leaves pleasantly astir all about them, doves cooing overhead,
and flowers sweetly gossiping together through the summer afternoon. Nelly wove her smooth, green rushes, Tony pored over
his pages, and both found something better than fairy legends in
the family histories of insects, birds, and beasts. All manner of
wonders appeared, and were explained to them, till Nelly felt as
if a new world had been given to her, so full of beauty, interest,
and pleasure that she never could be tired of studying it. Many
of these things were not strange to Tony, because, born among
plants, he had grown up with them as if they were brothers and
sisters, and the sturdy, brown-faced boy had learned many
lessons which no poet or philosopher could have taught him, un-
less he had become as childlike as himself, and studied from the
same great book.

When the baskets were done, the marked pages all read,
and the sun began to draw his rosy curtains round him before
smiling "Good night," Nelly ranged the green beds round the
room, Tony put in the screens and the hospital was ready. The
little nurse was so excited that she could hardly eat her supper,
and directly afterwards ran up to tell Will how well she had succeeded with the first part of her enterprise. Now brother Will
was a brave young officer, who had fought stoutly and done his
duty like a man. But when lying weak and wounded at home,
the cheerful courage which had led him safely through many
dangers seemed to have deserted, and he was often gloomy, sad,
or fretful, because he longed to be at his post again, and time
passed very slowly. This troubled his mother, and made Nelly
wonder why he found lying in a pleasant room so much harder
than fighting battles or making weary marches. Anything that
interested and amused him was very welcome, and when Nelly,
climbing on the arm of his sofa, told her plans, mishaps, and suc-
cesses, he laughed out more heartily than he had done for many
a day, and his thin face began to twinkle with fun as it used to

do so long ago. That pleased Nelly, and she chatted like any affectionate little magpie, till Will was really interested; for when one is ill, small things amuse.

"Do you expect your patients to come to you, Nelly?" he asked.

"No, I shall go and look for them. I often see poor things suffering in the garden, and the wood, and always feel as if they ought to be taken care of, as people are."

"You won't like to carry insane bugs, lame toads, and convulsive kittens in your hands, and they would not stay on a stretcher if you had one. You should have an ambulance and be a branch of the Sanitary Commission," said Will.

Nelly had often heard the words, but did not quite understand what they meant. So Will told her of that great and never failing charity, to which thousands owed their lives; and the child listened with lips apart, eyes often full, and so much love and admiration in her heart that she could find no words in which to tell it. When her brother paused, she said earnestly: "Yes, I will be a Sanitary. This little cart of mine shall be my amb'lance, and I'll never let my water barrels go empty, never drive too fast, or be rough with my poor passengers, like some of the men you tell about. Does this look like an ambulance, Will?"

"Not a bit, but it shall, if you and mamma like to help me. I want four long bits of cane, a square of white cloth, some pieces of thin wood, and the gum-pot," said Will, sitting up to examine the little cart, feeling like a boy again as he took out his knife and began to whittle.

Up stairs and down stairs ran Nelly till all necessary materials were collected, and almost breathlessly she watched her brother arch the canes over the cart, cover them with cloth, and fit in an upper shelf of small compartments, each lined with cotton-wool to serve as beds for wounded insects, lest they should hurt one another or jostle out. The lower part was left free for any larger creatures which Nelly might find. Among her toys she had a tiny cask which only needed a peg to be water-tight; this was filled and fitted in before, because, as the small sufferers needed no seats, there was no place for it behind, and, as Nelly was both horse and driver, it was more convenient in front. On each side of it stood a box of stores. In one were minute rollers, as bandages are called, a few bottles not yet filled, and a wee doll's jar of cold-cream, because Nelly could not feel that her outfit was complete without a medicine-chest. The other box was full of crumbs, bits of sugar, bird-seed, and grains of wheat and corn, lest any famished stranger should die for want of food before she got it home. Then mamma painted "U.S. San. Com." in bright letters on the cover, and Nelly received her charitable playthings with a long sigh of satisfaction.

"Nine o'clock already. Bless me, what a short evening this has been," exclaimed Will, as Nelly came to give him her good-night kiss.

"And such a happy one," she answered. "Thank you very, very much, dear Will. I only wish my little ambulance was big enough for you to go in,—I'd so much like to give you the first ride."

"Nothing I should like better, if it were possible, though I've a prejudice against ambulances in general. But as I cannot ride, I'll try and hop out to your hospital tomorrow, and see how you get on,"—which was a great deal for Captain Will to say, because he had been too listless to leave his sofa for several days.

That promise sent Nelly happily away to bed, only stopping to pop her head out the window to see if it was likely to be a fair day to-morrow, and to tell Tony about the new plan as he passed below.

"Where shall you go to look for your first load of sick folks, miss?" he asked.

"All around the gardens first, then through the grove, and home across the brook. Do you think I can find any patients so?" said Nelly.

"I know you will. Good night, miss," and Tony walked away with a merry look on his face, that Nelly would not have understood if she had seen it.

Up rose the sun bright and early, and up rose Nurse Nelly almost as early and as bright. Breakfast was taken in a great hurry, and before the dew was off the grass this branch of the S.C. was all astir. Papa, mamma, big brother and baby sister, men and maids, all looked out to see the funny little ambulance depart, and nowhere in all the summer fields was there a happier child than Nelly, as she went smiling down the garden path, where tall flowers kissed her as she passed and every blithe bird seemed singing a "God speed!"

"How I wonder what I shall find first," she thought, looking sharply on all sides as she went. Crickets chirped, grasshoppers leaped, ants worked busily at their subterranean houses, spiders spun shining webs from twig to twig, bees were coming for their bags of gold, and butterflies had just begun their holiday. A large white one alighted on the top of the ambulance, walked over the inscription as if spelling it letter by letter, then floated away from flower to flower, like one carrying the good news from far and wide.

"Now every one will know about the hospital and be glad to see me coming," thought Nelly. And indeed it seemed so, for just then a blackbird, sitting on the garden wall, burst out with a song full of magical joy, Nelly's kitten came running after to stare at the wagon and rub her soft side against it, a bright-eyed toad looked out from his cool bower among the lily-leaves, and at that minute Nelly found her first patient. In one of the dewy cobwebs hanging from a shrub nearby sat a fat black yellow spider, watching a fly whose delicate wings were just caught in the net. The poor fly buzzed pitifully, and struggled so hard that the whole web shook; but the more he struggled, the more he entangled himself, and the fierce spider was preparing to descend that it might weave a shroud about its prey, when a little finger broke the threads and lifted the fly safely into the palm of the hand, where he lay faintly humming his thanks.

Nelly had heard much about contrabands, knew who they were, and was very much interested in them; so, when she freed the poor black fly, she played he was her contraband, and felt glad that her first patient was one that needed help so much. Carefully brushing away as much of the web as she could, she left small Pompey,* as she named him, to free his own legs, lest her clumsy fingers should hurt him; then she laid him in one of the soft beds with a grain or two of sugar if he needed refreshment, and bade him rest and recover from his fright, remembering that he was at liberty to fly away whenever he liked, because she had no wish to make a slave of him.

Feeling very happy over this new friend, Nelly went on singing softly as she walked, and presently she found a pretty caterpillar dressed in brown fur, although the day was warm. He lay so still she thought him dead, till he rolled himself into a ball as she touched him.

"I think that you are either faint from the heat of this thick coat of yours, or that you are going to make a cocoon of yourself, Mr. Fuzz," said Nelly. "Now I want to see you turn into a butterfly, so I shall take you, and if you get lively again I will let you go. I shall play that you have given out on a march as the soldiers sometimes do, and been left behind for the Sanitary people to see to."

In went sulky Mr. Fuzz, and on trundled the ambulance till a golden green rose-beetle was discovered, lying on his back, kicking as if in a fit.

---

*Pompey was a popular name for fictional African-American characters. It drew on a tradition in the South of naming slaves after classical or mythological characters.

"Dear me, what shall I do for him?" thought Nelly. "He acts as baby did when she was so ill, and mamma put her in a warm bath. I haven't got my little tub here, or any hot water, and I'm afraid the beetle would not like it if I had. Perhaps he has pain in his stomach; I'll turn him over, and pat his back, as nurse does baby's when she cries for pain like that."

She set the beetle on his legs, and did her best to comfort him; but he was evidently in great distress, for he could not walk, and instead of lifting his emerald overcoat, and spreading the wings that lay underneath, he turned over again, and kicked more violently than before. Not knowing what to do, Nelly put him into one of her soft nests for Tony to cure if possible. She found no more patients in the garden except for a dead bee, which she wrapped in a leaf, and took home to bury. When she came to the grove, it was so green and cool she longed to sit and listen to the whispers of the pines, and watch the larch-tassels wave in the wind. But, recollecting her charitable errand, she went rustling along the pleasant path till she came to another patient, over which she stood considering several minutes before she could decide whether it best to take it to her hospital, because it was a little gray snake, with a bruised tail. She knew it would not hurt her, yet she was afraid of it; she thought it pretty, yet could not like it; she pitied its pain, yet shrunk from helping it, for it had a fiery eye, and a keep-quivering tongue, that looked as if longing to bite.

"He is a rebel, I wonder if I ought to be good to him," thought Nelly, watching the reptile writhe in pain. "Will said there were sick rebels in his hospital, and one was very kind to him. It says, too, in my little book, 'Love your enemies.' I think snakes are mean, but I guess I'll try and love him because God made him. Some boy will kill him if I leave him here and then perhaps his mother will be very sad about it. Come, poor worm, I wish to help you, so be patient, and don't frighten me."

Then Nelly laid her little handkerchief on the ground, and with a stick gently lifted the wounded snake upon it, and, folding it together, laid it in the ambulance. She was thoughtful after that, and so busy puzzling her young head about the duty of loving those who hate us, and being kind to those who are disagreeable or unkind, that she went through the rest of the wood quite forgetful of her work. A soft "Queek, queek!" made her look up and listen. The sound came from the long meadow-grass, and, bending it carefully back, she found a half-fledged bird, with one wing trailing on the ground, and its eyes dim with pain and hunger.

"You darling thing, did you fall out of your nest and hurt your wing?" cried Nelly, looking up into the single tree that stood near by. No nest was to be seen, no parent birds hovered overhead, and little Robin could only tell his troubles in that mournful "Queek, queek!"

Nelly ran to get both her chests, and sitting down beside the bird, tried to feed it. To her great joy it ate crumb after crumb as if it were half starved, and soon fluttered nearer with a confiding fearlessness that made her very proud. Soon baby Robin seemed quite comfortable, his eyes brightened, he "queeked" no more, and but for the drooping wing would have been himself again. With one of her bandages Nelly bound both wings closely to his sides for fear he should hurt himself by trying to fly; and though he seemed amazed at her proceedings, he behaved very well, only staring at her, and ruffling up his few feathers in a funny way that made her laugh. Then she had to discover some way of accommodating her two larger patients so that neither should hurt nor alarm the other. A bright thought came to her after much pondering. Carefully lifting the handkerchief, she pinned the two ends to the roof of the cart, and there swung little Forked-tongue, while Robin lay easily below.

By this time Nelly began to wonder how it happened that she found so many injured things than ever before. But it never

Nelly spies a patient for her little hospital. From Our Young Folks.

entered her innocent head that Tony had searched the wood and meadow before she was up, and laid most of these creatures ready to her hands, that she might not be disappointed. She had not yet lost her faith in fairies, so she fancied they too belonged to her small sisterhood, and presently it did really seem impossible to doubt that the good folk had been at work.

Coming to the bridge that crossed the brook she stopped a moment to watch the water ripple over the bright pebbles, the ferns bend down to drink, and the funny tadpoles frolic in quieter nooks. There the sun shone, and the dragon-flies swung among the rushes. When Nelly turned to go on, her blue eyes opened wide, and the handle of the ambulance dropped with a noise that caused a stout frog to skip into the water heels over head. Directly in the middle of the bridge was a pretty green tent, made of two tall burdock leaves. The stems were stuck into cracks between the boards, the tips were pinned together with a thorn, and one great buttercup nodded in the doorway like a sleepy sentinel. Nelly stared and smiled, listened, and looked about on every side. Nothing was seen but the quiet meadow and the shady grove, nothing was heard but the babble of the brook and the cheery music of the bobolinks.

"Yes," said Nelly softly to herself, "that is a fairy tent, and in it I may find a baby elf sick with whooping cough or scarlet-fever. How splendid it would be! Only I could never nurse such a dainty thing."

Stooping eagerly, she peeped over the buttercup's drowsy head, and saw what seemed a tiny cock of hay. She had no time to feel disappointed for the haycock began to stir, and looking nearer, she beheld two silvery gray mites, who wagged wee tails, and stretched themselves as if they had just waked up. Nelly knew that they were young field-mice, and rejoiced over them, feeling rather relieved that no fairy had appeared, though she still believed them to have had a hand in the matter.

"I shall call the mice my Babes in the Woods, because they are lost and covered up with leaves," said Nelly, as she laid them in her snuggest bed, where they nestled close together, and fell asleep again.

Being very anxious to get home, that she might tell her adventures, and show how great was the need of a Sanitary Commission in that region, Nelly marched proudly up the avenue; and having displayed her load, hurried to the hospital, where another applicant was waiting for her. On the step of the door lay a large turtle, with one claw gone, and on his back was pasted a bit of paper, with his name,—"Commodore Waddle,

U.S.N." Nelly knew this was a joke of Will's, but welcomed the ancient mariner, and called Tony to help her get him in.

All that morning they were very busy settling the newcomers, for both people and books had to be consulted before they could decide what diet and treatment was best for each. The winged contraband had taken Nelly at her word, and flown away on the journey home. Little Rob was put in a large cage, where he could use his legs, yet not injure his lame wing. Forked-tongue lay under a wire cover, on sprigs of fennel, for the gardener said that snakes were fond of it. The Babes in the Wood were put to the bed in one of the rush baskets, under a cotton-wool coverlet. Greenback, the beetle, found ease for his unknown aches in the warm heart of a rose, where he sunned himself all day. The Commodore was made happy in a tub of water, grass, and stones, and Mr. Fuzz was put in a well-ventilated glass box to decide whether he would be a cocoon or not.

Tony had not been idle while his mistress was away, and he showed her the hospital garden he had made close by, in which were cabbage, nettle, and mignonette plants for the butterflies, flowering herbs for the bees, chickweed and hemp for the birds, catnip for the pussies, and plenty of room left for whatever other patients might need. In the afternoon, while Nelly did her task at lint-picking, talking busily to Will as she worked, and interesting him in her affairs, Tony cleared a pretty spot in the grove for the burying ground, and made ready some small bits of slate on which to write the names of those who died. He did not have it ready an hour too soon, for at sunset two little graves were needed, and Nurse Nelly shed tender tears for her first losses as she laid the motherless mice in one smooth hollow, and the grey-coated rebel in the other. She had learned to care for him already, and when she found him dead, was very glad she had been kind to him, hoping that he knew it, and died happier in her hospital than all alone in the shadowy wood.

The rest of Nelly's patients prospered, and of the many added afterward, few died, because of Tony's skillful treatment and her own faithful care. Every morning when the day proved fair the little ambulance went out upon its charitable errand; every afternoon Nelly worked for the human sufferers whom she loved; and every evening brother Will read aloud to her from useful books, showed her wonders with his microscope, or prescribed remedies for the patients, whom he soon knew by name and took much interest in. It was Nelly's holiday; but though she studied no lessons, she learned much, and unconsciously made her pretty play both an example and a rebuke for others.

At first it seemed a childish pastime, and people laughed. But there was something in the familiar words "Sanitary," "hospital," and "ambulance" that made them pleasant sounds to many ears. As reports of Nelly's work went through the neighborhood other children came to see and copy her design. Rough lads looked ashamed when in her wards they found harmless creatures hurt by them, and going out they said among themselves, "We won't stone birds, chase butterflies, and drown girls' little cats any more, though we won't tell them so." And most of the lads kept their word so well that people said there never had been so many birds before as all that summer haunted wood and field. Tender-hearted playmates brought their pets to be cured, even busy fathers had a friendly word for the small charity, which reminded them so sweetly of the great one which should never be forgotten; lonely mothers sometimes looked out with wet eyes as the little ambulance went by, recalling thoughts of absent sons who might be journeying painfully to some far-off hospital, where brave women waited to tend them with hands as willing, hearts as tender, as those the gentle child gave to her self-appointed task.

At home the charm worked also. No more idle days for Nelly, or fretful ones for Will, because the little sister would not neglect the helpless creatures so dependent upon her, and the big brother was so ashamed to complain after watching the patience of these lesser sufferers, and merrily said he would try to bear his own wound as quietly and bravely as the "Commodore" bore his. Nelly never knew how much good she had done Captain Will till he went away again in the early autumn. Then he thanked her for it, and though she cried for joy and sorrow she never forgot it, because he left something behind him which always pleasantly reminded her of the double success her little hospital had won.

When Will was gone and she had prayed softly in her heart that God would keep him safe and bring him home again, she dried her tears and went away to find comfort in the place where he had spent so many happy hours with her. She had not been there before that day, and when she reached the door she stood quite still and wanted very much to cry again, for something beautiful had happened. She had often asked Will for a motto for her hospital, and he promised to find her one. She thought he had forgotten it; but even in the hurry of that busy day he had found time to do more than keep his word, while Nelly sat indoors, lovingly brightening the tarnished buttons on the blue coat that had seen so many battles.

Above the roof, where doves cooed in the sun, now rustled a white flag with the golden "S.C." shining on it as the west wind tossed it to and fro. Below, on the smooth panel of the door, a skillful pencil had drawn two arching ferns, in whose soft shadow, poised upon a mushroom, stood a little figure of Nurse Nelly, and underneath it another of Dr. Tony bottling medicine, with spectacles upon his nose. Both hands of the miniature Nelly were outstretched, as if beckoning to a train of insects, birds, and beasts, which was so long that it not only circled round the lower rim of this fine sketch, but dwindled in the distance to mere dots and lines. Such merry conceits as one found there! A mouse bringing the tail it had lost in some cruel trap, a dor-bug with a shade over its eyes, an invalid butterfly carried in a tiny litter by long-legged spiders, a fat frog with gouty feet hopping upon crutches, Jenny Wren sobbing in a nice handkerchief, as she brought dear dead Cock Robin to be restored to life. Rabbits, lambs, cats, calves, and turtles, all came trooping up to be healed by the benevolent little maid who welcomed them so heartily.

Nelly laughed at these comical mites till the tears ran down her cheeks, and thought she never could be tired of looking at them. But presently she saw four lines clearly printed underneath her picture, and her childish face grew sweetly serious as she read the words of a great poet, which Will had made both compliment and motto:

> "He prayeth best who loveth best
> All things both great and small;
> For the dear God who loveth us,
> He made and loveth all."*

---

*From Samuel Taylor Coleridge, "The Rime of the Ancient Mariner" (1798), pt. vii.

4

The Roll Call of the Brave

Loss and Sacrifice

Americans of all ages discovered that war demanded sacrifices of everyone. Editors of children's magazines tried to educate their readers about the losses that children suffered during the war, particularly of beloved fathers, brothers, uncles, and friends, by publishing letters from bereaved youngsters. Sacrifice was also a major theme in wartime poetry and stories, which often featured affecting, if sometimes maudlin, images of the youngest victims of war. According to the middle-class gospel of the time, nothing was worth having if it could be gained without sacrifice.

Years before the war, the juvenile magazine *Youth's Companion* had filled its columns with inspiring obituaries and vignettes of youngsters accepting Jesus on their deathbeds. As late as the 1860s, *The Little Pilgrim* still featured the occasional pious death of a treasured reader. The children's literature of the time, even when it avoided the subject of death, was so laden with moral rectitude that readers could hardly fail to perceive the necessity for self-denial and piety in their own lives.

Many Americans—in both sections—believed that the war had been brought on them by a God angry at their continued bickering, at their grasping for economic gain, and at their enslavement of other human beings. The sacrifice and loss that loomed so large in their theology was reflected in the insistence by authors and editors for children that they, too, might be called upon to pay for their country's sins. Perhaps, as Abraham Lincoln suggested in his Second Inaugural Address, God would permit the war to "continue until all the wealth piled by the bondman's two hundred and fifty years of unrequited toil shall be sunk, and until every drop of blood drawn with the lash shall be paid by another drawn with the sword."

SOLDIERS' ORPHANS

In his Second Inaugural Address, President Lincoln accepted on behalf of the government responsibility "to care for him who shall have borne the battles, and for his widow, and his orphan." Even before the war ended the plight of war orphans and half-orphans, and the country's duty to provide for them as a kind of memorial to their dead fathers, had inspired patriotic rhetoric. A *Harper's Weekly* cartoon in August 1862 showed Uncle Sam, standing with a crowd of women and children waving to departing soldiers and assuring the men, "I'll take care of the Wives and Babies."

Congress eventually passed a small pension for children whose fathers had died in the army (those whose mothers were still living were often called "half-orphans"), but much of the effort to memorialize slain soldiers came in the form of state soldiers' orphans' homes. Some were started even before the guns fell silent, with names such as the New York State Volunteer Institute, a military school for male orphans; the Union Home School for the Children of Volunteers; and the Patriot Orphan Home. By the late 1860s almost every Northern state had founded at least one institution for these orphans. Pennsylvania, with a major contribution from a railroad company, had established a system of more than a dozen soldiers' orphans' schools.

Orphans were potent symbols of the cost of war. Although the poems that follow may bring to mind the morbid fourteen-year-old poet Emmeline Grangerford in Mark Twain's *Huckleberry Finn*, who "made poetry about all the dead people," they nevertheless were an important element of the war lessons disseminated by children's magazines.

"The Soldier's Baby"
C. Chauncey Burr
The Student and Schoolmate 12 (August 1865), 239

A baby was sleeping,
Its mother was weeping,
Pale vigil was keeping,
For slumber had fled.

Sad news from the battle,
Where death's cannon rattle,
Of news from the battle!
Its father was dead.

The wife still is weeping,
The baby is sleeping,
Good angels are keeping
Watch over its bed.

Too young to know sorrow,
Or life's woes to borrow,
Must learn some to-morrow,
Its father is dead.

"The Soldier's Little Boy"
Holly Clyde
The Little Pilgrim 10 (August 1863), 110

Who will care for you now, mother,
Who will care for you now?
For the shadows of death are gathering fast
On your little Willie's brow.
I have felt it was coming a long, long time,
And you have felt it too,
For I saw it was breaking your very heart
To know I was leaving you.
I did what I could, you know, mother,
But my hands were young and weak,
And you have toiled for our daily bread
Till the bloom has left your cheek.
And your eyes were once very bright, mother—
Is it weeping that changes them so?
Ah! mother, don't grieve for your little boy,
He is ready and willing to go.

If father were only here, mother,
I would never shrink from the grave;
But the pain of leaving you here alone
Is the sharpest pain I have;
For I know you will never smile again,
And no little boy will be nigh

To wipe the tears on your cheek away,
And whisper—"Dear mother, don't cry!"

Talk to me about father, now—
We could not bear it before;
But now that I am going to him,
Dear mother, you'll tell me more.
I only knew that he fell, mother—
I could not ask for the rest,
There was such a pain within my heart,
And a choking in my breast.

Oh! those sad, dark days of Antietam, mother,*
The darkest I ever knew!
They made your Willie a fatherless boy,
And almost a motherless, too;
For you were so cold, and still, and white,
When my father's name was read,
I put my ear close down to your heart,
To be sure you were not dead.

Kiss your Willie again, mother,
His life is going so fast
I am not afraid to die, mother,
For the fear of death is past;
But mother—oh, mother, you must not grieve,
We'll meet again by and by—
Where every tear shall be wiped away—
Father, and you, and I.

"The Soldier's Little Daughter"
The Student and Schoolmate 11 (April 1862), 131

The night was stormy, dark, and cold;
My way led through the city,
Where wretched buildings, gray and old,
Seemed stained with tears of pity.

A little bird unblest with wings,
Her dark, sad eyes all tearful;
And God! to see such tender things
Out in the storm is fearful.

---

*The battle of Antietam, fought near Sharpsburg, Maryland, on September 17, 1862, was the bloodiest single day of fighting of the war, with over 26,000 total casualties.

And thus she 'plained—"Oh! stranger hear
I never begged before;
But mother has been dead a year,
And father's gone to war.

"And yesterday the work gave out
By which I earned a penny;
Last night I had a crust of bread;
To-night I haven't any.

"And I am very hungry, sir";
I bought her bread—to spare—
Then up into the old gray house
Climbed by the broken stair.

I asked her name, her tender age;
Intensest pity won her;
A little maid of seven years
And all this woe upon her!

"My name is Nellie Grover, sir;
My father loved me dearly;
And is it true as people say,
That the war is ended, nearly?"

'Twas strange, but as she spoke, I chanced
To look my paper over;
And there I read,—*"shot through the heart,*
A private, William Grover."

O! awful hour! can I forget
Her tears, her broken sobbing—
The little heart I pressed to mine
With bitter anguish throbbing!

And as the light grew dimmer,
And the wild cries fainter fell,
Unto my soul there came a voice,
I marked its cadence well.

"I sleep beneath the traitor's sod—
I died for Liberty;
I gave my spirit unto God—
My little child to thee.

"Teach her to hold as sacred trust,
Her patriot father's doom:
Teach her to pray that from his dust
Freedom's fair flower may bloom."

Thus to my home, most tenderly,
With loving words I brought her;
Ah! only death could tear her from me
That soldier's little daughter.

"Home News in Battle-Time"
Forrester's Playmate 23 (July 1864), 120

Dying! Along the trodden bloody field,
Along the field where still the tide of battle ran,
The Night came down with flaming spear and shield,—
Came down with starry legions mourning in our van;
Came down and touched the rows of mangled dead,
Across the knolls and by the little ridges lying,
With loving smile, and silent bowed her head,
Like some pale mourner o'er other brave ones dying.

Just on the edges of the stormy fight,
As the soft night came down, a group of soldiers knelt
Around a comrade, lying calm and white:
A stain of flowing blood upon his bayonet-belt.
Close by him, on the trampled meadow grass,
Beside his musket, an unopened letter lay—
A message from home, which now, alas!
Must be forever dark, because of this sad day.

"Read to me, corporal," he said at last;
"Read to me what Mary says—I shall die happier so";
Then, while across his face a spasm passed,
He sadly moaned: "It only came to-day, you know;
Just as I came a-field 'twas given me;
I could not pause to read it then, but comrade, hark!
I'm going now—the long dim way I see—
Read me what Mary says; 'twill cheer me in the dark."

They read him, as he wished, the precious lines—
The words of love, of brave encouragement and cheer—
Read him how Mary, 'mid her household shrines,

Was hopeful and content; how baby, "little dear,"
Had learned to walk; how Tom had won the prize
At school, last term; how he, the dear one, far away,
Was prayed for nightly; how, with straining eyes,
They waited his return, as for a festal day.

They ceased. Upon the pallid, vacant face,
A deeper shadow fell, and with a weary cry,
The dying soldier sobbed—"Give them Thy grace,
Oh blessed Father! shield them till the storm goes by!"
His voice grew faint, then ceased—but one who bent
Close to the fading lips heard this: "Good night, my dears!"
As if with death's cold chill and pains were blent
Sweet memories of home-dreams of life's brighter years.

And still the battle throbbed along the hills,
And still the dying and the dead in billows lay
Along the slopes and by the crimson rills—
The night-shades folding all in mantles dim and gray.
There, where he fell, they scooped a shallow grave,
And with her letter on his heart, so cold and calm,
Left him to wait the roll-call of the brave,
The summons to receive the victor's crown and palm.

DEAD DRUMMER BOYS

Americans during the Civil War loved to hear about the youngest heroes, the drummer boys whose job it was to signal troop movements. Although they were technically not combat soldiers, many did come into harm's way. Chucking their drums, they seized rifles and entered the fighting. The most famous, of course, was John Clem, a drummer who rallied the Union troops at Shiloh, shot a Confederate colonel, and after the war rose to the rank of major general in the regular army. Both adult and children's literature were filled with images of drummer boys. They were heroes of adventure stories, reformers of grizzled and sinful veterans, and subjects of numerous poems and drawings. The children's book *Frank Manly, the Drummer Boy,* by J. T. Trowbridge, even showed the hero temporarily succumbing to the temptations of gambling and liquor before regaining his virtuous balance.

More typical, perhaps, was "The Drummer-Boy's Burial," a poem that appeared in *Harper's New Monthly Magazine* during the bloody summer of 1864. In the aftermath of a terrible battle, two girls come upon the serene body of a young drummer, smiling in death, his "broken drum beside him all his life's short story told:/How he did his duty bravely till the death-tide o'er him rolled." They bury him, doing their own duty as patriotic children, but also, with their simple, dignified, silent service, inspiring much older adults with their pious courage. So ubiquitous were images of slain drummers that one child, at least according to a letter from his mother to *The Little Pilgrim*, wished that he could go off to war with his father and become "the dead drummer boy"!

The hero of "The Boy of Chancellorsville" actually survives his encounter with death. The most notable part of this representative account of a drummer boy's tribulations is his confrontation with none other than Robert E. Lee, whom the patriotically biased author depicts without the admiring, almost worshipful tones that even Northerners began to apply to him shortly after the war.

Heroic drummer boys were frequently called upon as examples of patriotism, piety, and heroism. From "The Drummer-Boy's Burial," Harper's New Monthly Magazine *(July 1864), 145.*

"The Drummer-Boy of Fort Donelson"
J. C. Hagen
The Student and Schoolmate 12 (September 1863), 278-79*

[Among those who lost their lives at the taking of Fort Donelson† was a drummer boy of about fifteen years of age, much esteemed by his comrades. He had passed unharmed through the fiercest of the struggle, exhibiting great courage and intrepidity, but was found dead on the field the morning after the battle, having perished during the night from cold and exhaustion.]

No more shook the earth with the *cannon's* dread thunder;
The *shriek* and the *war*-cry clashed wildly no more,
Nor *shells*, madly bursting, rent *columns* asunder;
The *night* had set in, and the *battle* was o'er.

The weary young drummer-boy saw now before him
No *foe* on the field, save the *dying* or *slain*;
And he sank down to rest, when a *slumber* came o'er him,
The *slumber* from which he should *wake* not again.

He laid himself down, with the *dying* around him,
The *sky* for his tent, and the *field* for his bed;
And *there*, at the dawn of the morning, we found him,
As *lifeless* and *cold* as the stone at his head.

No *shot* for its victim his young heart had chosen;
Unharmed he had passed through the heat of the fray;
But the cold, wintry *night-wind* his life's blood had *frozen*,
And his *spirit* had passed without murmur away.

His *drum* and his *sabre* we buried beside him,
And paid him the honors befitting the brave!
And knew that, though Fate length of *days* had denied him,
His comrades, in pride, would his *memory* save.

---

*Although this poem was published as a declamation piece by Oliver Optic, the distracting symbols indicating gestures, which appear in several selections in Chapter Three, have been omitted.

---

†Fort Donelson, a Confederate post on the Cumberland River, was captured by Gen. Ulysses S. Grant on February 16, 1862, during the campaign in which he won the nickname "Unconditional Surrender" Grant.

And there let him *rest*, on the battle-field fearful,
Where *heroes*, in *thousands*, repose at his side;
And we'll think on his doom with a feeling less tearful,
To know that for *justice* and *freedom* he died.

"The Boy of Chancellorsville"
Edmund Kirke
Our Young Folks 1 (September 1865), 600-608

On the second and third days of May 1863 was fought the great
and terrible battle of Chancellorsville, and not until men beat
their swords into ploughshares, and boys exchange their drums
for Jews-harps and penny-whistles, will it be forgotten.* But I do
not propose to write about it, for I cannot. No one can describe a
battle without seeing it, and I did not see the battle of
Chancellorsville. But I did see, more than a year after it was
fought, a little boy who was in it, and who, nearly all the inter-
vening time, was a prisoner in the hands of the Rebels.

He was only twelve years old, and you may think that
what such a little fellow did, at such a time, could not be of
much consequence to anybody. But it was. He saved one or two
human lives, and lighted the passage of a score of souls through
the dark valley; and so did more than any of our great generals
on those bloody days. He saved lives, they destroyed them.

You know that, if you break a small wheel in a cotton-
mill, the entire machinery will stop; and if the moon—one of the
smallest lumps of matter in the universe—should fall from its
orbit, the whole planetary system might go reeling and tumbling
about like a drunken man. So you see the great importance of little things,—and little folks are of much greater importance than
little things. If they were not, the little boy I am writing about
would not have done so much at Chancellorsville, and I should
not now be telling you his story.

The battle was raging hotly on our left, when this little
drummer-boy was ordered to the rear by his Captain. "Go," the
Captain said; "you're in danger here; back there you may be of

---

*The Battle of Chancellorsville was one of Gen. Robert E. Lee's greatest victories.
Fought over several days in May 1863, his Army of Northern Virginia defeated the
much larger Army of the Potomac. The key to his victory was the famous flanking attack by Gen. Thomas "Stonewall" Jackson, after which Jackson was mortally wounded
by his own troops.

use to the wounded." The little fellow threw his musket over his shoulder,—his drum he left behind when the battle began,—and, amid the pelting bullets, made his way back to the hospital. Our forces were driving the enemy, and all the ground over which they had fought was strewn with the dead and dying. Here and there, men with stretchers were going about among the wounded; but the stretchers were few, and the wounded were many; and as the poor maimed and bleeding men turned their pitiful eyes on the little boy, or in low, faint tones asked him for water, he could not help lingering among them, though the enemy's shells were bursting, and their bullets falling like hailstones all about him. Gray jackets were mingled with blue; but in a generous mind the cry of suffering dispels all distinction between friend and enemy; and Robert—that was his name—went alike to the wounded of both armies. Filling his canteen from a little stream which flowed through the battle-field, he held it to many a parched lip, and was rewarded with many a blessing from dying men,—blessings which will be to him a comfort and a consolation when he too shall draw near to death.

He had relieved a score or more, when he noticed, stretched on the ground at a little distance, his head resting against a tree, a fair-haired boy of not more than seventeen. He was neatly dressed in gray, and had a noble countenance, with a broad, open forehead, and thick, curly hair, which clustered all about his temples. His face wore the hue of health, his eyes were bright and sparkling, and only the position of his hands, which were clasped tightly above his head, told that he was in pain and wounded.

"Can I help you?" asked Robert, as he approached him.

"Thank you. Yes," he answered, clutching the canteen, and taking a long draught of the water. "Thank you," he said again. "I saw you. I knew you would come to me."

"Why! have the rest passed you by?"

"Yes; for, you see, I'm a Rebel," he replied, smiling faintly. "But you don't care for that."

"No, I don't. But are you badly hurt?"

"Pretty badly, I fear. I'm bleeding fast,—I reckon it's all over with me";—and he pointed to a dark red stain on his jacket, just under his shoulder. His voice had a clear, ringing tone, and his face a calm, cheerful look; for to the brave death has no terrors. To the true man or boy it is only passage upward to a higher, better, nobler life in the heavens.

Robert tore open the young man's clothes, and bound his handkerchief tightly about his wound; then, seeing an empty stretcher coming that way, he shouted to its bearers: "Quick! Take him to the hospital. He's bleeding to death!"

"I don't like the color o' his clothes," said one of the men, as the two moved on with the stretcher. "I guess he kin wait till we look arter our own wounded."

His face flushing with both shame and anger, Robert sprang to his feet, and, turning upon the men, said in an imperious tone, which sounded oddly enough from such a little fellow: "He can't wait. He will bleed to death, I tell you. Take him now; if you don't I'll report you,—I'll have you drummed out of the army for being brutes and cowards."

The men set down the litter, and the one who had spoken, looking pleasantly at Robert for a moment, said: "Well, you are a bully boy. We don't keer for no reportin'; but for such a little chap as you, we'll do anything,—I'm blamed if we won't."

"I thank you very much," said Robert, in an altered way, as he hastened to help the men lift the wounded youth upon the stretcher.

The hospital was an old mill at a cross-roads, about a quarter of a mile away. It was built of logs, without doors or window-panes, and was fast falling to decay; but its floor, and nearly every square inch of shaded ground around it, were covered with the wounded and the dying. Thither they bore the Rebel boy, and, picking their way among the many prostrate and bleeding men, spread a blanket under a tree, and laid him gently on it. Then Robert went for a surgeon.

One shortly came, and after dressing the wound, he said in a kindly way: "It's a bad hurt, my lad, but keep up a good heart, and you'll soon be about. A little pluck does more for a wound than a good many bandages."

"Oh! Now you've stopped the bleeding, I shan't die. I won't die—it would kill mother if I did."

And so, you see, the Southern lad, even then, thought of his mother! and so do all brave boys, whether well or wounded. They think of her first, and of her last; for no other hand is so gentle, no other voice is so tender, no other heart so true and faithful as hers. No boy ever grew to be a great and good man, who did not love and reverence his mother. Even the Saviour of the world, when He hung upon the cross, thought of his, and said to John, "Behold thy Mother!"

With so many needing help, Robert could do little more for the Southern youth. He saw him covered warmly with a blanket, and heard him say, "Whether I get well or not, I shall never forget you." Then he left him, not to see him again till long afterwards.

The surgeon was a kind-hearted man, and told Robert he should not go again upon the battle-ground; so he went about among the wounded in the hospital, tending them, writing last words to their loved ones at home, or reading to them from the blessed Book which God has given to be the guide of the living and the comfort of the dying.

So the day wore away, until the red tide of battle surged again around the old mill at the cross-roads. The Rebels came on in overpowering force, and drove our men, as autumn leaves are driven before the whirlwind. Numbers went down at every volley; and right there, not a hundred yards away, a tall stalwart man fell, mortally wounded. A Rebel bullet had entered his side, and as the fallen man pressed his hand upon it, a dog which was with him began to lap the wound, as if he thought he could thus stay the crimson stream on which his master's soul was going to its Maker.

Robert saw the man fall, and the dog standing by amid the leaden storm which was pouring in torrents all around them. Admiring the bravery of the dog, he stepped out from behind the tree where he had stood out of range of the bullets, and went to the wounded man. Gently lifting his head, he said to him, "Can I do anything for you?"

"Yes!" gasped the man. "Tell them that I died—like a man—for my country."

"Is that all? Nothing more?" asked Robert quickly, for he saw that the soldier was sinking rapidly.

The dying man turned his eyes to the little boy's face, clasped his arm tightly about the neck of his dog, made one or two efforts to speak, and then, murmuring faintly, "Take care—of—Ponto!" passed upward to that world where there are no wars and no fighting.

The battle by this time had surged away to the northward, and a small party of cavalry-men had halted before the doorway of the hospital. Robert had closed the eyes of the fallen soldier, and was straightening his limbs upon the blood-dampened ground, when one of the horsemen called out to him: "What,—my little fellow! What are you doing out here, so far away from your mother?"

Robert looked up, and, amid the group of officers, saw a tall, broad-shouldered, grave-looking man, with handsome, regular features, and hair and beard streaked with gray, but almost as white as cotton. He wore a high felt hat, an old gray coat, and blue trousers tucked into high-top boots; and rode a large, handsome horse, whose skin was as soft and glossy as a leopard's. He

An angry Gen. Robert E. Lee banishes the hero of "The Boy of Chancellorsville" to Libby Prison. From Our Young Folks.

carried no arms, but the three dingy stars on his collar showed that he held high rank among the Rebels. All this Robert had time to observe, as he very deliberately answered: "I came out here, sir, to help fight the wicked men who are trying to destroy their country."

The officer's placid face flushed with anger; and, turning to an aide, he said, in a harsh, grating tone: "Take that boy to the rear. Send him to the Libby with the other prisoners."

Robert did not then know that this officer was the famous General Lee,—the man who neither smokes, drinks, nor chews tobacco; who has, in short, none of the smaller vices, but all of the larger ones; for he deliberately, basely, and under circumstances of unparalleled meanness, betrayed his country, and, long after all hope of success was lost, carried on a murderous war against his own race and kindred.

It was nearly sunset before Robert was sent off to the rear, and meanwhile a narrow trench was scooped in the ground, and the dead soldier was placed in it. Robert set a small stake at the head of the grave, and it stands there still; but no one knows who rests below, and no one will know till the morning of the resurrection; and yet it may be that even now, in some far-away Northern home, hearts are heavy, and eyes are red, with waiting and weeping for the father and the husband who never again will return to his loved among the living.

Early on the following day, with about three hundred poor fellows, one half of whom were wounded, Robert was marched off to Richmond. The soldier's dog, when he saw his master laid away in the ground, howled and took on piteously, but soon afterwards grew friendly with Robert, and the two made all the weary journey together.

It was in truth a weary journey, and I cannot find it in my heart to tell you about it, for I do not want to make you sad; and it would draw tears from hearts of stone to know all that the poor boy endured. It seemed more than human nature could bear, and yet it was only what thousands of our tired, footsore, wounded, and starving men have suffered on their long, dusty, and muddy march to the Richmond Bastille. Time and again the little boy would have fallen by the way, had not the poor dumb dog sustained him. They shared their meagre crust together; and often, when Robert's spirits drooped on the march, Ponto would gambol about him, and make him cheerful in spite of himself; and often, too, when he lay down to sleep on the damp ground, the dog would stretch his huge paws across his breast, and cover him, as well as he could, from the cold air, and the unhealthy night dew.

At sunset, on the fourteenth day of May, the column, wayworn and footsore, with haggard faces and uncombed hair, was set down from the cars of the Virginia Central Railroad, and marched into the city of Richmond. Down the long, grass-grown streets they were hurried with clouded faces and heavy hearts; but when at last the cold, brown walls of the Libby rose before them darkly outlined on the gray sky, they almost shouted for joy,—for joy that their toilsome journey was over, though it had ended in prison. If they had known of the many weary months of cold and hunger and misery which some of them were to pass there, would they not rather have died than have entered the dark doorway of that living grave?

All of you have read descriptions, or seen pictures, of the gloomy outside of this famous prison, so I need not tell you how it looks. It is indeed gloomy, but the inside is repulsive and unsightly to the last degree. The room into which Robert and his companions were taken was a long, low apartment on the ground floor, with naked beams, broken windows, in whose battered frames the spider had woven his web, and bare, brown walls, from which hung scores of torn, dingy blankets, every one of them filled with a larger caravan of wild animals than any ever seen in a Northern town. The weary, travel-soiled company was soon ranged in four files along the floor of this room, and there they were made to wait two long hours for the Inspector. At last he came,—a coarse, brutal fellow, with breath perfumed with whiskey, and face bloated with drink and smeared with tobacco-juice.

"Yer a sorry set!" he said, as he went down the lines, taking from the men their money and other valuables. "A sorry set!" he added, as he looked down on their ragged clothes, through which here and there the torn flesh was peeping. "A sorry set! Sorrier nur purtater-tops in September; but yer green though,—greener nur laurel-bushes, and ye bar [bear] better," again he said, as he stuffed a huge handful of United States notes into his pocket, and went on with his dirty work. At last he stopped before a coatless officer, with matted hair, only one boot, a tattered shirt, and no hat or neck-tie, but in their stead a stained bandage, from under which the blood still was trickling. "Who'd ha' thought o' raisin' sich a crop from sich a hill o' beans!" he said, as he drew from the pocket of this officer a roll larger than usual, and in his greed paused to count the money.

"We reap what we sow," said the officer, with a look of intense loathing; "you are sowing theft, you'll reap hell-fire—if I live to get out of this prison."

"Yer sowin' greenbacks, and ye'll reap a dungeon, if ye don't keep a civil tongue in yer head," responded the fellow, with a brutal sneer, as he went on down the column.

Ponto had kept close at the heels of Robert, and, following him into the prison, had crouched down behind the line, and remained unobserved until the robbery was over. Then a dozen sentinels were ordered to take the prisoners to their quarters, and when they began to move, the dog attracted the notice of the Inspector. "Whose dog is that?" he roared, as Ponto started up the stairway, a little in advance of his young master.

Robert was about to answer, but a kind-hearted sentinel, seeing from his looks that the dog was his, touched him on the shoulder, and whispered: "Not a word, sonny! It mought git ye inter trouble."

"Stop him! Cotch that dog!" shouted the Inspector, as Ponto, hearing the inquiry, and seeming to know by instinct that it referred to him, darted forward and disappeared in the room above. The Inspector and two or three sentries pursued him, and bounding after them two steps at a time, Robert soon saw what followed.

The room was of the same size, and furnished in much the same way, as the one below stairs; but scattered about it, in messes of fifteen or twenty, were more than two hundred prisoners. In and out among these prisoners, ran the dog and his pursuers. It was an exciting chase; but they might as well have tried to catch a sunbeam, or a bird without salting its tail, as to take Ponto in such a crowd of friends. In and out among them—crouching behind boxes, leaping over barrels, running beneath benches, right under the legs of his pursuers—went Ponto, as if he were a streak of lightning out on a frolic; while the prisoners stood by, laughing, and shouting, and getting in the way as much as possible, to keep the loyal dog from the clutches of his Rebel enemies. Half an hour the chase lasted. Then the patience of the Inspector gave out, and puffing with heat and anger, he shouted, "One of you, shoot the ____ critter."

A sentinel levelled his musket, but a Union man threw up the barrel. "Don't fire here," he said, "you'll kill some of us."

"Fire, ____ you, fire! Don't mind him," shouted the enraged Inspector.

"Do it, Dick Turner," said the man, planting himself squarely before him, "and I'll brain you on the spot," and Turner prudently omitted to order the shooting.

Taking advantage of this momentary lull, Ponto darted up into the officers' room, and was soon snugly hid away in the third story. Baffled and exasperated, Turner turned to the man, and growling out, "I'll have my revenge for this, my fine fellow," strode down the stairway.

Robert's quarters were in the room where this scene occurred, and his new messmates received him very kindly. They gave him food, bathed his aching, swollen limbs, and soon made him a bed on the floor, with a blanket for a mattress, and Ponto for a coverlet. He was just falling into a doze, when he heard a voice at the landing ask, with an oath, "Where is that dog?" The lights were out, but by the lantern which the man carried, the boy saw that he was a short, slight, dapper individual, with a beardless face, a sneaking look, and a consequential air, which seemed to say: "Get out of my way, sir; I am Thomas P. Turner, by profession a Negro-whipper, but now keeper of Libby Prison, and I take my hat off to nobody." With him was the other Turner,— his tool, and the fit instrument of his contemptible tyranny.

No one answered the question, and the two worthies groped their way about the room with the lantern. They caught sight of Robert's mess just in time to see Ponto again take himself off up the stairway. The sagacious creature had heard the un-gentlemanly allusion to himself, and like a sensible dog, deter-mined to keep out of such low company.

With the aid of his Union friends, that night and for a week afterwards, Ponto baffled his pursuers; but at last he was taken, and, much against his will, was set free,—for, you know, it is only men that deserve to be shut up in prison. What became of him Robert does not know; but if he is living, he is a decent dog; if dead, he has gone where the good dogs go,—that is certain.

"So, he is your dog?" said Turner, halting before Robert, who had risen to his feet.

"He is, sir," answered the little boy in a respectful tone, "and you will be cruel if you take him away from me."

"Cruel! do you call me cruel!" cried Turner, flying into a passion. "I'll teach you manners, you young whelp." Turning then to his subordinate, he asked for the "other Yankee."

The prisoner who had forbidden the firing was pointed out, and soon he and Robert were escorted to a dungeon, down in the cellar, under the sidewalk. The members of Robert's mess told Turner of his exhausted condition, and begged him not to consign a tired, sick boy to so horrible a place,—at least to let him rest where he was till the morning; but all they said was of no avail. They might as well have talked to an adder, for an adder is not more deaf, more venomous, than was that man!

So Robert's long, weary journey ended in a dungeon. It was a horrid den,—a low, close, dismal place, with a floor en-crusted with filth, and walls stained and damp with the rain, which in wet weather had dripped down from the sidewalk. Its every corner was alive with vermin, and it seemed only a fit habitation for some ferocious beast, which had to be shut out from the light of day, and kept from contact with all things human. Yet into it they thrust a sick, fragile boy; and he would have died there but for the kind-hearted soldier who went with him. He wrapped him in his blanket; gave him every morsel of his own food; stretched himself on the naked floor, and held him for hours clasped to his own warm breast; and, in all ways, nursed and tended him as if he had been his own mother. So Robert lived through it, and, at the end of forty hours, God soft-ened the hearts of his keepers.

For a month afterwards Robert was confined to the hos-pital. The occupant of the next cot to his own was a Union Colonel, who, when they were well enough to go back to the prison, procured for him admission to the officers' quarters in the third story. This secured for him no better fare or accommo-

dations than he would have had below with the private soldiers, but it gave him more air and larger space to move about
in. There he lived for seven long months; sleeping, at night, on
the hard floor; idling, by day, through the large rooms, or gazing out on the narrow prospect to be seen from the prison windows. But his time was not altogether idled away. Under the
eye of the good Colonel, he went over his arithmetic and grammar, and learned French and Spanish. But it was a weary time.
Exchanges were suspended, and there seemed to be no hope;
yet at last deliverance came.

Robert went seldom from his own floor, but one cold
day in January 1864 he was called by a simple errand to the
lower story. He was about returning, his foot was even on the
stairway, when he heard some one call his name. Looking
around, he saw it was the sentinel,—a young man, with light,
wavy hair, and an open, handsome countenance. His left coat-
sleeve was dangling at his side, but he seemed strong, and otherwise capable of military duty. "Did you call me?" asked Robert.
"Why!" cried the other, grasping his hand, "don't you know me?
don't you remember Chancellorsville?" It was the Rebel youth
whose life Robert had saved on the battle-field. The musket
dropped from his hand, and he hugged the little boy as if he had
been his own brother. The other sentries, and even an officer,
stood by, and said nothing; though all this was against prison
regulations. After all,—after even the atrocities the Rebels have
committed,—it is true that the same humanity beats under a
gray coat that beats under a blue one.

The next day a gentleman came into the room where
Robert was quartered, and asked to see him. He was a stoutly
built man, rather above the medium height, with a full, open
face, large pleasant eyes, and an agreeable manner. He was
dressed in dark-gray clothes, wore a broad felt hat, and everything about him seemed to denote that he was a kind-hearted
gentleman. He asked Robert how old he was; where his home
was; how long he had been in prison; and all about his mother;
and, when he rose to go away, gave him his hand, and said:
"You're a brave boy. I am sorry I haven't known of you before.
But you shall go home now,—in a few days I shall be going to
the lines, and will take you with me."

Robert's eyes filled with tears, and he stammered out: "I
thank you, sir. I thank you very much, sir."

"You need not, my boy," said the gentleman, placing his
hand kindly upon his head. "It is only right that we should let
you go,—you saved the life of one of our men."

In three days, with money in his pocket, given him by this gentleman, Robert was on his way to his mother. He is now at his home, fitting himself to act his part in this great world, in this earnest time in which we are living; and the kind-hearted man who set him free, charged with dishonest meanness and theft, is now shut up in that same horrid prison. Robert does not think him guilty, and he has asked me to tell you this about him, which I do gladly, and all the more gladly because I know him, and believe that, if there is an honorable, high-minded man in all Virginia, that man is Robert Ould.

5

"Some Day I Shall Be with You Again"

Children and Soldiers

Southern children were terrified when they found out that Yankee troops were bearing down on their homes. The frightening stories about children captured by "savage" Native Americans in Peter Parley's *Child's History* haunted one Southern girl. "My hair 'stood on end,'" remembered Sallie Hunt, "when I thought of the Yankees tying the children up in bags and knocking their brains out against a tree." As Northern armies approached New Orleans, Grace King shuddered when she recalled the "pictures of captured cities of the Bible where men and women were cut through with spears and swords, and children were dashed into walls."*

The children soon realized, however, that mass murder was not federal policy. The friendly Union soldiers setting up camp outside Gallatin, Tennessee, chatted and laughed with the boys who clustered around them. A Wisconsin soldier told Opie Read about killing a bear, and the young Rebel smuggled him a piece of peach pie. Throughout the South, Union soldiers acted as faithful guards, shared rations, and made presents of worn-out horses that could be nursed back to health and used by hard-strapped Southern families.

The readiness with which "enemy" soldiers attached themselves to children was directly related to their loneliness for their own young ones. When Federal forces occupied Front Royal, Virginia, in May 1862, a local family "made themselves

---

*Sallie Hunt, "Boys and Girls in the War," in *Our Women in the War: The Lives They Lived, the Deaths They Died* (Charleston: News and Courier Book Presses, 1885), 45; Grace Elizabeth King, *Memories of a Southern Woman of Letters* (New York: Macmillan, 1932), 5.

great favorites with their new acquaintances." The soldiers freely handed out candy and oranges, while the officers, according to the oldest daughter, "seem glad to be in the midst of little children again." The men's loneliness often made them desperate for affection. An officer whose unit occupied Dosia Williams's plantation in Louisiana offered to let her peek into a gold locket in return for a kiss. "I must have descended from Pandora," wrote Dosia years later, "for I could not stand it." She pecked him on the cheek, and he showed her a "miniature of a lovely little girl about my age." He and the Williams girls soon became "great friends, and his aides brought us candy and made much of us." After learning how badly "they wanted to see their children back up North," the Williams girls "excepted these particular Yankees from our fear and hatred."*

Any parent can identify with these soldiers' urgent desire to see their children, to temporarily adopt other children as stand-ins for their own little girls and boys. This relationship unites the selections in this chapter. Although none of them deals with encounters between Union soldiers and Southern children, they each show the interaction between grizzled veterans and wide-eyed youngsters.

"YOU MUST BE VERY GOOD": SOLDIERS' LETTERS

Children's magazines occasionally shared the most intimate communications between soldiers and their offspring. Like men in any war, Civil War soldiers worried about their offspring, fretted when they could not be with them during times of crisis and joy, and hoped that their little ones would not forget them during their long absence. To keep their memories alive in their children's minds, soldiers sent home letters detailing camp life, describing the great battles they had fought, and offering advice, encouragement, and instruction. They also assured their children that they had not forgotten them. One Union officer, writing home from Vicksburg, described how he had arranged photographs of his children around him as he sat on the ground scratching out a letter to them. Children tried to comfort their fathers with the knowledge that they were eagerly awaiting

---

*William P. Buck, ed., *Sad Earth, Sweet Heaven: The Diary of Lucy Rebecca Buck during the War between the States* (Birmingham: Cornerstone, 1973), 68, 72; Carol Wells, ed., *War, Reconstruction, and Redemption on Red River: The Memoirs of Dosia Williams Moore* (Ruston, La.: McGinty, 1990), 21–22.

their return, that everything was all right, and that they were minding their mothers.

The heart-tugging correspondence that follows reveals many elements of the relationships between soldiers and their children. Editors at the time offered them as examples of the sacrifices that adults and children alike had to make on behalf of their country. For modern readers, they provide familiar-sounding declarations of love, concern, and grief.

"To the Very Little Children"
The Little Pilgrim 10 (July 1863), 89

Little Flora's papa is a soldier away down in Nashville, Tenn., and she often writes letters to him, and then reads them to her mamma, to tell him in her letter what Flora says. Florence does not like it at all that papa cannot read her writing as well as he can mamma's, for she says she writes just like mamma. Of course she don't, for she is but four and a half years old, but she thinks she does. She makes her letters sound very well when she reads them, quite like "grown up" letters, so when she can "truly" write, I hope she will always be ready to write to her friends.

Her papa was very sick for a long time, in Nashville, and had to board with a "secesh" family, for there are few Union folks down that way. When he was better, he wrote her a little letter which perhaps you would like to hear. This is it.

My Dear Little Flora,

Papa has been very happy to see your nice little letters when he was sick, and thinks they deserve an answer.

You must be a good girl, and be kind to your mamma, your little brother, and all the "folkses"; and learn to read, and play on the "panno," (as you used to call piano, before you could speak plainly), so when papa comes home, he can hear you read and play.

There is a little girl not so big as you, lives here; she comes to see me every day, and her name is Mary, but she says it is "Mamy." And she says she is "fourteen years old," when she is only just four. Her grandfather lives here where your papa boards. I asked her the other day if she was a little Yankee, and she said, "No, sir, I am a little webel"; she thinks that is right, you see. She is a nice little girl, and I tell her about you almost every day. I had not seen her for about two days, until yesterday she came into my room, and she looked pale. I asked her what was the matter, and she said she had "berry much high feber."

Now papa must stop, and you must write me another letter when mamma does. Good-bye, my little girl, kiss mamma, brother, grandma and grandpa, and all the folks, and your little cousins, for your Dear Papa.

"Correspondence"
The Little Pilgrim 10 (June 1863), 74

Dear Pilgrim: This letter to little Nettie, from her papa in the army, came from Tennessee, all alone, in an envelope directed to herself. She thinks this proves that she is now too large to be considered "one of the good-for-nothings." You may read it, and if you like, show it to your friends.

Camp By-the-way, Oct., 1862

My Little Nettie, Busy Bee:

What are you doing, I wonder, to-night? Sitting on mother's knee, telling her a story about papa, living in his white house, and sleeping nice and warm in his blankets, on his cot, or some clean straw? I suppose so. And sometimes I wish I had Harry, or Fred, to curl down close to me and tell me all that has happened at home during the day. But some day I shall be with you again, and when Harry and Fred have done all the work mamma wants them to do, and eaten their suppers, we shall all sit down by the fire, and Harry will crack nuts for us, and Fred will parch some corn, while Nettie will ask me all sorts of questions. Fanny will be home from school, and mamma will look on while she sews, and we all will be very happy.

As we came here, I saw, early in the morning, a very beautiful house; and up stairs a little girl in a white night-gown, pushing aside the window curtains and looking out wonderingly at the long line of soldiers, as we surged along. I thought how my Nettie would have looked out so, if the soldiers had passed our home. We see a great many things which are interesting, and which will be so to you, some day, when you are older.

You must try to be a very good girl indeed, and when I come home, I shall be sure to bring you the china dishes I promised.

Kiss mamma and the boys for me. Good night, my Nettie.

From Papa

To Nettie, with the blue eyes.

"Correspondence"
The Little Pilgrim 10 (May 1863), 67-68

Pilot Knob. (From a letter of an officer in the army to his children.)

My dear boys—
    This is a hilly country, and there are hills all around our camp. In the rear there is a rise of probably one hundred and fifty feet, with a fort upon the summit, to which, if necessary, all our forces could retire, and where we could keep the ground for days against thousands of foes. Crowning another eminence, forty rods off, and forty feet above, is another small fort.
    A mile and a half from us, in a direct line towards Murfreesboro [Tennessee], is Pilot Knob, which I mentioned to you in my last letter. In company with one of the surgeons here, I rode up there a day or two ago. Riding around, and rising the hill gradually, we got within seventy-five feet of the summit, and then tying our horses, took the foot-path. The top of the hill gained, we found a spot of ground nearly level, and giving room for the six or seven tents occupied by sixty men. This place is used as a signal station and look-out, for many miles away. There are several large trees on this summit, and at the cool height of sixty feet they had erected a scaffold in the forks of one of them, from which of course the eye could command an immense extent of country. To me, the view from the ground was sufficiently enchanting. For miles upon miles I could see cultivated fields and flourishing farms, with their clusters of buildings. Rock river was to be seen through the trees, two miles away; but away to the west I could indistinctly see a large collection of tents and buildings. The gentlemanly Lieutenant handed me his glass, and there, in plain view, was Murfreesboro; and, clustering around it, the camps of whole divisions of the army. To our surprise we are told it is ten miles distant. With the aid of a telescope, they read messages signalled from the station at Murfreesboro. While we were talking with the Lieutenant commanding the post, the Lieutenant in charge of the signal corps came out to give a message. The flag man had a flag, say five feet square, white with a black centre, on a staff ten feet long. The officer calls out certain numbers; what they mean, no one can tell but the few initiated. The men know nothing of it, except what motions of the

flag represent the numbers given. The flag is held up straight before the flag man; the officer calls some number, say "21," and the man brings the flag down to the ground on his right, and up again twice. Another number is given, and down goes the flag once to the left. A third, and it dips away in front of the flag man, and so on. As each number represents a sentence, or many do, a good deal can be said in this way. Our forage train was out, and at head-quarters at Murfreesboro they were inquiring about it. Thus every movement is known at once; and if there were a movement among the hills five miles from us which looked suspicious, it is telegraphed at once to the station in our fort, up above us, and a reinforcement would, if necessary, be sent at once to our train.

My companion, Dr. L., said he would take a view from the look-out in the tree; so he started up the ladder, made by nailing strips across a flatted stick, fifty feet long. He got up ten feet, and stopped to pull off his spurs, lest he should trip. At twenty feet, he stops to ask a question, getting very careful, I notice; thirty feet, and he remarks that the wind blows like the mischief. I extol the fine view doubtless to be enjoyed above. He starts again, very slowly. Forty feet, and a dead stop; says he don't think the aperture in the platform above is large enough to admit of his passing through. Big signal fellow says he climbs through, every day. Doctor finally reaches the point where the ladder touches the tree, and halts. I ask if he is reflecting "how not to do it?"—says he thinks he is. I think so too. He inquires if the platform above is secure, as if it is, he may as well go down! He is assured it is quite safe, so he starts back, and in due time reaches the ground.

We are invited to peep through the telescope, and then taking leave of our courteous entertainers, make our way out of the entrenchments, and get to our horses.

It is warm here as May in Ohio. I can hardly think it is only February.

Good bye, my boys.

Your Father.

"A Soldier's Letter to His Little Sister"
The Little Pilgrim 10 (May 1863), 39

Sperrysville, Va., July 22d, 1862.

Dear Sister Fannie:

I received a letter not long ago from a certain very young lady, and I guess thee knows her too. She has black eyes, brown hair, and I believe is about nine years old. She is a kind, good-natured little girl. I wish thee would, when thee sees her, if thee has guessed who I am talking about, tell her that I want to find her just as nice a girl when I come back as when I left. Please kiss her for me, right on the mouth too, if thee can, and tell her that her soldier brother would like to receive another letter from her very well. Since I last saw you folks at home, I have done a great many queer things, and seen a great many queer sights.

I have been away on the tops of high mountains, where you could see away far, far off. See the houses down below. They look like little chicken-coops away down there; and there is an orchard, and a little creek running down the mountain side and winding away out of sight.

I have crossed over five big mountains since I saw thee; and one of them in the night, most of the way. It was so dark you could not see any farther than your horse's head. I have travelled many a night, till I got so sleepy that it was as much as I could do to keep on my horse, and once I did not stay on. We had been travelling all day over the mountains, and were going down the other side, when the wagons stopped for about fifteen minutes, and, as I sat there on my horse, though I tried my best, I could not keep awake, and the first thing I knew, I was lying in the mud, right under my horse. I had gone to sleep, and just naturally rolled off. It was lucky that my horse was sleepy too, for if he had not been almost asleep himself, he would very likely have done me some harm. I managed to keep awake the rest of that journey. We stopped at about two o'clock A.M., and I hitched my horse to a sapling, took my saddle for a pillow, my saddle blanket to lie on, and my overcoat for covering, laid down and went to sleep in the twinkling of an eye. About six o'clock the next morning, I awoke and found there had been a very hard rain since I laid down, and that I, of course, was soaked through and through, but was so tired that I had slept through it all, as soundly as I ever slept on a comfortable bed at home. That morning I had nothing for breakfast but a cup of coffee, with a hard cracker broken into it, and then had to start on, wet as I was, and ride that way all day.

This is a true and faithful specimen of many of the marches we have gone through. How would thee like it, dear sister Fannie? How would thee like to see a train of wagons ten miles long? I have seen them, and, as Quartermaster, had to be along with them, to look after my wagons which were in the train. And then just think of standing on the side of the road for three or four hours, and seeing soldiers marching by continually!

I used to think that I would like to take a horse-back ride once in a while, when I was at home. I have had plenty of it since

I came into the service. I have often been on my horse from twelve to fifteen hours at a time, going without my dinner, except some hard crackers, which I carried in my pocket. These are what are called forced marches, and we have had a great many of them in the last two months. Sometimes on these marches the road would run along the bank of a river, with a high wall of rock on one side, and the river on the other.

Near a town called Edinburgh, the bridge was burnt over the creek and it was high, but we had to ford it. The water came nearly to my knees, while sitting on the horse, and it was hard work for him to stand the current, but he succeeded in doing it, and bringing me across safely, with my boots full of water. There was one place we passed between Moorefield and Strasburg, where a creek, called "Lost Creek," runs right into the mountain, and comes out again, they say, ten miles off.

But I cannot remember all my adventures, and I will wait till I come home and see thee, and then I can tell thee more. I am well and hearty, and like this kind of life, and if only had the right kind of companions, could enjoy it well.

I wish thee, and father and mother, and Annie, could all come out to my tent some day, and bring a good dinner with you, and spend an hour or so. We'd have a nice time I'll bet. Well, good bye, dear sister Fannie—write again—thee and Annie write a letter together. I'll answer it.

Love to father, mother and Annie. Kiss them all for me. With many kisses for thee, I am thy loving soldier brother

Tom.

FROM HOME FRONT TO BATTLE FRONT

Children took it upon themselves to lighten the burdens of the soldiers they knew or came across. Throughout the North and South, soldiers' aid societies collected food, sewed clothing, knit socks, rolled bandages, and raised money to help soldiers in the Union and Confederate armies. Children frequently took part in these efforts. "Even little children worked" with their mothers at Soldiers' Aid Society meetings at the Baptist Church in a small town in Wisconsin. One girl recalled years later that she and the other children felt "very important . . . as we scraped away at the linen, making fluffy piles of the soft lint 'for the soldiers.'" Working with the older women helped the girls feel a part of the effort in other ways, too. Throughout the long afternoons of volunteer work, "they tried to comfort one another for the absence or the loss of dear ones. Long letters . . . were some-times read aloud, describing camp scenes, or battle experiences, or hair-breadth escapes from Libby Prison." The stories, the work, the sense of belonging to the community's war effort "thrilled us and left indelible memories."*

"A Box for the Soldier" describes one family's effort to pack the perfect combination of necessities and sentimental me-mentos into a box to be sent to their father in the army. The boys choose a miniature carved gun and a useful knife, while the girls offer handmade items to keep their father warm in his cold tent. The second selection, "Soldier, Are You Hungry?" became something of a legend during the war, reprinted in several chil-dren's and adult magazines; it represents the highly personal approach to supporting the war effort favored by many authors and philanthropists.

"A Box for the Soldier"
Mrs. Phebe H. Phelps
The Student and Schoolmate 13 (March 1864), 71–74

They were "making up a box" for the soldier gone to war. One of the daughters was knitting a pair of socks, soft and thick, for the weary feet that must stand all day in the cold, wet trenches; or drag themselves painfully on the march, mile after mile, long, slow, hard miles, over the rough and muddy roads of a strange country.

Another was knitting mittens; warm mittens for the hands that had lifted and carried her before she could use her own, the kind hands that had fed her, and held her clasped in tender love. Dear hands! if she could only grasp them now! Rough as they might be, how would she kiss them! warm them in her own! Oh, how many times she thought thus, as she picked up and slid from her needles the almost innumerable stitches with which she made the mittens.

The youngest daughter, only five years old, the darling, the pet of the household, was trying her little unskillful fingers on a cap, a cap for papa to sleep in on cold nights, a cap to keep his precious head from the frosty ground. "Ah," she kept saying, "poor, dear papa! how I would like to have papa's head close to mine, on my little pillow! I don't like to have him sleep on the bare ground!"

---

*Clara Lenroot, *Long Long Ago* (n.p., 1929), 14.

What were the boys doing for their father? What were they going to put in the box? What could boys put in? What could they make? One of them put in his knife,—the knife he prized so much,—all the knife he had, for he thought that father might have lost his and would want one, and his love to his father was more, even, than his pleasure in whittling, and the convenience and satisfaction which the real boy always finds in the ownership of a valuable knife.

Another sent nuts gathered by himself expressly for the loved and absent one, fresh, home-grown shell-barks and sweet chestnuts, that would make the once-mountain-boy smile, perhaps weep and smile together, as he recalled the far away hills whereon they grew; hills when a bold, brave boy he had climbed and gathered nuts, and where he had rejoiced to see his young boys, bold and brave like him, at their adventurous sports.

They picked the apples over to find rare ones to send; the best were not good enough, nor the largest, large enough to send to father. And one of the boys had carved a little miniature gun and a sword and a cannon, and they must be sent, for father would know all about such soldier things, better than anybody

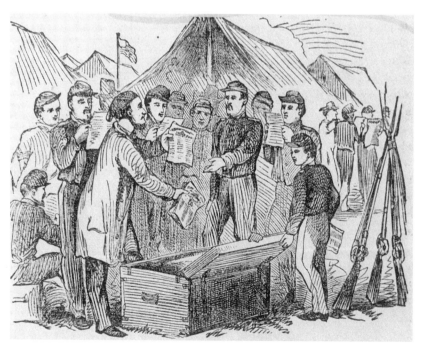

Soldiers found treasured keepsakes, newspapers, and homemade food in boxes sent from home. From The Student and Schoolmate.

else, and the young carver wanted his praise and high approval. Oh, there was plenty even for the boys to send; no one but has something to give, if he has a heart inclined.

The young people were discussing whose gift was best, would be most acceptable, most valued.

"I'm sure," said one of the knitters, "that father will like my socks the best of anything, for there's nothing so bad as cold feet. What can you do when your feet are frozen? Why, father would have to lie in his tent all the whole time, or perhaps be sick in hospital, if he had not good warm socks. Now, see if father don't like my present best. He may not say it right out, but see if he don't speak of the warm socks coming good, the very first thing."

The mitten-knitter argued for her work. "Why, father's fingers would stick fast to the cold iron of his gun in the sharp, stinging, wintry mornings, without mittens. Without them, he could never load and fire his gun in time to save himself from being shot by a rebel picket or a bloody guerrilla." She admitted that socks were very good for soldiers, but insisted that mittens were better; especially, mittens like hers, with an exclusive, isolated place for the forefinger.

John knew a knife would be a most acceptable gift. Father always wanted a knife; he used a knife a hundred times a day; no other man used one so much; and ten chances to one he had lost his, or it had been stolen. And the generous boy, who knew well how to use and value a knife and who also knew how much he should miss his own, was satisfied that his father would not fail to appreciate his gift, and give it the preference; for could he not get stockings and mittens and caps from the Sanitary Commission and other charitable societies, but they never sent knives.

So the children talked and discussed their offerings. "Why, we never thought of the things that mother is going to send! Of course, father will like them best," exclaimed one of the children. "She sends so many nice things; flannels and other clothes, and jellies, and cakes, and everything she can think of. And then I saw her writing such a long letter, with the tears on her cheeks! I know it's a beautiful letter, and I know father'll like that letter better than everything else in the box. You see if he don't."

"Of course he will," was the ready answer.

"How I wish I could write him a real good letter, as good as I can feel. I can feel it all, but when I come to write, I'm ashamed to put it down. I hate writing letters."

"What's grandmother going to send?" was asked.

Grandmother heard the inquiry and answered, "I'm going to send some socks, my child."

"Ain't you going to send anything else, grandmother?"

"What else can I send?" she slowly said, looking fixedly at her work. She seemed for a long time in deep thought; then covered her eyes with her hand, and bent her head as if in prayer.

"Ah!" the children whispered to each other, "grandmother will send plenty of prayers."

Everything was ready, and the soldier's box was being packed, the children looking on glad and hopeful, each desirous that his gift should be in a safe place.

Grandmother came slowly and totteringly into the room, holding out in her withered, trembling hands, her old and well-worn Bible. "Here, Susan," she said to the wife, "pack this; I send this to my dear son,—the best thing I've got. The best I've got is not too good for him. It's the very Bible his father read out of; the Bible I've read out of for fifty years; the Bible that he himself read out of when a child. No other one is like it, nor can be— to me and to him too. And he'll never want it more than now, when he's every day looking death so close in the face."

"But you'll miss your Bible so, mother!"

"Pack it, Susan, and tell William that with it go my prayers, my very heart. And it seems to me, that God himself will go to my son, with that blessed book; surely, he will, for is it not his own Holy Word?"

All was hushed and solemn among the children and tears stood in their eyes as they saw the sacred book carefully wrapped and deposited in the box. Then one of them whispered, "Grandmother has sent the best thing; better than all the rest."

Grandmother caught the whisper. "It is God's gift, more than mine, my child."

"Soldier, Are You Hungry?"
New Church Magazine for Children 2 (February 1864), 252–53

It was a bleak day in the month of March 1862. A cold, biting wind was astir: now it whistled round corners, causing gentlemen to pull their hats over their eyes; then it would send shutters to with a bang, startling quiet people. But few ladies were abroad, and these had veils tightly drawn over their faces to keep out the cold and dust.

It was on the afternoon of this day, that a train of cars, heavily laden with troops, might have been seen slowly entering the city of B——. They had been called to the defense of the capital of the nation, and were on their way.

When the cars stopped, the soldiers alighted, and, gathering their things up, prepared to march to the other depot, when they were told that a delay of some hours was unavoidable. So the colonel ordered them to stack arms, and make themselves as comfortable as possible.

Some of the men began to talk; others sat upon the curb, and clapped their hands to get some warmth in them. But one stood alone: very sad he looked, as he stood there in the wind, his hat pulled over his eyes. Perhaps he was thinking of his home so far away, and of those who were in that home; or may be he was cold and tired.

It chanced that a little boy had heard that some soldiers were passing through; and, gaining permission from his mother, he went out to see them.

He came slowly up the street,—his hands in his warm coat-pockets, a bright woolen comforter about his neck, and his cap securely fastened on.

When he came near where the soldiers were, he stopped to look at them; when suddenly he saw the one who looked so sad and lonely. Going up to him, he laid his hand upon his arm, and said, "Soldier, are you hungry?"

The soldier looked up, smiled, and said "he was both hungry and tired."

"Come with me," said the boy: "my home is near, and I will give you something to eat."

The soldier went with him. They soon came to the house; and his little friend took him to the dining-room, found his mother, told the story, and the table was soon spread with a substantial meal.

When he had finished, the soldier rose, thanked the boy and his mother for their kindness, and left them. In a few hours, he was on board the cars on his way to Washington.

Months passed; and the soldier, battling for his country's honor, often thought of his little friend. By his good conduct, he won the esteem of his officers, and was promoted to the rank of captain.

One day last fall, his regiment passed through B—— en route for home, their term of enlistment having expired; and the soldier, having a few hours to spare, determined to visit his little friend.

His ring at the bell was answered by a girl, of whom he inquired "if Frank was at home."—"Yes," was the answer: "walk in." He did so; and, in a few minutes, Frank was standing beside him, talking eagerly.

"I am going home," said the captain: "but I could not pass through without seeing you; and I have brought you something to remember me by."

As he finished speaking, he handed him a large package. With eager, trembling hands, the boy untied the string, and out came a beautiful photographic album. Frank undid the massive clasps, and looked inside, and saw that every page had a picture of the most distinguished Union generals: then he looked on the back, and saw in beautiful gilt letters the words, "Soldier, are you hungry?"

CHILDREN IN CAMP

The gruff exteriors of most soldiers melted when they came into the presence of children. This was not just a literary conceit; many Southern children recorded exactly that reaction when they encountered Yankees. Two stories from *Our Young Folks* show soldiers welcoming children into their camps. As in real-life encounters, the children here serve as reminders of the soldiers' own sons and daughters, as symbols of the future they are fighting to preserve, and as hints of the homes and hearths worlds away from the rough and dangerous existence they lead in the army.

These are charming stories, but they also contain threads of the themes of class and race that run through many of the selections in this book. Little Freddy and his widowed mother are unbearably poor, and his fascinating New Year's Day in camp is just a brief respite from grinding poverty. Still, he remains cheerful and refuses to challenge his place in the world. Even the lovely summer in the country that restores his mother's health does not mean that their status will change. Thomas Wentworth Higginson's portrayal of the African-American troops in his First South Carolina Volunteers remains one of the most objective and least biased of any contemporary description of black soldiers.* The relative absence of condescension toward blacks highlights his entertaining description of a peaceful winter in the South Carolina Sea Islands, showing young readers the equanimity and generosity that they should direct toward members of other races and cultures. Even more to the point, Higginson stresses that little Annie, the "baby of the regiment," is completely indifferent to racial differences, as is the little African-American baby who also spends a few weeks in winter camp with the First South Carolina.

---

*Also published in *Army Life in a Black Regiment* (1870).

The authors of the stories in this section were two of the period's most accomplished writers for children. Going back to her days as editor of the *Juvenile Miscellany* from 1826 to 1836, Lydia Maria Child had introduced young readers to the issues of race, class, and reform. A maverick Unitarian minister, educator, and abolitionist, Higginson was also a prolific author of essays, Latin translations, and fiction. A decade after the war he published the *Young Folks' History of the United States*, which was an even-handed but pro-Northern history of the country. In the stories that follow, Child's and Higginson's obvious affection for children transcends their rather conventional writing.

"Freddy's New Year's Dinner"
Lydia Maria Child
Our Young Folks 1 (July 1865), 421–29

Freddy Lincoln was the son of a widow, and, because he was born on the First of January, she called him her New Year's Present. A charming present he was, the bright, loving little fellow! His mother was not very well. She was not strong enough to earn much money. But Freddy grew stout on boiled potatoes, and good sweet bread and milk. His clothes were patched; but he liked them, because mother mended them nicely. He had no money to buy playthings; but he did not need any. He could amuse himself all day with chips and shavings, and his little frisky kitten, and tin cow that he picked up in the street. The cow had her feet broken off, but his mother bored four holes in a piece of wood, and put the cow's legs into the holes, and then she stood as well as any cow in the barn-yard; but she could not give any milk, you know, because she was made of tin. Kitty was a live thing, that wouldn't break, and Freddy liked her much better than anything made of tin or wood. She was a white kitten,— all white, except a little black spot on her nose. That black spot made her look as if she had been smelling of crocking kettles. When boys peeped in through the open fence, they called her Smutty Nose. Freddy did not like to have them laugh at his kitten. One day he took a basin of water and a piece of sponge, and tried to wash the black spot off. The kitten cried, "Miou!" and kicked her hind legs very hard against his wrists. But he held her tight, and scrubbed poor Kitty's nose till he almost rubbed the skin off. Perhaps he would have rubbed the skin quite off, if his mother had not called him. But as soon as he heard her sweet voice calling, "Freddy dear!" he ran to see what was wanted. His

Freddy and his new friend celebrate New Year's together.
From Our Young Folks.

mother said to him, "Here is Bobby Spring come to see you. He is going to have a Christmas party, and he wants you to come." "O Mother, do let me go!" exclaimed Freddy; and when mother said he might go, he jumped up and down, and shook his elbows, and laughed out loud, he was so glad. When Kitty saw him jumping about, she began to jump too. She ran round and round as fast after her own tail; but she didn't catch it; for the tail ran round fast as she did. "What a little fool!" said Bobby Spring. "She don't know that her tail is tied on." Freddy clapped his hands, and laughed to see how fast the kitten ran round. "So it is tied on," said he; "and Kitty don't know it. She thinks she can catch it, but she can't never catch it. Mother, when is Christmas? Is it to-night? May I wear my blue jacket?"

When he was told that the next night would be Christmas Eve, he thought it was a long time to wait. All the next day he kept asking, every hour, how long it would be before sunset. The sun went down at last, and Freddy went to the Christmas party. There he saw wonderful things. There was an evergreen tree on the table, lighted up with little candles; and dogs, and dolls, and birds, and all sorts of pretty things were on the branches. Every little girl and boy had something from the tree. Freddy had a small flag with stars and stripes on it, and on top was a bright gilded eagle and yellow tassel. And he had a paper full of sugared almonds, and a book full of pretty pictures. He jumped round with a little black-eyed girl, and called it dancing. Mrs. Spring played on the piano, and they had a merry time.

When Freddy's mother came for him, he could not believe it was nine o'clock, though he never sat up so late before. His mother told him it was time his little peepers were shut. But his peepers were open for two hours afterward; and when he fell asleep, he went to the Christmas party again. He dreamed that he saw his white kitten up in the Christmas tree, stretching her paw down to catch the dolls, that were dancing on the branches to the tune of Yankee Doodle. He remembered it when he woke up, and talked to his mother about it. When she told him the kitten did not go to the party, he said, "Yes, she was there, mother, for I did see her." Then he turned to puss, who was sleeping on the hearth-rug, and said, "Kitty, you know you was there. I did see you trying to catch the dolls." The kitten winked her eyes sleepily, and didn't seem to remember anything about the Christmas tree. But Freddy always thought that puss was at the party, though she couldn't talk about it. He talked it over to her ever so many times.

A week after the party it was New Year's Day. Freddy came down stairs barefoot, his little toes all red with the cold. He jumped and skipped about, for he was never still. And he hugged and kissed his mother and said, "I woke up first! I did wish you a happy New Year first! Didn't I, dear mother?" Then looking at his cup of milk and crust of bread, he began to think of the nice things at the Christmas party. And he said, "Mother, I don't think that is a very good breakfast for New Year's Day. It's my birthday, too. All the boys have things New Year's Day. Bobby Spring said he was going to have lots of things. His father, and his mother, and his grandfather, and his grandmother are all going to give him something."

Freddy's mother kissed him, and said, "My little boy has no father, and no grandfather, and no grandmother; and mother is not well, and can't earn much money to buy things. But she has made her dear little son a nice cap, just such a one as he wanted. See! It is like a soldier's cap. There are two bright buttons and a tassel. Isn't that a pretty New Year's present?"

Freddy seized it with both hands, pushed it down on his head, and began to march about the room. His mother smiled to see how tall he felt. "I wish I had a feather in it," he said.

"Well, here is the cockerel's feather you picked up; I will put that in," said his mother.

Freddy was delighted to have it, and as soon as it was fastened in, he began to march about again.

"But isn't my little son going to give mother a New Year's present?" said she.

He stopped marching at once, and said sorrowfully, "I don't know what to give you, dear mother. I haven't got anything. I am sorry I did eat up all my sugared almonds."

His mother kissed him, and said, "You are my New Year's present, sonny. Give mother a kiss. She will like that better than almonds."

When they had kissed each other many times, his mother said, "Now my little boy must be dressed, and eat his breakfast."

Freddy jumped down and looked out of the window. "It did snow while I was asleep," said he. "Let me have on my copper-toed shoes, and go out in the snow."

"But you must eat your breakfast first," said his mother.

Freddy nibbled away at the crust; then he laid it down, and looking up coaxingly in his mother's face, he said, "You know once, when I did look into the baker's window, he comed out and did give me a gingerbread rabbit, with two black currants for eyes. P'raps, if I wish the baker a happy New Year, he will give me another gingerbread rabbit. May I go and wish the baker a happy New Year? Do let me go, mother."

She smiled and said, "You may go and wish Mr. Wheaton a happy New Year, my son; but you mustn't ask him for a gingerbread rabbit. If he gives you a cake, make a bow, and say, thank you, sir; and if he does not give you a cake, make a bow and say, Good morning sir, and come right away, like a little man."

"But mother, if the baker don't give me a cake," said Freddy, "I should like to stop outside one little minute, just to look into the window and see the gingerbread rabbits. I won't ask for a rabbit. I will only look at 'em."

"Well, you may look at them, darling," said his mother. "But drink your cup of milk before you go."

He took the tin cup with both his plump little hands, and held back his head, and poured every drop into his mouth, and then set the cup down, smacking his lips. "Now, mother," said he, "please put on my coat, and my new cap, with the brass buttons and cockerel's feather; and I'll take my little flag, and then I shall look like a soldier." When his coat and cap were on, he gave his mother a smacking kiss, and said, "If the baker gives me a gingerbread rabbit, I will give you half of it." And away he went, saying, "March! March!"

His mother looked after him with a smile, but the tears were in her eyes; for Freddy was her darling boy, and she felt sad because she had no New Year's cake to give him. It was a beautiful winter morning. There was snow on the ground, and a sprinkling of snow on the trees, and bright sparkles of frost in the air. Freddy went marching along, making the snow fly with his little copper-toed shoes. His eyes were blue as the sky, his cheeks were rosy with cold, and the curls of his soft yellow hair blew about in the wind. He felt very tall, with a flag on his shoulder and a feather in his cap. He saw a man coming toward him dressed in a blue coat, with bright brass things on his cap. But he did not mind that. He kept marching along. When the man came up to him, he stopped and said, "What are you doing, my fine little fellow?"

"Playing soldier, sir," said Freddy, looking up into the man's face with his clear blue eyes.

The man caught him up in his strong arms, and hugged him and kissed him. "Bless your heart, I wish you were my little boy," said the man. "Your eyes are just like my little Lucy's. Whose boy are you?"

"I'm Mrs. Lincoln's boy. Whose boy are you?" said Freddy, with a roguish smile. His mother had taught him to say so, for fun; and he said it to the stranger man because he thought he would think it funny.

The man did think it was funny. He laughed, and chucked Freddy under the chin, saying, "You little Rogue! I'm one of Mister Lincoln's boys." He said that because he was a soldier in President Lincoln's army.

"Please let me get down," said Freddy; "I'm going to the baker's, to wish him happy New Year; and p'raps he will give me a gingerbread rabbit. He did give me a gingerbread rabbit once."

"You had better come with me," said the soldier. "I will give you a cake. You will see ever so many soldiers, and they will play Yankee Doodle for you on the drum and the fife."

"I would like to see the soldiers, and hear the drum and the fife," said Freddy. "Is it a great ways? Will you bring me back? I don't want to go a great ways from my mother."

"I will bring you safely back, my boy," said he. "So come with me and see the soldiers." He kissed him again, and set him down on the ground very tenderly.

Freddy liked this new friend very much. Sometimes he looked up in his face and smiled; and the soldier smiled to see him marching along by his side, with his little copper-toed shoes, and the flag on his shoulder, and the feather in his cap.

Freddy felt very safe, and very grand, marching along with a real live soldier. He thought it was a great deal better than playing with tin soldiers at the Christmas party. When his friend asked him if he had ever been to see the soldiers, he said he had played with a whole company of tin soldiers. Then he told him all about the Christmas party, how he danced with a little girl, and how Santa Claus put a little flag and a picture-book, and some sugared almonds, in the tree for him.

"I should like to see you dance with my little Lucy," said the soldier. "She has great blue eyes and curly yellow hair, just like you. She is a pretty little puss, and I love her dearly."

"Is she a kitten?" asked Freddy.

"No indeed. She is my little girl," said the soldier. "What made you think she was a kitten?"

"Because you did call her a pretty little puss; and that is what mother calls my kitten," said Freddy. Then he began to tell about his kitten; how she was all white, except a smutty spot on her nose, that he couldn't wash off.

The big soldier was as much pleased with his prattle as if he himself had been a little boy. It sounded very pleasantly to his ears, for his own dear little Lucy at home was just such a chatterbox. They had not walked very far before they came to a large building, and in front of it there were a great many men wearing blue coats and soldiers' caps. Some were singing, some talking, and some cleaning their guns. Freddy had never seen so many men together before. He began to wish his mother was with him. He nestled close to his new friend, and took hold of his coat.

"You needn't be afraid," said the man. "These are all Mr. Lincoln's boys, and they'll all be glad to see you. Come with me. I'll take good care of you."

"Hilloa, Sergeant!" shouted one of the soldiers, "who is this?"

"He is a little boy I found in the street," said the Sergeant. "I brought him here to see the soldiers. He wants to hear you play Yankee Doodle on the drum and the fife."

"That we will!" said the drummer. "Come here, my little fellow."

"Wish you happy New Year! Wish you happy New Year!" said the soldiers.

"It's my birthday, too," said Freddy, who began to feel that he was among friends.

They gave him apples and peanuts, and told him about the little girls and boys they had left at home. Then they began to play Yankee Doodle, with a big drum and a little drum, and big fife and a little fife; and some of the soldiers sang Yankee Doodle, and snapped their fingers to the music; and one of the men danced, and another made up droll faces. All this made Freddy so merry, he didn't know what to do with himself. He jumped up and down, and rolled over in the snow, and laughed, and laughed. Then he got up and marched about with his little flag, and tried to sing Yankee Doodle. He forgot all about the baker, and the gingerbread rabbit, and his little white kitten, and everything. The soldiers thought he was a charming little fellow, and he thought they were charming great fellows; and they had all manner of fun together.

Presently there was the rolling sound of a big drum, and somebody called out that dinner was ready. Then little Freddy stopped jumping about, and said, "I must go right home to my mother."

But his friend the Sergeant said, "You couldn't find the way home, my boy. Come and eat dinner with us, and as soon as I have done dinner, I will carry you home."

"I don't want to be carried," said Freddy. "I am a great, large boy, and I can walk home alone."

"What a big tail our kitten's got!" said one of the soldiers.

"Where is the kitty?" asked Freddy.

When the soldiers saw him looking all round for a kitten, they laughed; but Freddy didn't know what they were laughing at.

An officer came up and told the soldiers to form into a line. So they marched, two and two, to the dinner-tables; and Freddy took hold of the friendly Sergeant's hand, and marched along, with the cockerel's feather in his cap, and the little flag on his shoulder. The drums and the fifes sounded so merrily, that he wanted to jump and skip; but the Sergeant told him he must march like a little soldier, because he had the flag to carry. So he marched along very steadily, and his little copper-toed shoes made marks on the snow exactly alongside the sergeant's big shoes. Freddy felt as if he was a man.

The ladies of the town had sent the soldiers a great many good things for a New Year's dinner. They all seemed to think that Freddy was king of the feast. They mounted him on a tall box, so that he was as high as any of them. They put on his plate a slice of roast turkey, and squash, and potatoes, and gravy. He was in a hurry to have his friend the Sergeant cut up the turkey for him; for he had never had roasted turkey but twice before in his life. It tasted wonderfully good; but when he had eaten two or three mouthfuls, he stopped, and, looking up in the Sergeant's face, he said, "If you please, sir, I should like to put this nice dinner in a paper, and carry it home for my mother. My mother isn't very well, and she doesn't get much money to buy good things."

"That's right! Always be good to your mother, my brave boy," said the Sergeant. "But you may eat the turkey on your plate. I will give you another slice to carry home to your mother."

Then Freddy ate his turkey with great appetite. And when he had eaten it, they gave him a slice of plum-pudding with sweet-sauce. He looked at the big raisins, and laughed, and began to sing,

"Little Jack Horner sat in a corner,
Eating a Christmas pie;
He put in his thumb and pulled out a plum,
And cried, 'What a good boy am I!'"

He wanted to pull out a plum; but the pudding looked so good, he said, "If you please, I would like to put this in a paper and carry it home for my mother."

"Eat your pudding, my boy," said one of the soldiers. "I will go out presently and buy a basket, and we will fill it full of nice things for your mother."

So he ate his pudding, and all the sweet sauce on his plate. Then he took a little tin cup of water with both hands, and drank it all, and said he had had dinner enough.

The soldier went out and bought a basket, as large as he thought such a little boy could lift, and they filled it full of nice things. Then Freddy was in a great hurry to go home to show his mother what a New Year's present the soldiers had sent her. His friend the Sergeant put a bow of ribbon in his cap, red, white and blue, with a bright gilt eagle in the middle. The long ends of the ribbon hung down about his ears, and mixed with his yellow curls; and it all looked as nice as a picture. Freddy was in a great hurry to go and show his mother; but the soldiers all wanted to kiss him. It took a long while to go round among them all; and his friend the Sergeant said, "Make haste. The boy ought to go home. His mother will think he is lost."

Freddy hurried through his kissing, and heaved a big sigh when he said, "Good by, Mr. Lincoln's boys. I wish I could come again to-morrow."

"We are going to march away to-morrow," said the men; "and we don't know whether we shall ever see little Freddy again. Good by. Remember Mr. Lincoln's boys."

Some of them felt tears coming in their eyes, for they were thinking of their own dear little children at home.

"Good by," said Freddy. "Thank you for my nice dinner, and for the nice things you have sent my mother."

"Good by, Good by, Good by," they all said; and Freddy did not see them any more.

He felt sorry they were going away; but when the Sergeant began to whistle Yankee Doodle, he became merry again; and as they walked along, he shook his little head to the music, till the cockerel's feather in his cap, and the red and white and blue ribbons, and the yellow curls all seemed to be dancing the jig. There never was a little boy so happy as Freddy was that day.

When they came in sight of his mother's house, the Sergeant said, "Now you can carry the basket the rest of the way. Good by, dear little fellow." He took him up in his arms, and looked into his face, and kissed his mouth, and both cheeks, and both his eyes. When he sat him down on the ground, tears fell on his yellow curls, for the kind soldier was thinking of his own little blue-eyed Lucy at home.

Freddy did not see the tears, and he did not know what his friend was thinking of when he kissed him so many times. He was in a great hurry to show his mother the present he had brought her, and he tugged the basket along as fast as he could. His mother opened the door and said, "Why Freddy! Where have you been all this while?"

He was all out of breath, but as soon as he could speak, he said, "O mother, I did have such a darling New Year's Day! I did see such a many, many soldiers! And they did give me roast turkey, and they did give me plum pudding; and they did send a New Year's present to you."

"But Freddy," said his mother, "you have been naughty. Poor mother has been much troubled about you. She thought her little boy was lost."

"Was I naughty?" said Freddy, sorrowfully. "I didn't know I was naughty."

"Why only think how long you have been gone!" said his mother. "You went away at breakfast-time, and now it is after dinner."

"So I did!" said Freddy. He was very much surprised. He did not know where the day had gone to, it had gone so quick. When his mother told him she had been frightened about him, he felt sorry, and began to make up a lip to cry.

But his mother patted him on the head and said, "Don't cry. You didn't mean to be a naughty boy. You didn't mean to stay away from poor mother so long; did you? How was it? Tell me about it."

But Freddy was busy unpacking the basket. "O mother," said he, "see what lots of things the soldiers did send you! Here is a great piece of mince pie, and a great piece of apple-pie, and a great piece of plum pudding, and great piece of turkey, and four red apples; and see this great, big, large orange!"

His mother smiled, and said, "But where is the gingerbread rabbit you went out to get his morning?"

Freddy laid down the big orange, and seemed very much surprised again. "Why, mother," said he, "I did forget all about the gingerbread rabbit! How funny! But I did have a darling New Year's Day."

"You have not told me where you have been," said the mother. "Come, sit in my lap, and tell me all about it."

Then he began to tell how he met a soldier, who took him up in his arms and kissed him and told him he looked like his little blue-eyed Lucy at home. And how he asked him to go and see the soldiers; and how they played Yankee Doodle on great drums and little drums, and a big fife, and a little fife. How his tongue did run! It seemed as if he could never go to sleep that night. And when at last his peepers were shut, his mother saw him smiling in his sleep. He was dreaming about the soldiers that made such funny faces. He was awake bright and early in the morning, and the first words he said were, "Hark, mother! Don't you hear the drums and fifes? I guess the soldiers are marching away. O mother, let me get up and be dressed, and march a little way with 'em."

She put her arm round him and said, "My little boy don't want to go away and leave his poor mother all alone, does he?"

"No, dear mother, I don't." He nestled close up to her, and began to tell her over again all the wonderful things he had seen and heard. Freddy was a chatterbox.

When the winter passed away, something else happened. A lady in the country invited his mother to come and stay at her house; for she thought the fresh air and the smell of the new hay would be good for her. Freddy was delighted to go. He was always delighted with everything. The lady had a neighbor, whose little blue-eyed daughter was named Lucy; and they lived alone, because Lucy's father had gone to be a soldier.

One day, when Lucy was picking up chips, Freddy helped her to fill her little basket; and when it was full, he took hold of one side of the handle, and she took hold of the other, and they carried it into the house to her mother. The lady asked him whose little boy he was; and when he told her he was Lincoln's boy, she smiled, and asked him if he didn't go to see Mr. Lincoln's boys on New Year's Day. Freddy began to tell about the charming time he had with the soldiers. The lady took him up on her lap and kissed him, and told him her husband was the soldier who met him in the street. "And is that his little Lucy?" asked Freddy. "Yes, that is his little Lucy," said the lady. Then Freddy felt as if he was very well acquainted with the little girl. They played together every day. He told her, over and over again, what great times he had on Christmas Eve and New Year's Day; and he told her about his white kitten with a smutty nose; and she told him all about her chickens and her lambs. They made houses of cobs, and rode see-saw on the boards. He called her Sissy, and she called him Bubby. They have very pleasant times together.

When summer was gone, he did not want to go back to the city. He said, "I shall have nobody to play with me, mother. I wish Lucy would go with me. I wish she was my Sissy." "I wish so too," said his mother. "But Lucy must not leave her mother all alone, you know. And we must go home now, and see what has become of puss." "O yes," said Freddy, "I want to see puss again."

He found that she had grown to be a great puss; and he told his mother he did not like her half so well as he did Lucy.

"The Baby of the Regiment"
Thomas Wentworth Higginson
Our Young Folks 1 (February 1865), 102–9

They were in our winter camp on Port Royal Island, South Carolina. It was a lovely November morning, soft and spring-like; the mocking-birds were singing, and the cotton fields still white with fleecy pods. Morning drill was over, the men were cleaning their guns and singing happily; the officers were in their tents, reading still more happily their letters just arrived from home. Suddenly I heard a knock at my tent-door, and the latch clicked. It was the only latch in the camp, and I was very proud of it, and the officers always clicked it as loudly as possible, in order to gratify my feelings. The door opened, and the Quartermaster thrust in the most beaming face I ever saw.

"Colonel," said he, "there are great news for the regiment. My wife and baby are coming by the next steamer!"

"Baby!" said I, in amazement. "Q.M., you are beside yourself." (We always called the Quartermaster Q.M. for shortness.) "There was a pass sent to your wife, but nothing was ever said about a baby. Baby, indeed!"

"But the baby was included in the pass," replied the triumphant father-of-a-family. "You don't suppose my wife would come down here without her baby. Besides, the pass permits her to bring necessary baggage, and is not the baby six months old necessary baggage?"

"But my dear fellow," said I, rather anxiously, "how can you make the dear little darling comfortable in a tent, amidst these rigors of a South Carolina winter, when it is uncomfortably hot for drill at noon, and ice forms by your bedside at night?"

"Trust me for that," said the delighted papa, and went off whistling. I could hear him telling the same news to three others, at least, before he got to his own tent.

That day the preparations began, and soon his abode was a wonder of comfort. There were posts and rafters, and a raised floor, and a great chimney, and a door with hinges,— every luxury except a latch and that he could not have for mine was the last one that could be purchased. One of the regimental carpenters was employed to make a cradle, and another to make a bedstead high enough for the cradle to go under. Then there must be a bit of red carpet beside the bedstead, and thus the progress of splendor went on. The wife of one of the colored sergeants was engaged to act as nursery-maid. She was a very respectable young woman; the only objection being to her, that she smoked a pipe. But we thought that perhaps Baby might not dislike tobacco; and if she did, she would have excellent opportunities to break the pipe in pieces.

In due time the steamer arrived, and Baby and her mother were among the passengers. The little thing was soon settled in her new cradle, and slept in it as if she had never known any other. The sergeant's wife soon had her on exhibition through the neighborhood, and from that time forward she was quite a little queen among us. She had sweet blue eyes and pretty brown hair, with round, dimpled cheeks, and that perfect dignity which is so beautiful in a baby. She hardly ever cried, and was not at all timid. She would go to anybody, and yet did not encourage any romping from any but the most intimate friends. She always wore a warm long-sleeved scarlet cloak with a hood, and in this costume was carried, or "toted," as the colored soldiers said, all about the camp. At "guard-mounting" in the morning, when the men who are to go on guard duty for the day are drawn up to be inspected, Baby was always there, to help inspect them. She did not say much, but eyed them very closely, and seemed fully to appreciate their bright buttons. Then the Officer-of-the-Day, who appeared at guard-mounting with his sword and sash, and comes afterward to the Colonel's tent for orders, would come and speak to Baby on his way, and received her orders first. When the time came for drill, she was usually present to watch the troops; and when the drum beat for dinner, she liked to see the long row of men in each company march up to the cookhouse, in single file, each with tin cup and plate. During the day in pleasant weather, she might be seen in her nurse's arms, about the company looking very pretty amidst the shining black cheeks and neat blue uniforms of the soldiers. At "dress-parade," just before sunset, she was always an attendant. As I stood before the regiment, I could see the little spot of red out of the corner of my eye, at one end of the line of men; and I looked with so much interest for her small person, that, instead of saying at the proper time, "Attention, Battalion! Shoulder arms!"— it is a wonder that I did not say, "Shoulder babies!"

Our little lady was very impartial, and distributed her kind looks to every body. She had not the slightest prejudice against color, and did not care in the least whether her particular friends were black or white. Her especial favorites, I think, were the little drummer-boys, who were not my favorites by any means, for they were a roguish set of little scamps, and gave more trouble than all the grown men in the regiment. I think Annie liked them because they were small, and made a noise, and had red caps like her hood, and red facings on their jackets, and also because they occasionally stood on their heads for her amusement. After dress-parade the whole drum-corps would march to the great flag-staff, and wait till just sunset-time, when they would beat on their drums what is called "the retreat," and then the flag would be hauled down,—a great festival for Annie. Sometimes the Sergeant-Major would wrap her in the folds of the flag, after it was taken down, and she would peep out very prettily from amidst the stars and stripes, like a little new-born Goddess of Liberty.

About once a month, some inspecting officer was sent to the camp by the general in command to see to the condition of everything in the regiment, from bayonets to buttons. It was usually a long and tiresome process, and when everything else was done, I used to tell the officer that I had one thing more for him to inspect, which was peculiar in our regiment. Then I would send for Baby to be exhibited, and I never saw an inspecting officer, old or young, who did not look pleased at the sudden appearance of the little, fresh, smiling creature,—a flower in the midst of war. And Annie in her turn would look at them, with the true baby dignity in her face,—that deep, earnest look which babies often have, and which people think so wonderful when Raphael paints it, although they might often see just the same expression in the faces of their own darlings at home.

Meanwhile, Annie seemed to like the camp style of housekeeping very much. Her father's tent was double, and he used the front apartment for his office, and the inner room for parlor and bedroom; while the nurse had a separate tent and wash-room behind it all. I remember that, the first time I went there in the evening, it was to borrow some writing paper; and while Baby's mother was hunting for it in the front of the tent, I heard a great cooing and murmuring in the inner room. I asked if Annie was still awake, and her mother told me to go in and see. Pushing aside the canvas door, I entered. No sign of anybody was seen; but a variety of soft little happy noises seemed to come from an unseen corner. Mrs. C. came quietly in, pulled away the counterpane of her own bed, and drew out the rough cradle where lay the little damsel, perfectly happy, and wider awake than anything but a baby can possibly be. She looked as if the seclusion of a dozen family bedsteads would not be enough to discourage her spirits, and I saw that camp life was likely to suit her very well.

A tent can be kept very warm, for it is merely a house with a thinner wall than usual; and I do not think that Baby felt the cold much more than if she had been at home during the winter. The great trouble is, that a tent-chimney, not being built very high, is apt to smoke when the wind is in a certain direction; and when that happens, it is hardly possible to stay inside. So we used to build the chimneys of some tents on the east side, and those of others on the west, and thus some of the tents were always comfortable. I have seen Baby's mother running in a hard rain, with little Red-Riding-Hood in her arms, to take refuge with the Adjutant's wife, when every other abode was full of smoke; and I must admit that there were one or two windy days that season, when nobody could really keep warm, and Annie had to remain ignominiously in her cradle, with as many clothes on as possible, for almost the whole time.

The Quartermaster's tent was very attractive to us in the evening. I remember that once, on passing near it after nightfall, I heard our Major's fine voice singing Methodist hymns within, and Mrs. C.'s sweet tones chiming in. So I peeped through the outer door. The fire was burning very pleasantly in the inner tent, and the scrap of new red carpet made the floor look quite magnificent. The major sat on a box, our surgeon on a stool; "Q. M." and his wife, and the Adjutant's wife, and one of the captains, were all sitting on the bed. Baby had retired for the night, was overshadowed, suppressed, sat upon; the singing went on, and the little thing had wandered away into her own land of dreams, nearer to heaven, perhaps, than any pitch their voices could attain. I went in, and joined the party. Presently the music stopped, and another officer was sent for, to sing some particular song. At this pause the invisible innocent waked a little, and began to cluck and coo.

"It's the kitten," exclaimed somebody.

"It's my baby!" exclaimed Mrs. C. triumphantly, in that tone of unfailing personal pride which belongs to young mothers.

The people all got up from the bed for a moment, while Annie was pulled from beneath, wide awake and placid as usual; "and she sat in one lap or another during the rest of the concert, sometimes winking at the candle, but usually listening to the songs, with calm and critical expression, as if she could make as much noise as any of them, whenever she saw it fit to try. Not a sound did she make, however, except one little soft sneeze, which led to an immediate flood-tide of red shawl, covering every part of her, but the forehead. After a little while, I hinted that the concert had better be ended, because I knew from observation that the small damsel had carefully watched a regimental inspection and a brigade drill on that day, and that an interval of repose was certainly necessary.

Annie did not long remain the only baby in camp. One day, on going out to the stables to look at a horse, I heard a sound of baby-talk addressed by some man to a child near by, and looking around the corner of a tent, I saw that one of the hostlers had something black and round, lying on the sloping side of a tent, with which he was playing very eagerly. It proved to be his little baby, a plump little shiny thing, younger than Annie; and I never saw a merrier picture than the happy father frolicking with his child, while the mother stood quietly by. This was Baby Number Two, and she stayed in camp several weeks, the two little innocents meeting each other every day, in the placid indifference that belonged to their years; both were happy little healthy things, and it never seemed to cross their minds that there was any difference in their complexions. As I said before, Annie was not troubled by any prejudice in regard to color, nor do I suppose that the other little maiden was.

Annie enjoyed the tent-life very much; but when we were sent out on picket soon after, she enjoyed it still more.

When a regiment is on picket, the main camp is usually much smaller, because most of the companies are scattered about at outposts, and but few are left at head-quarters. Our head-quarters were at a deserted plantation house, with one large parlor, a dining room, and a few bedrooms. Baby's father and mother had a room up stairs, with a stove whose pipe went straight out at the window. This was quite comfortable, though half the windows were broken, and there was no glass and no glazier to mend them. The windows of the large parlor were in much the same condition, though we had an immense fire-place, where we had a bright fire whenever it was cold, and always in the evening. The walls of this room were very dirty, and it took our ladies several days to cover all the unsightly places with wreaths and hangings of evergreen. In this performance Baby took an active, or rather a passive part. Her duties consisted in sitting in a great nest of evergreen, pulling and fingering the fragrant leaves, and occasionally giving a little cry of glee when she had accomplished some piece of decided mischief.

There was less entertainment to be found in the camp itself at this time; but the household at head-quarters was larger than Baby had been accustomed to. We had a great deal of company, moreover, and she had quite a gay life of it. She usually made her appearance in the large parlor soon after breakfast; and to dance her for a few moments in our arms was one of the first daily duties of each one. Then the morning reports began to arrive from the different outposts,—a mounted officer or courier coming in from each place, dismounting at the door, and clattering in with jingling arms and spurs, each a new excitement for Annie. She usually got some attention from any officer who came, receiving with her wonted dignity any daring kiss or pinch of the cheek. When the messengers had ceased to be interesting, there were always the horses to look at, held or tethered under the trees beside the sunny piazza. After the various couriers had been received, other messengers would be despatched to the town, seven miles away, and Baby had all the excitement of their mounting and departure. Her father was often one of the riders, and would sometimes seize Annie for a good-bye kiss, placing her on the saddle before him, gallop her around the house once or twice, and then give her back to the nurse's arms again. She was perfectly fearless, and such boisterous attention never frightened her, nor did they ever interfere with her sweet, infantine self-possession.

After the riding-parties had gone, there was the piazza still for entertainment, with a sentinel pacing up and down before it; but Annie did not enjoy the sentinel, though his breast-plate and buttons shone like gold, so much as the hammock which always hung swinging between the pillars. It was a pretty hammock, with great open meshes; and she delighted to lie in it, and have the netting close above her, so that she could only be seen through the apertures. I can see her now, the fresh little rosy thing, in her blue and scarlet wrappings, with one round and dimpled arm thrust forth through the netting, and the other grasping an armful of blushing roses and fragrant magnolias. She looked like those pretty little French bas-reliefs of Cupids imprisoned in baskets, and peeping through. That hammock was a very useful appendage; it was a couch for us, a cradle for Baby, a nest for the kittens; and we had, moreover, a little hen, which tried to roost there every night.

When the mornings were colder, and the stove up stairs smoked the wrong way, Baby was brought down in a very in-complete state of toilet, and finished her dressing by the great fire. We found her bare shoulders very becoming, and she was very much interested in her own little pink toes. After a very slow dressing, she had a still slower breakfast out of a tin cup of warm milk, of which she generally spilt a good deal, as she had much to do in watching everybody who came into the room, and seeing that there was no mischief done. Then she would be placed on the floor, on our only piece of carpet, and the kittens would be brought in for her to play with.

We had, at different times, a variety of pets, of whom Annie did not take much notice. Sometimes we had young par-tridges, caught by the little boys in trap-cages. The children called them "Bob and Chloe," because the first notes of the male and female sound like those names. One day I brought home an opossum, with her blind bare little young clinging to the droll little pouch where their mothers keep them. Sometimes we had pretty little green lizards, their color darkening or deepening, like that of chameleons, in light or shade. But the only pets that took Baby's fancy were the kittens. They perfectly delighted her, from the first moment she saw them; they were the only things younger than herself that she had ever beheld, and the only things softer than themselves that her small hands had grasped. It was astonishing to see how much the kittens would endure from her. They could scarcely be touched by anyone else without mewing; but when Annie seized one by the head and the other by the tail, and rubbed them violently together, they did not make a sound. I suppose that a baby's grasp is really soft, even if it seems ferocious; and so it gives less pain than one would think. At any rate, the little animals had the best of it very soon; for they entirely outstripped Annie in learning to walk, and they could soon scramble away beyond her reach, while she sat in a sort of dumb despair, unable to comprehend why anything so much smaller than herself should be so much nimbler. Meanwhile, the kittens would sit up and look at her with the most provoking indifference, just out of arm's length, until some of us would take pity on the young lady, toss her furry playthings back to her again. "Little baby," she learned to call them; and these were the very first words she spoke.

Baby had evidently a natural turn for war, further cultivated by an intimate knowledge of drills and parades. The nearer she came to actual conflict, the better she seemed to like it, peaceful as her own little ways might be. Twice, at least, while she was with us on picket, we had alarms from the Rebel troops, who would bring down cannon to the opposite side of the Ferry, about two miles beyond us, and throw shot and shell over upon our side. Then the officer at the Ferry would think that there was to be an attack made, and couriers would be sent, riding to and fro, and the men would all be called to arms in a hurry, and the ladies at head-quarters would all put on their best bonnets and come down stairs, and the ambulance (or, as some of the men called it, "the omelet") would be made ready to carry them to a place of safety before the expected fight. On such occasions, Baby was in all her glory. She shouted with delight at being suddenly uncribbed and thrust into her little scarlet cloak, and brought down stairs, at an utterly unusual and improper hour, to a piazza with lights and people and horses and general excitement. She crowed and gurgled and made gestures with her little fists, and screamed out what seemed to be her advice on the military situation, as freely as if she had been a newspaper editor. Except that it was rather difficult to understand her precise directions, I do not know but the whole Rebel force might have been captured through her plans. And at any rate, I should much rather obey her orders than those of some generals whom I have known; for she at least meant no harm, and would lead one into no mischief.

However, at last the danger, such as it was, would be all over, and the ladies would be induced to go peacefully to bed again; and Annie would retreat with them to her ignoble cradle, very much disappointed, and looking vainly back at the more martial scene below. The next morning, she would seem to have forgotten all about it, and would spill her bread-and-milk by the fire as if nothing had happened.

I suppose we hardly knew, how large a part of the sunshine of our daily lives was contributed by dear little Annie. Yet, when I now look back on that pleasant Southern home, she seems as essential a part of it as the mocking-bird or magnolias, and I cannot convince myself that in returning to it I should not find her there. But Annie came back, with the spring, to her Northern birthplace, and then passed away from this earth before her little feet had fairly learned to tread its paths; and when I meet her next, it must be in some world where there is triumph without armies, and where innocence is trained in scenes of peace. I know, however, that her little life, short as it seemed, was a blessing to us all, giving a perpetual image of serenity and sweetness, recalling the lovely atmosphere of far-off homes, and holding us by unsuspected ties to "whatsoever things are pure."

6

Home Guards

Virtue and the War Effort

The war intruded on more than the imaginations of children. With fathers and brothers absent in the army, many Civil War children had to take on greater responsibilities. As one soldier reminded his son, "Fate has ordained that we should be *actors* in this dark chapter of the World's history—*You and I*—'*Ma*' and sister . . . perhaps the little ones—all are actors—all have some *part* to perform." Girls and boys both had to take on unfamiliar responsibilities such as caring for younger siblings, performing heavy farm chores, or working in factories. Twelve-year-old Marion Drury had "to assume the work and responsibilities" of a man because most farmhands had gone into the army, while future comedian Eddie Foy helped his widowed mother make ends meet by singing and dancing with a wandering fiddler in the bars and streets of New York. When Anna Howard's father and brothers rushed into the army, they left Anna, her mother, and her younger sisters to support themselves in the backwoods of Michigan. Anna helped her mother sew, wash laundry, take in loggers as boarders, and teach school just to bring in a bare living. She still remembered that life, fifty years later, as "a strenuous and tragic affair."*

In addition to pitching in to support their families, children contributed to the war effort by sending mittens, socks,

---

*Edward Pye to Neddie Pye, November 7, 1864, "Letters from the Confederate Medical Service in Texas, 1863–1865," ed. Frank E. Vandiver, *Southwestern Historical Quarterly* 55 (April 1952): 465–66; Marion Richardson Drury, *Reminiscences of Early Days in Iowa* (Toledo, Iowa: Toledo Chronicle Press, 1931), 45; Anna Howard Shaw, *The Story of a Pioneer* (New York: Harper and Brothers, 1915), 34.

One of dozens of patriotic songs published by Oliver Optic during the war.
From The Student and Schoolmate.

and food to soldiers in the field. They also raised money for soldiers' hospitals and other good causes by staging tableaux,
pinching pennies, and hosting fairs where they sold toys and
needlework. The proceeds of at least a dozen "children's fairs"
in Philadelphia in the fall of 1862 bought bandages, lint, fans,
handkerchiefs, food, soap, tobacco, combs, brandy, food, and
cash to a local army hospital. Schools sometimes adopted individual hospitals and canvassed neighborhoods for donations.
In Philadelphia's 18th Ward, children gathered two large wagons of food and linen in a single week. In the same city, black
children from the Bethel African Methodist Episcopal Sabbath

School sent money to the local Soldiers' Aid Society and to the hospital of a local black regiment.

The large sanitary fairs held throughout the North during the last two years of the war were a focus for Northern children's fund-raising. At New York's 1864 fair, a separate "children's department" offered booths and displays of toys and crafts made by boys and girls from a wide variety of backgrounds: soldiers' orphans; inmates at the Deaf and Dumb Asylum and the Blind Asylum; students at the Wilson Industrial School and the Birch Church Mission School; the "girls of the House of Refuge"; members of the Hebrew Orphan Asylum and the "Colored Home"; and the "Children of the Sacred Heart" in Harlem. At many fairs, young girls, including Gen. Ulysses S. Grant's daughter Nellie, took turns sitting in giant shoes and selling dolls as "The Old Woman Who Lived in a Shoe."

Sanitary fairs also offered tremendously interesting entertainment for children. The Great Central Fair in Philadelphia, for instance, offered stereopticon views, magic shows, ventriloquists, and an indoor playground adjacent to the sprawling restaurant. Children caught up in war excitement could tour the huge Military Department at the New York Metropolitan Fair, which featured a musket fired at the Battle of Bunker Hill, a pistol that had been owned by Cornwallis and captured at Yorktown, and the Marquis de Lafayette's camp kettle. Even more fascinating were the racks of firearms, fragments from a shell fired into Fort Sumter and splinters from a Union monitor, the battle flags of perhaps seventy New York regiments, and a number of captured Rebel banners.

Wartime stories did show children having fun, and a few mentioned local sanitary fairs. Affluent children raised money for penniless "contrabands" and various soldiers' causes, and middle-class youngsters also found ways to be useful. But even as these stories reflected and, no doubt, inspired children's desire to participate in the war effort, they emphasized that there was a right way and a wrong way to give. The war provided authors—and children—with the opportunity to learn the value of age-old virtues such as thrift, generosity, humility, and hard work.

In keeping with the antebellum convention of posing "good" and "bad" child models in counterpoint to one another, some characters displayed stellar behavior instinctively while others had to overcome innate deficiencies—laziness, selfishness, or carelessness—on their way to becoming the sort of thoughtful, kind, and determined children that authors had invented for generations. As a recent study of children's literature suggests, one prerequisite for being a "good" boy "was that he should have at one stage been a bad one."* Boorish, or selfish, or disloyal behavior could be just as instructive as virtue, as long as the culprit was eventually reformed.

MATERIAL FOR BRAVE AND HONEST MEN: LESSONS OF WAR

Even in wartime, children had to learn that there were many forms of duty, that it was not enough simply to spend a few minutes a day picking lint or cheering for the Union. *Kathie's Soldiers*, an obscure juvenile novel, showed children that they must not get caught up in the excitement of war to the extent that they forget what is really important. Every character in the middle-class family at the center of the book finds out that merely being patriotic and supporting the war effort is easy; they learn that other virtues are much harder to attain—and, perhaps, much more valuable. The main character, a teenager named Kathie Allston, not only works at the local sanitary fair and watches over the motherless daughter of a soldier but also fulfills her larger moral duty by refusing to engage in the constant gossip and backbiting going on among the fashionable girls at her school and persevering against the condescending daughter of a dishonest army contractor. Kathie's little brother Freddie shows his patriotism by trotting around in his soldier's outfit, but his chief duty—his contribution to the war effort, readers are supposed to believe—is to stay out of trouble and mind his mother. Sometimes, the story argues, even enlisting in the army is not the best way to do one's duty. Kathie's Uncle Rob decides against going off to war. In fact, although he is subject to the draft, like thousands of real-life Northerners, he hires a "substitute" to go in his place so that he can remain at home to support his widowed sister and her family. His nephew Rob fulfills his duty by submitting to his mother's wishes that he attend a boarding school rather than become a drummer in the army. The poem and stories that follow reveal how readers could begin to do their "duty" by being good Christian children, by living up to their parents' expectations, and by refusing to give up in the face of adversity. Their "wars" were not on the battlefield, but in their hearts.

---

*Gillian Avery, *Behold the Child: American Children and Their Books, 1621–1922* (Baltimore: Johns Hopkins University Press, 1994), 197.

"The Home Guard"

The Little American 1 (July 15, 1863), 159

My father's gone down with the army, to fight;
My brother's a sailor, away on the sea;
And now where my mother sits quiet at night,
There's no one to look at but Annie and me.
Rub-a-dub!

Sometimes when I beat an alarm on my drum,
Annie folds her arms tight and declares she won't yield;
For we are at play that the rebels have come,—
But I'd just like to see them come into our field!
Rub-a-dub!

Little Annie's my sister; and though she's a girl,
She's almost as brave and as good as a boy;
And I really believe, if her very last curl
Could help our dear Country, she'd give it with joy.
Rub-a-dub!

We were talking about that one day, she and I,
And trying to make up our minds what to do;
For when father and brother are willing to die,
It seems as if we ought to do something too.
Rub-a-dub!

"You know, Willie," said Annie, "I've hemmed a good deal,
And I've got a grey stocking all nicely begun;
But then I can't knit half as fast as I feel,
And the war may be over before it is done."

"Yes, Annie," said I, "I dare say it will be;
but all girls can do is the best that they can.
But this is the point—I am sure I can't see
Why a boy shouldn't fight, just as well as a man."
Rub-a-dub!

"Now if General Burnside would make me his aide,
I'd never give aid to the rebels—not I!
And as to this talk about being afraid,
Why, if the right time came, I guess I could die."
Rub-a-dub!

Then Annie's blue eyes like our spring over flowed,
(Girls' tears come so easy!) "O Willie," said she,
"If you marched away with the men down the road,
Then who would take care of poor mother and me?"
Rub-a-dub!

So we went and asked mother—and mother cried too;
At least for a minute she couldn't just speak;
And then she said, "Children, there's plenty to do,
If work for the Country is all that you seek."
Rub-a-dub!

"But look at these dear little hands—and you'll see
The Lord did not fit them for sabre and gun;
And when we would soldiers and conquerors be,
With arms of his giving the work must be done.

"You cannot go into the battle, my dears,
But kneel down and pray for the hosts that have gone!
That God may give victory unto our tears,
Nor leave our brave soldiers to fight on alone.

"Pray, pray for your Country! that God would be nigh,
And with these deep fires burn out all her dross,
And give to the people his peace from on high,
And joy out of weeping, and gain out of loss.

"In each of our hearts there's disorder to quell,
And rebels enough to be put to flight there;
And none serve their Country so truly, so well,
As those who fight Satan by faith and by prayer.

"So little ones, pray!—even very small hands
Are strong when uplifted to heaven's great King:
some fight for their Country in fierce armed bands,
But we on our knees must the victory bring."

Then mother rose up and went quickly away,
With oh such a sob coming up from her breast!
And I wish I could be with my father to-day,—
And we'd give them a lesson, Jeff, Lee, and the rest!
Rub-a-dub!
Rub-adub-dub, Rub-adub-dub!
Rub-a-dub, dub-a-dub, dub-a-dub-dub!

"Small Fighting"
Gail Hamilton

The Student and Schoolmate 11 (January 1862), 7–11

"Holley is as cross as two sticks this morning," said Janet, confidentially, as she settled down in one corner of the sofa, by the side of her sister.

"Qu'a-t-il—what's the matter with him?" asked Cappie, quietly, continuing to "rummage" her bag for certain silk pieces necessary to the trimming of her doll's dress.

"I don't know. I just asked him to button my boot, and he said, 'O! get out!'"

"And you got out, I suppose, like the goose you are. Why don't you stand up for your rights? Everybody imposes on you, Janet, because you let 'em. Holley wouldn't have answered me in that way. Pour-quoi? Parceque, I should have boxed his ears." Cappie was very much interested in her French, which was as yet a novelty; so you must excuse her peculiar style of talking.

"I suppose he thinks it is his right not to have to button girls' boots," said Janet, philosophically from her head, and exculpatingly from her sweet little heart, which was always making allowances for everybody else, and sacrificing her own comfort to other people's selfishness.

"It's boys' duty to do what their sisters want to have them, when it's reasonable," said Cappie, decidedly. Cappie was always inclined to severity, particularly when boys were in the case. She desired them to keep to the letter of the law. "It is no use, Janet, for you to let them set up that they are going to do just what they like, and make girls do it too. Don't you and I have to mend all Holley's stockings, and make his bed, and dust his room, and sew on his buttons? And I should like to know if he's to set up and not button your boots! I should think! Open that door! I'll give him a lesson or two."

Janet obediently threw open the door of the library where Holley sat with his feet on the fender, and his jack-knife in his hands, and Cappie sang out, "Venez ici: Come here, mon garcon."

"What do you want?" growled Holley.

"You, my jewel," responded Cappie, sweetly.

"What of me, then?" and Holley stood lowering and scowling in the doorway.

"N'est-ce pas que vous etes un sweet creature? Scolding his little sister who takes care of him, and snubbing her when she just asks him to do a little thing for her. Look at her feet.

Now she'll have to go and bother papa to get her feet decent; and you with no earthly thing to do but make yourself agreeable."

"Agreeable! how is a fellow to make himself agreeable with everything going to smash generally?"

"Que vouiez-vous dire? Who's gone to smash now?"

"We are—all of us. Every time there's a fight, we are defeated, and we don't have any fights to speak of, either. Little catch-penny, one-horse affairs—a handful here and a handful there, and running away at that! My stars! I guess if I was a soldier, if I wouldn't have more pluck!"

"Why you horrid, vile slanderer! Didn't our soldiers fight like heroes at Ball's Bluff?* What are you talking about?"

"Some of 'em did, and some of 'em didn't. If they fought so splendidly, how came there to be five or six hundred taken prisoners? Tell me that! do you think if I was in a battle I would be taken prisoner? No, sir. I'd fight to the last. I'd kill every man that asked me to surrender. I'd do as Lieut. Hooper did. I'd never surrender! I'd die a thousand times first."

"O! now you hush up, Holley Tremaine. Do you expect you are going to make me believe that you are braver and smarter than anybody else in America? You tell about you wouldn't surrender! Suppose you could not help yourself? There's Col. Lee,—I think he was brave and splendid too—because he might have got off, but he let the poor wounded soldiers go, and staid himself—"

"Well, Col. Lee—yes—but when they came up to take him prisoner, why didn't he turn round and shoot them—what did he go with them for? Why didn't he fight? instead of walking off like a lamb?"

"I don't know—I wasn't there. Perhaps he had lost his gun, or hadn't got any, or wet his powder. Perhaps they got hold of him so he couldn't shoot. I don't know anything about it, and you don't know anything about it—and for you to sit here at home, lolling and lazy, and talk about what you would do, and what you wouldn't do—it's my opinion you are a great—Gascon—that's English for humbug, dear, only humbug is coarse, and I don't like to say it."

"Oh! you better set up for refined," muttered Holley, somewhat nettled.

"When you set up for a hero," answered the imperturbable Cappie. "I think we'd better both of us mind our business, and let soldiers alone."

---

*A disastrous little battle fought in northwestern Virginia in late October 1861. Of the 1,700 Union troops engaged, over 700 were captured.

"If I was a few years older, I'd mind my business without letting the soldiers alone. I'd go there and let them see how things ought to be done. Oh! I wish I was old enough to fight."

"Plenty old enough," said Uncle Arthur, coming forward and joining in the conversation to which he had hitherto been a silent and unobserved, but interested listener. "There's plenty of fighting for you to do, too, without going to the Potomac to find it."

"Yes, Cappie is always on hand," said Holley, doubtfully, making a lunge in the dark, but sure of hitting something.

"Oh! let Cappie alone," laughed Uncle Arthur. "You have a more formidable foe than Cappie. She's nothing but a scouting party, compared with the great army that lies in wait."

"A conundrum," whispered Cappie to Holley.

"I saw a skirmish last night, and if I am not deceived, the great Commander-in-Chief, the knight, sans peur et sans reproche—is that correct, Cappie?—the Chevalier Tremaine did not come off victorious."

Holley looked puzzled, and his uncle continued:—

"It was a conflict between certain rules and axioms, and Major-Gen. Holley. The x's, y's and z's were drawn up in line on the one side, and Gen. Holley's forces on the other. There was sharp skirmishing for ten minutes. Figures flew as thick as hail on all sides. The rattling of the pencil against the slate was terrific. Then there came a lull. Gen. Holley gradually relaxed fire. He lost presence of mind, equanimity, self-possession. And this brave young soldier, who will never surrender, no, never—who will die a thousand deaths before he will give up—he gave up to—what do you think? to a problem in Algebra. He let himself be conquered by it. Yielded ignominiously—said he couldn't do it—wouldn't try—SURRENDERED!"

"Oh pshaw! Now Uncle Arthur, that isn't fighting now, you know. There's no fight in Algebra."

"Begging your pardon, my dear Lieutenant, there is a great deal. A mathematical problem is your enemy till you have grappled with it, captured it, possessed yourself of it. Then it becomes your friend. It marshals itself on your side, and is a faithful ally when you attack the next problem. But this doughty knight has been defeated in other battles. He resolved to get up at six o'clock in the morning, so as to have an hour for study before he went to school. He woke before six, but Gen. Self-Indulgence attacked him, and there was a desperate battle under the bed clothes, in which Gen. Holley was defeated with great slaughter. 'It's too confounded cold,' muttered the General, as he laid down his arms, made an unconditional surrender, and with-drew under cover of the counterpane."

"Oh! con-found it!" jerked Holley; but Uncle Arthur had not quite done with him. "I was an eye-witness of another en-gagement in which this invincible warrior came off second best. He was making a reconnaissance in force, and suddenly fell in with his shoe-string. It was knotted, and refused to straiten at his summons. He and his temper fought manfully about twelve sec-onds, then the shoe-string got the better of them both. He pulled and twitched, broke out the eyelet of his shoe, and his temper was actually taken prisoner and carried off."

"Well," said Holley, arching his eye-brows and shrug-ging his shoulders, "all I have to say is—if that is fighting it's mighty small fighting. 'Tisn't the kind of thing I'm after."

"But the small fighting is the prelude of large fighting, my boy," said Uncle Arthur, seriously. "You long for the battle field, but if you lose battles now, what prospect is there that you will ever win them?"

"Sure enough," chimed Cappie, senatorially.

"Ho! you shut up shop, Miss," pouted Holley, under his breath.

"Taisez-vous," rejoined Cappie, in the same subdued tone.

"When a man boasts loudly of his bravery," continued Uncle Arthur, "he is certainly a braggart, and probably a cow-ard. But if, while he thus boasts of conquering the foe whom he never sees, he yields to the foe who does appear, there is no un-certainty about it. He is a braggart and a coward."

"Oh! Uncle Arthur!" exclaimed Cappie, who loved to browbeat Holley herself, but did not choose to have anybody else do the same.

"Both a braggart and a coward," repeated Uncle Arthur, calmly, though Holley's eyes were filled with tears of rage. "I think Holley's braggadocio and cowardice are youthful follies. I believe he has the material for a brave and modest man; but his fierce talk and his feeble deeds show neither the one nor the other. If he means to be a hero, let him begin now. The best preparation to be a good soldier is to do unflinchingly every duty. Let every task and every temptation be looked upon as a foe. Indolence, petulance, passion, impatience, gluttony, vanity, falsehood, self-indulgence—these are the enemies which are drawn up against you now, Holley, my lad. These are the rebels that want to batter down the citadel of your manhood. You can't go to Virginia, but you can throw out your pickets at home, and give battle manfully. Show whether you have the stuff of a soldier in you here. Conquer your algebra, your Latin, conquer your temper, and if the war lasts till you are old enough, go down and conquer the rebels, and you won't find it half so hard work as this 'small fighting.' But so long as every little whipper-snapper of a provocation or a difficulty conquers you, don't let us hear any more magnificent talk about your never surrendering."

"That means, you see," said Cappie, who had a turn for exegesis, "that when I torment you, il vous faut, take it lovingly,—because if you get angry and torment me again, you are no soldier. For instance, if I pull your hair—" and she gave it a smart twitch, "you mustn't——" but Holley was upon her, and away they rushed over the sofa, over Uncle Arthur, pell-mell, harum-scarum, and whether Holley will be a hero or a coward, remains to be seen.

YOUNG MEN

Children had to take up the slack for their absent fathers and brothers. Horatio Alger, the author of the famous "rags to riches" dime novels of the 1870s and 1880s, also wrote a book about one boy's contribution to the Union war effort. In *Frank's Campaign* the title character manages to keep his family's farm running, enabling his father to enlist in the army, safe in the knowledge that his young son is taking care of things back home. Along the way, Frank also befriends a family of fugitive African Americans and helps foil the evil plans of a shady army contractor.

Few children enjoyed such drama in their lives, but tens of thousands did men's work and took on men's responsibilities. Their contribution to their families went beyond plowing fields and keeping shops open. Frank Rogers of Iowa, whose father was a surgeon in the army, packed a pistol when he accompanied his mother to the home of a particularly nasty local "copperhead" and stayed up all night during an Indian scare. When nine-year-old Levi Keeler's mother became seriously ill, he nursed her back to health. Jane Keeler wrote her husband that Levi "sat up with me all night and every little while he would ask Mother do you want anything." In the middle of the night, he made an emergency trip for the doctor. Recognizing the adult role her little boy had assumed, she declared, "Levi was my man."*

---

*Helen Klaas, ed., *Portrait of Elnathan Keeler, a Union Soldier* (Wappingers Falls, N.Y.: Golflief Reproductions, 1977), 20–21.

The main character of Emily Huntington Miller's serial "The House that Johnny Rented" is the story of another boy filling a man's role. When the Reverend White agrees to become an army chaplain, he leaves an invalid wife and seven children without a home, as the new minister will require the parsonage. His son, Johnny, finds a comfortable little cottage for them to live in, but that is just the beginning of their wartime adventures. They enthusiastically manufacture tall-tale war stories, raise money for soldiers, send boxes of provisions to the Reverend White and, when he finally returns home to recuperate from an illness contracted while nursing sick soldiers, adopt the young African American who has come home with him, teaching the boy to read and fending off racist attacks from less tolerant children.

"The House that Johnny Rented"
Emily Huntington Miller
The Little Corporal 1 (July 1865), 6–9

If you had looked into the great south chamber of the parsonage at Dunham, almost any evening after tea, you might have thought all the children of a charity school had been turned loose there. And on this particular night of which I'm going to tell you, there was such a chattering and laughing, that you might have fancied there was a score of new comers, but if you had contrived to count them you would have found, after all, only the seven children of the White family, taking their usual romp after supper. What they were all doing, I'm sure I cannot tell. Johnny White was standing on his head, and turning somersaults, after a fashion he had learned at school. Lucy and Will were trying to teach Jock, the dog, to perform some remarkable feats with a cane, but after trying in vain to comprehend them, he invariably finished by seizing the stick in his teeth and trotting off with it to his corner. One thing they were all agreed in, and that was, in making as much noise as possible, till all at once a bell rang in the hall below, and that was the signal for quiet. Even Jock understood that, for he marched away gravely to the rug, and the children seated themselves around the fire and prepared to tell stories.

"Let me tell, to-night," said Gerty, "I can make a splendid story about my campaign in Virginia, like Jo. Webster."

"I don't think much of Captain Webster," said Hatty, gravely. "He says babies are a nuisance."

"All gentlemen think so," said Master Johnny, "it's only women and girls that like 'em."

"I should like to know if papa isn't a gentleman," said Hatty, indignantly.

"Never mind, Gerty," said Will, "let's hear about the campaign." So Gerty ran her fingers through the curly locks on her little black head and began her story.

"You see it was when we were in the retrenchments before Richmond—"

"En-trenchments, Gerty," interrupted Johnny, giving a sly pinch to Jock's ear.

Gerty gave him a dignified glance and went on:

"General McClellan he came over to my house—my tent, I mean—and says he, 'Captain White, I do wish you'd take some men and go out foraging; they have such mean stuff to eat at my boarding house, that I'm half starved.' So I called out my regiment and started."

"A regiment!" said Johnny, again, "that's a thousand men!"

"Is it?" said Gerty, "well, then this was a very small one: not more'n about thirty soldiers. We mounted our horses and filled our knapsacks with powder!" Exclaimed Johnny, once more, "Oh, my eyes!"

"Johnny White," said Gerty, emphatically, "you don't treat me with the least respect. I was there, and it's likely I know what happened, and then you never heard Jo. Webster talk. Let me see, where was I?"

"Filling your knapsack with powder and shell," said Johnny, gravely.

"Yes; well, it was a splendid moonlight night, and we rode away from camp out into the country, miles and miles, till we came in sight of a great house, almost as grand as a palace, with elegant gardens all around it, and carriage drives all shaded with orange trees, hanging full of ripe oranges."

Johnny whistled softly at hearing of oranges in Virginia, but when Gerty looked at him he was gazing into the fire so innocently, that she went on with her story.

"The house was all lighted up, and we hitched our horses under the trees, and crept softly up to the windows. What should we see but General Lee and General Beauregard, and all their staffs and head-quarters, all fixed up in their uniforms and dress parades, a-having a grand ball."

Here Johnny rolled over on the carpet laughing with all his might.

"What are you laughing at, Johnny White?" demanded Gerty.

"O, nothing," said Johnny, recovering himself, "only it must have been so jolly to see 'em."

"Yes, it was," said Gerty; "they had four brass bands a-playing, and all the officers were dancing with the ladies, and all the negro servants stood in the hall looking at the door. So we crept around to the dining room, and there was the splendidest supper, all set on the table, and nobody at all to watch it. There was three or four little pigs, roasted alive, with sweet potatoes in their mouths, and roast turkeys, and chickens, and oysters; and all sorts of cakes, and pies, and jellies. We just slipped into the kitchen and got a great lot of market baskets—they had 'em too—to pick corn in—and we took all the things off from the table, and hurried till we got back to camp, and came riding over the pickets just as the bell was ringing for breakfast. Dear me, you ought to have seen how pleased General McClellan was, and he promised to have me chosen a Brigadier, but he never did."

"Well," said Johnny, "seems to me I should have tried to nab some of those old rebs, instead of carrying off their supper."

"Humph," said Gerty, "of course we might have taken 'em prisoners, but I should like to know what would have become of General McClellan's breakfast?"

While Johnny was pondering over this unanswerable argument, the door of the chamber opened and Jimmy White came in with the baby. Jimmy wasn't a boy, as I dare say you are thinking, but, just the wisest, gentlest, most patient of sisters, that ever such an unruly little troop was blessed with. In the family Bible her name was written Jemina, just as dear old Grandpa White had named her fifteen years before, when she was a little red-faced baby, but Uncle Will had always insisted on shortening it to Jimmy, and so, after a while, all the rest had fallen into the same habit, till you might have lived at the parsonage a year, and never guessed that the quiet little girl who washed the children's faces, did up their cut fingers, dressed their dolls and covered their balls, had any other name but Jimmy.

When she came in there was a general rush for the baby, and Gerty succeeded in carrying him off over the heads of the others. Jimmy was always quiet, but to-night she did not speak a word. She busied herself with laying out the night clothes for the little ones, and then reached down the Bible from the shelf and laid it on the stand.

"Where's mamma?" asked Hatty, wonderingly, "isn't she coming to read to us to-night?"

"Mamma isn't well to-night," said Jimmy, "and I'm going to read to you."

They all saw that Jimmy looked grave and sad, and Lucy whispered to Will that she did believe she had been crying.

Jimmy's voice trembled a little at first, but the Psalm seemed to comfort her, and well it might, for, whatever her trouble was it was surely good to read—

"He that dwelleth in the secret place of the Most High, shall abide under the shadow of the Almighty."

Jimmy loved God, and she could trust him for herself, but she had a new lesson to learn now, and that was, to trust him for others, and that is often very hard to learn. After the Psalm was finished they all knelt down and repeated the Lord's Prayer together; then they remained kneeling while each one prayed for a moment in silence, and then the older ones went away to their rooms, while Jimmy undressed the two youngest and stowed them into their trundle-bed beside her own. Then she sat down by the fire to rock the baby, and, sitting there alone, she soon began to cry softly, and did not hear that Gerty had stolen back in her night dress, till she put her arms around her neck, and asked:

"O, Jimmy, what is it? something has happened!"

"It's about Father," said Jimmy, presently, "you know how long he's been thinking about going into the army as Chaplain, and now it's all settled, and he's going in a week. O, Gerty, how can we let him?"

Gerty was usually an excitable little creature, but this news came with such a sudden shock that it sobered, and almost bewildered her. She sat down on the floor by Jimmy's feet, with her hands folded over her knees, and after a moment of silence, asked anxiously:

"What does mamma say about it?"

"She tries to think it's best," said Jimmy, "and says she has been expecting it all along, but it will be hard to give him up, after all. You see, the young men that went into the army from papa's church, were determined to get him for Chaplain in their regiment, and they worked till they got the appointment for him, and now papa says he feels as if his duty called him to go."

"Chaplains don't fight, do they?" asked Gerty.

"No," said Jimmy, "I suppose not."

"And even the rebels wouldn't be mean enough to shoot a Chaplain, would they?"

"Perhaps not," said Jimmy, rather doubtfully.

"And he'll always have a tent to sleep in, and a horse to ride on," went on Gerty, talking more to herself than Jimmy; "well, I don't think it is so bad as it might be; I think I can give him up to my country if I must"; and Gerty rested her dismal little face on her hands and tried to look very heroic. "There's one thing about it," said she, "I shall have somebody in the army to talk about, as well as Jenny Webster. She's been putting on airs, and making herself mis'able about Jo. ever since he went away, and I know she never has a minute's peace of her life for his teasing, when he's at home."

"Gerty White," said Jimmy, as nearly out of patience as she ever got, "you are the most ridiculous child I ever saw. Anybody would think you was glad to have papa go away. Supposing he should get sick, working night and day on the battle fields and in the hospitals; and, supposing he should die away there, with nobody to take care of him."

The thought was too much for Jimmy, and she hugged the baby up closer and sobbed bitterly, and Gerty joined her most heartily, till all at once she woke up to the idea that she was likely to get a headache and Gerty had a bad cold, so she put the baby in its crib, at once, and then said to Gerty:

"God can take care of papa in camp, just as well as here at home. You know what we read to-night:

> 'Thou shalt not be afraid for the terror by night; nor for the arrow that flieth by day; nor for the pestilence that walketh in darkness; nor for the destruction that wasteth at noonday. A thousand shall fall at thy side, and ten thousand at thy right hand; but it shall not come nigh thee.'"

And so Gerty nestled back into bed, greatly consoled by the promises of heavenly guardianship; and, thinking the whole matter over, she could not help a little lingering feeling that, after all, it was grand to have "somebody in the army.". . .

If there was abundance of anything in the Dunham parsonage, it certainly was not money. Aunt Dorcas White used to say that nothing was plenty there except children, but Aunt Dorcas was rheumatic, and took snuff, and didn't like children so well as she did cats, so how should she know if there was a plenty.

One thing you may be sure of: with so many mouths to feed, and only a small salary to do it with, there was need to look very carefully after the pennies; and if Mamma White had not been a wonderful woman for making new things out of old, she never could have managed to keep them all so neat and tidy. But, as it was, Jimmy's dresses were cut down for Gerty, and then cut over for Hatty, and then turned upside down for Lucy, and inside out for the baby till the poor things must have been quite in despair of ever being hung away in the garret—that asylum for aged and infirm apparel—or even being honorably consigned to the rag-bag. This was when papa was at home, but what was to become of them now that he was away, for the new minister must have the parsonage. I ought to have told you before this time that Mamma White was an invalid, and so a great deal of the care of the family came upon Jimmy, and of all the children the only one that she ever depended on for help was Johnny. So when it was necessary to hunt up a new home, and Jimmy could hardly be spared from the old one, she sent Johnny out to begin the search. She gave him a list of a dozen houses that he was to examine, and he went out on his errand, feeling as grand as any boy of twelve would, at being entrusted with such business.

"Remember, Johnny," said his mother, "that we want a cellar, plenty of water, the kitchen and dining room on the same floor, and if possible a small garden."

"And, Johnny," said Gerty, "be sure and get a piazza, with grape vines all over it, and a summer house in the garden."

"Yes, and a garret, Johnny, with a swing in it, where we can play on rainy days," added Lucy, eagerly.

"And, oh Johnny," implored Will, at the gate, "do get a barn; I've been wanting one all my life."

"Now," thought Johnny, "if I don't suit 'em all it won't be because they haven't given directions enough. Let me see— 26 Pine Street—that is the nearest, and I'll go there first."

No. 26 proved to have neither cellar nor garden, and the next place had an up-stairs dining room, and so on through the whole list, there was some objection to every one that Johnny felt sure would spoil it for them. Then at several places Johnny was decidedly snubbed by people who didn't seem to fancy the liberty he was taking in looking at their houses, and though he was as polite as papa himself could have been, yet somebody's Biddy called him a "saucy little upstart."

But going home to dinner, with a very strong feeling that house-hunting wasn't such fun after all, he chanced to see a notice, "This House to Let," put up over the gate of a little old-fashioned looking cottage, with the queerest wings and gables running out in all sorts of unexpected corners, and great dormer windows in the roof.

"There's the piazza and summer-house, any way," thought Johnny, and after a moment's hesitation, he went in and began to make inquiries of a very deaf old lady, who sat grasping her cane with both hands as if she took him to be a robber. When she understood, however, that his mother was sick, and his father in the army, she was very gracious, and showed him all about the house. The rooms were small and low, but there seemed to be plenty of them, and the nice little garden was well stocked with fruits and berries. On the whole it seemed very promising to Johnny, in spite of the rent, which was a trifle above what Jimmy had given him as the limit of the family purse, and he went home in great delight to report progress. After two or three visits from Jimmy and one from Mamma White after innumerable family councils and measurements of rooms that must be covered with carpets that wouldn't cover them, the decision was given in favor of taking the house, and for at least a year from that time Johnny was never known to lose an opportunity of boasting about "the house that I rented."

Early in May the old lady and her cane hobbled out at the front door, and the White family came trooping in. The dear old chairs and tables, and books and pictures, wandered around uncomfortably for a little while, and then settled down in nooks and corners, and came to look as much at home as if they had grown up there in the queer little rooms. And all this time where was papa? In the first place it was only three weeks since he left home, and only two letters had been received from him, for the Regiment to which he had gone was in Tennessee, and the guerrillas often broke up the mail routes, so that letters were very uncertain. He had just reached the camp when his last letter was written, and he told them all about the long rows of tents where the soldiers lived, and the long huts that were the officers' quarters. The Regiment had been there all winter, and so they had built up a sort of village, and made themselves quite comfortable. Now they were just going to march somewhere; papa didn't know where, only the Colonel knew, for they never tell the men. . . .

I will not tell you any more of this letter, though it was very interesting to those for whom it was written, for I want to tell you about the Aid Society that the children formed themselves into, to try and raise money and hospital stores to send to papa for his soldiers. It was Jimmy who first proposed it, and she planned and arranged the whole matter, though even little Susy had a hand in carrying it out. The garden was divided by a gravel walk into two parts; one for flowers, next to the street, and the other for fruit and vegetables. Jimmy's plan was to make a "hospital fund" out of the garden. Will and Johnny were to take charge of the vegetables, and the girls attend to the flowers.

"We can give up all the fruit," said she, "and at least half of the vegetables, and if we can only manage to sell the flowers, I think we can raise quite a nice little sum for papa."

The children were delighted with the arrangement, and never were gardens more neatly laid out, or more carefully tended. . . .

I cannot tell how many charming bouquets found their way that summer from the children's garden to Friend Williams' store, or how many baskets of fruit and vegetables the boys carried to market; but the hospital fund grew bravely, and received frequent additions in ways that never would have occurred to any one whose heart was not full of love and interest for the soldiers. They learned to color photographs and skeletonize flowers; they made vases of shells and pebbles, and baskets of cones and acorns; they made picture frames from pine twigs, and carved brackets out of cigar boxes; and when their stores were full, they would hold a fair or an auction, and sell the articles to those of their friends whom they could induce to buy. At first they were unwilling to do anything with the proceeds except to send boxes of things directly to papa. But when he assured them that the safest way was to send through the Sanitary Commission, and trust to the wisdom of the managers to apply the things where there was the greatest need, they gave it up at last, but it was quite a disappointment. One box they did have the pleasure of filling especially for papa and his soldiers, and sending it to him by the Quartermaster of the Regiment, who came north on business. That was a wonderful box, and it seemed as if it would never be full, for just as it was packed, somebody was sure to find something that must go in; and so mamma would crowd the things a little closer, and rearrange them till she would find room for it. The very last thing that went in was a picture that Will drew, called "The Sanitary Commission Raising Funds."

There were Gerty and Hatty on their way to sell their flowers, with great baskets heaped up with sunflowers and marigolds, and after them came Johnny with a donkey loaded with cabbages and potatoes, while Will marched by his side, with a load of all kinds of fancy articles on his head, which he was crying along the streets. At home Jimmy was seen hoeing corn, and the little ones weeding, while mamma sat on the piazza scraping lint. Jock, the dog, was standing guard over the strawberry bed, and Tabby was just coming in with a basket of catnip hung about her neck.

There was nothing in the box that papa treasured more carefully than that comical little picture, for it seemed to bring the merry faces of his children right before him. He was not with the army when he got this box. As the terrible heats of summer came on, the men began to be stricken down with fevers, and they were constantly left behind on marches to be sent back to hospital, till by and by the hospitals began to be crowded, and the surgeons and nurses so overworked that there were many of them obliged to give up and stop for rest. This made matters still worse, and when Chaplain White went into one of the hospitals and found some of his own boys suffering for care, he felt as if he was more needed there than anywhere else, and so he staid to help the surgeons. He was a strong, healthy man, and had studied medicine in his younger days, so he was just such aid as they needed, and many a poor fellow blessed the Chaplain who cared for his wants almost as tenderly as his mother could have done.

All this gave Mamma White and Jimmy a great deal of anxiety. They knew well enough that he would work without once thinking of himself as long as any strength was left him, and they greatly feared that such constant care and labor would be more than he could bear. But week after week the letters kept coming, and though papa sometimes spoke of being tired, he always said he was well, until at last the fall weather began to come on, and the fiercest heat was over. Then they all felt easier, and papa began to write about rejoining his Regiment.

One pleasant day in October, Gerty started for Mr. Williams' store with the very last of her flowers: a few bouquets of asters that the frosts had spared. It was a long walk to the store, and as Gerty had not been very well, mamma told her to go in the streetcars.

As she took her seat in the car, she noticed a gentleman in military uniform near her, one glance at whom set her little heart in a flutter.

"That's Colonel Richardson," thought Gerty, "and he must have just come from the army."

Now Gerty had never seen the Colonel, but they had a large photograph of him at Dr. Webster's and she knew him in a moment. He had just come in on the morning train, and several gentlemen were making inquiries of him about his regiment.

Gerty did not hear the first of the conversation, and when she did begin to listen, her heart was thumping away so loud she thought they must all hear it.

"I've seen some pretty poor Chaplains since I've been in the army," said the Colonel, "but they are exceptions to the general rule. There was Chaplain White—he went right into the hospitals and worked among the men harder than any nurse on the ground. He endured an astonishing amount of labor, but when he did give up, he was completely prostrated. I would rather have lost any man in the Regiment than him; he had such an influence over the men."

Gerty heard every word of this, but no more, for she sat in her corner fairly rigid with horror, and with only one thought in her mind, as she kept saying over and over,

"Papa is dead! Papa is dead !"

The cars went jingling on past Mr. Williams' fruit store, but Gerty didn't get out. Colonel Richardson shook hands with his friends and stepped off at the crossing near the eastern depot; all the rest of the people left the car, and finally it came to a stop at the further end of the route.

"Aren't you going to get off, Miss?" asked the conductor, looking in at the door as they were changing horses.

Gerty gave him a bewildered look, and then rose slowly and passed off from the car. As she was going down the street again, neither crying nor sobbing, but simply stupefied by the sudden blow, another car came down behind her. It stopped at a crossing opposite, and she heard a strange voice calling from the platform,

"Gerty! Gerty White come here!"

While she was looking at the conductor in wonder, he sprang from the car, caught her up in his arms, and carried her in, setting her down by the side of somebody who was no stranger to her, if the conductor was.

"O, papa! papa!" said Gerty, with both arms around his neck, "I thought you were dead."

"Not quite," said papa, hugging his little girl very close, "though I have been pretty sick for a live man. But how did you know anything about it?"

"I just saw Colonel Richardson in the car," said Gerty, "and he talked about losing you, and I thought he meant you were dead."

"We just came up the river together," said papa, "and as I was going down on the car I caught a sight of your face, and got Mr. Wallace to call you."

Then followed a long list of questions about mamma, and all the dear ones at home, in the midst of which they came to Walnut Street, and it was time to leave the car. Papa got up very feebly, and while Gerty was trying to load herself with his bundles and satchels, a queer looking little black boy came forward and took them all away from her.

"Bob will take care of my traps," said papa, as they left the car, and Bob disposed of them all to Gerty's astonishment, who thought he must have been made like a hat-rack, with hooks all over him.

"Papa," asked Gerty cautiously, when she felt sure that Bob was out of hearing, "is that a contraband?"

"Yes," said papa, "Bob was born a slave, but he has been with Lieutenant Camp over a year; he was our groom and housekeeper, and laundress, and errand boy, and almost everything else. I don't know how we could have got along without him, but he begged so hard to come north with me, that I brought him along."

"Let us go in through the alley," said Gerty, as they turned up to the house, "and then mamma won't see us all at once; she always sits on the piazza in the morning."

In the garden they encountered the boys, and if mamma and Jimmy had not been used to every imaginable kind of noise, they must have known that something had happened. But as it was, they went quietly on with their sewing, till Gerty came rushing over Susy's block house, and planted her foot squarely in Sally Snip's face. If Sally Snip had been a common doll, her stock of good looks would have been ruined, but as she was rubber, and used to such things, she only gave a doleful wheeze and gasp when Gerty's foot came down, and righted herself with a pop when it was raised. Mamma looked in wonder at Gerty's excitement, and papa, peeping through the crack of the door, could hardly help laughing to see how puzzled she was to tell the news without being too abrupt. At last she burst eagerly out—

"O, mamma! Jimmy! something has happened! *We've got a contraband!*"*

"A *what!*" said Jimmy in astonishment, but just then she spied Bob coming in at a gate, with his arms full of blankets and bundles, and she sprang up, exclaiming, "I do believe papa has come!"

And then papa opened the door and marched in, and the boys rushed after, pell-mell; and there was a general shouting and laughing, and hugging and kissing, and poor Sally Snip was so unmercifully trampled on that she gave one asthmatic groan and burst open across the top of the head, revealing the fact that she had no brains at all.

And then Jimmy helped Bob dispose of his luggage, Gerty, meantime, looking curiously on to see if he really had any hooks on his arms and shoulders.

---

*Although no statistics are available, it was apparently not uncommon for soldiers to bring home young contrabands (freed slaves) as servants. At least one Union soldier offered to send one home as a present to his children, while a surgeon from Iowa employed a black man whom he had befriended while serving in the South.

"Isn't he nice?" she whispered to Johnny with an admiring glance at his uniform.

"I don't know," said Johnny, a little doubtfully; "do you 'spose he can dance on his head, and turn somersaults on a rope like the negros in the circus pictures?"

"*Of course not*," answered Gerty, indignantly; "he isn't a circus boy, he b'longs to a minister, and he's just as respectable as anybody."

It is due to Bob to say that he never brought his character into disrepute by attempting any such indecorous performances as dancing on his head, but behaved on all occasions with proper regard to his own and his master's standing.

And now having brought the White family once more together, we will leave them in their home, as happy as we first found them in the old one. For papa was as well pleased with it as any of them, and Johnny had two new auditors to listen to his favorite theme—"*the house that I rented.*"

THE CRUCIBLE OF WAR

Two main categories of children emerge from the stories and books written for young people during the Civil War. One was characterized by obedience, kindness, piety, and hard work, all the character traits deemed important by middle-class society. But another class of children had to learn the value of those virtues. These boys and girls at first display greed or laziness or carelessness, but find out that fulfilling their duty to their country and their families demands a reformation of their character. Some have been raised in affluence, which temporarily blinds them to the needs of the less fortunate. Others, spoiled by affectionate parents and older siblings, have to overcome the inertia of selfishness. Still others need to be jarred from silliness and thoughtlessness by parents who finally seem fed up with their children's self-centeredness. Once again, contributing to the war effort went hand-in-hand with personal growth and enrichment. The war could be the crucible in which human dross could be skimmed to reveal the gold beneath; any patriotic gesture would be tarnished if unsupported by sincerity and true loyalty.

The stories that follow show children demonstrating their virtue and self-worth by pitching in to help the Union win the war. They contribute in many of the large and small ways that real-life children did; more important, they come face-to-face with challenges and hardships—their own, or those of others—and have to decide how they will respond. In every case, of course, generosity eventually wins out over selfishness. Some children—the heroine of "Katie's Sacrifice," for instance—seem instinctively good. Others—the smug youngsters in "The Contraband" or the family of children overcome with Christmas ennui in "The Two Christmas Evenings"—have to dig down for their true selves. Orphans and "contrabands" and devoted servants benefit from the benevolence of the newly wise and philanthropic heroes and heroines. In all of these stories, the war serves only as a backdrop, a crucial subplot, for the moral lessons being learned by characters and readers alike. Children might learn other virtues as well: to be grateful for any blessing, however small; not to challenge one's place in society, however low; to be kind even to people far removed from one's own experience, education, or status.

"Katie's Sacrifice"
E. N. H.
The Student and Schoolmate 14 (November 1864), 140–41

When I read in the papers the other day that Mr.—— had given ten thousand dollars to aid our suffering soldiers, my heart blessed him for his noble deed. But a single act which I heard of this morning seemed to me as truly noble, and as really worth relating, as the generous donation which I have named. Little Katie was the only child of a poor widow. She had not, like many children, a supply of books, pictures and toys. Yet she was a loving, happy child; and her gentle, unselfish disposition endeared her to all the neighborhood. Though this sweet girl was more than six years old, she had heard but little about the present war, or the sufferings of our sick and wounded soldiers, until last week. She lived among the hills, in a lonely part of the country, where no military display had been witnessed, and no hero in "army blue" had passed before her eyes.

But last week, her cousin Archie came from his distant home to spend the August vacation with Katie and her mother. A few other strangers also found their way to the quiet valley, it having somehow reached the ears of those in search of health or pleasure, that a beautiful lake which was nestled between the hills in that locality, afforded fine facilities for rowing and fishing. The new comers had not left all their home cares and duties behind them; especially had they not laid aside their patriotism. City belles and their high-bred mothers spent many a leisure hour in this rustic retreat, making army shirts and drawers, or pressing rare wild flowers for the Albums which should sell in the Sanitary Fair. Thus it happened that the poor widow and her quiet neighbors were stirred up to do their part in the noblest struggle of the age.

Katie's cousin Archie had gone one day from house to house to collect the rolls of old linen and cotton for hospital use, and to gather the socks for the worn and bleeding feet of soldiers on the march. Almost all found something to give, and bestowed it cheerfully. When the boy came home at night to his cousin's, he found Katie in tears.

"What's the matter?" he kindly asked.

"Oh, Archie! Archie! I have nothing to give for the dear soldiers," she said. "We do not get any money, and mother can only earn enough to keep us. I haven't anything in the world but Tippie, and she wouldn't be of any use to the army, if I could spare her."

"Perhaps," said Archie—"but no—it would be too bad, for Tippie is all you've got, and she sleeps with you and plays with you; you could not part with her, surely."

"What do you mean, Archie?" inquired the child, eagerly.

The boy did not like to say, but his little cousin would not be put off.

"Why, you see, Katie, that girl in white frock and blue ribbons, that stopped for a drink of water from your spring, yesterday, fell in love with Tippie, and teased her mother to buy her. The lady, Mrs. Ruskin, spoke to me about it this morning, and said she'd give a dollar for the kitten; but I told her it was all the play-fellow you'd got, and I knew you couldn't spare it; that's all";—and the boy looked down on the ground.

"Spare Tippie! Sell my kitten! the dearest thing in the world; of course I couldn't!" and the child, flushed and agitated, hugged her only treasure tightly to her breast, and bore it away to its place across her bed, where she was soon stretched beside it.

But when the morning came, and a little later than usual Archie rose, neither his cousin nor her pet were in the house.

"Katie has made her sacrifice," said her mother, in answer to the boy's inquiries. "She loved her kitten dearly, but she is willing to part with it that she may help the poor soldiers, who are doing and suffering so much. So she has gone to take it to Mrs. Ruskin, and before night it will be carried to its new home in A——."

Dear young readers, should you see that snow-white kitten, with the least possible touch of Malta gray on the corner of its ears and the end of its tail; should you watch its graceful antics and merry capers, and remember that it was Katie Daniel's only treasure, you would, I think, feel as I do, that the giving up of Tippie was a real and costly sacrifice.

"Christmas, After All"
Gail Hamilton
The Little Pilgrim 9 (April 1862), 50–52

A charming family, as you would say if you knew them. But let us have a more special introduction.

Master Ivers Arthurell, step up and make your bow, sir. A fine young gentleman, little friends, only he thinks it is almost time he was called "Mister," and already bullies the little ones into doing it when he happens to feel in the mood. He is just now making himself an especial nuisance in the family, by continually strutting about in his first long-talked-of and long-wished-for "tails," and persistently affirming that his beard is beginning to grow, though the most minute examination reveals nothing but a general dinginess. However, there is good blood in the boy, and when twenty years or so have stiffened him up, and toned him down, and filled him out, and evaporated, and strained, and distilled him, you shall see as fine a man as you could wish for.

Miss Muriel, a matronly little lady, sweeps you a graceful courtesy, and you think she is certainly the most dignified piece for one of her years that you ever saw; and so she is; but wait a moment, and you shall see a sparkle in her eyes, and a spring in her heels, which will show you that the kitten has not wholly died out of her yet; by no means. What a lively little thing she is, to be sure! Yes, the cares of life came upon her early, but not its perplexities; so the child goes hand in hand with the woman.

Pug-nosed Tim, what have you to say for yourself? How do the statistics look this morning? What tale does the yard-stick tell? For you must know, Little Pilgrim, that this pug-nosed Tim, with his shock of black hair, and the restless, mischievous fingers, measures himself every other day, to see how much he has grown, evidently fearful lest he may steal a march on himself some night, and shoot up four or five feet without discovering it. But time flies, and paper too, and I must not linger over this red-cheeked, fat-sided girl, whose high-sounding baptismal name, Christiana, is quite lost in such undignified sobriquets as "Puff-Ball"; "Chunkarthur," etc.; and little Robert, who answers to Robin, Bob, General Hi, and in fact, whenever there is an unusual noise about the house, he considers himself called, and runs. It is a sad family for nicknames, as you see; but they all seem to know, by a certain instinct, "who is who," and from the greatest confusion, invariably come out "right side up, with care."

Are there no others? Yes, a grave, sad father, who loves them with a pitying tenderness, and surrounds them with everything comfortable and beautiful, and rejoices to see them so happy, and strong, and good, and affectionate, but who can nevermore lift his heart from out the shadow that fell over it one sunny summer morning, years ago.

And one more, in the far-off, beautiful land, among the angels—a sweet-faced mother, her pure heart over-full of joy, yet watching and waiting for the hour that shall bring her darlings to her bosom once more. There is a well-worn path to the green grave in the sunset corner of the maple grove.

And so these children, who have been motherless ever since the day that Robert's chestnut eyes opened to the sunshine—who have never known a want that money could supply—who have never heard their father's voice toned with displeasure towards them, are growing up kind, brave, truthful and intelligent. In some way that I know not, the dying mother's prayer is answered.

"Papa," said little Chunk one morning, climbing over the arm of his chair, and laying her fat cheek against his, "Melly says"—she waited for him to lay down his pen, and look at her. The soft, sweet voice, had not long to wait.

"What does Melly say, daughter?"

"Melly says we can't have any Christmas." And the round face grew just as long as it could.

"No Christmas! Why, what has happened?"

"Oh, papa! Melly can't think. Melly says she has thinked and thinked, and she can't think any more. Oh, papa! can't you think?"

"Think what, pet?" for Mr. Arthurell could not "think" what she meant.

"Oh! something for Christmas, very great and grand," said Tim, who had come in and taken up his station on the other side of the study-chair.

"Something like St. Paul's Cathedral, for instance," said papa, placing a strong arm around each, and whisking them up on his knees.

The fact was, that a family council had been held that morning on the subject, Melly and Ivers being the active members, and the others agreeing with everything that was proposed to be done, and lamenting when anything was decided to be left out. But Muriel and Ivers could not fasten upon anything "nice" and novel.

"Of course, we don't want to do the same thing year after year, for a whole century," said Ivers, when a Christmas tree had been proposed.

"I'd just as soon do the same thing a hundred centuries as not, if it's a Christmas tree," moaned Chunk.

"Of course you would, Miss Roly-Poly," said Muriel, looking up from the coals which she had been meditatively poking, and "making at" Christy with the hot end of the poker, "of course you would. You had nothing to do but look at it after it was all made, and take down perpetual bags of sugar-plums. Just you have all the work, and the planning, and the care, and the trouble, and to keep the children away, and not get wax on the carpet, and set the house a-fire, and disturb papa, and then see how you would like it right over and over again."

But when Muriel got up and put away the poker, and said tragically, "Well, we can't have any Christmas at all, that I see, for I am sure I've thought till my brain is as hot as a coal, and I can't think any more," Christiana determined to appeal to a higher power for aid. No Christmas was a calamity which she could not calmly contemplate. Therefore, papa was requested to put on his thinking-cap, and begin. He had hardly had time, however, to turn the subject over in his mind, before Ivers sounded the tocsin at the head of the stairs.

"Girls! children! Tim! Chunk! Chunkarthur! Good land of Goshen! what is become of the family?" And, not reflecting that nobody had time to respond, he leaped over the baluster, swung himself to the floor below, popped his head into the library, and cried—"Aunt Thula is here! wants to see us!—Come along, every one of you!" and rushed off to drum up the rest of the absentees. No need of a second call. Even Christmas and its exigencies were forgotten. Christy and Tim tumbled down from their father's knees. Muriel left the canary that she was feeding, to fly about in the conservatory, Robin threw down the magnificent steam-engine that he thought he was building, but wasn't, and all rushed up to see Aunt Thula, the dear old negro nurse, who had done her best to pet and spoil them when they were babies, and kept it up still, as far as possible, through the holidays. They were all her "chil'n," and would be, all their days; and they hung around her, and hugged her, and warmed her old heart with their simple tenderness.

"Now, I suppose ye's gwine ter have high times Christmas an' New Year—no lessons nor work."

"Oh, Aunt Thula!" sighed Muriel, "of all days in the year, Christmas and New Year are the most trying."

"Lawsy, Miss Mury, honey, I al'us thought no oder days wan't no account wid you long o' dem."

"But the presents—the presents are such a trouble. Whatever to get for such a rabble? Papa will furnish the money, but who will furnish the brains, to think up anything new to get, or any nice way to do it, that is not as old as the world?"

"Oh, chile! I hope yer sweet heart'll never know not'in wuss." And Aunt Thula fetched a sigh from the very deeps of her heart—a sigh which had so much sorrow in it, that even the merry children were saddened.

"Oh, Aunt Thula! what is it?" asked Muriel, softly; and Christiana put up her chubby fist to the dark face, and echoed— "What is it?"

"I'se a mis'able ole woman to be a sorrowin' you on your play-days," replied Aunt Thula, apologetically; "but I'se so full, it will run over."

"I knew something was the matter, the moment you came in," said Ivers, his brave, boyish face, grown beautiful with sympathy. "Now you'd better tell us, and perhaps we can help you."

"No, honey, you can't. Nobody can help us but de Lor'; and sometimes He will, and sometimes He won't. Oh, bress de Lor'!" with sudden remorse—"yes, He al'us helps us; but 'tis in His own way. We'se a poor race, we niggers, an' de laws is strong; an' Peely's a slave, an' I can't get her, no how!" And honest Aunt Thula poured her sobs into her big bandanna, while the children stood by, awed into silence.

"I'se a mis'able ole woman, any how."

"But, dear old nurse," cried Muriel, "you darling Aunty, how came Peely a slave? You're not a slave."

"No honey; but I was a slave."

"Why, I didn't know it."

"Nor I, either," added Ivers; "we were so little, you know. I wish you would tell us all about it—if you don't mind."

"It's a bad ting to talk about, 'deed, honey. It b'longs to de devil. Don't b'long to de Lor', no how. I'se a slave, b'longed ter Massa Pete Gillus. He died, an' left us all, me an' de chil'n to Miss Mary and Miss Beulah. Dem was two old maid sisters. When dey died, I was to be free, an' de chil'n, dey wan't never to be removed; dey was al'us to stay roun' de ole place. Chloe, she was to go to one of the gran'sons, Parson Gillus, we call'd 'im. She was named for his gran'ma; an' dey all liked her; an' she was a little kitten for 'em sure. She was to be freed when she was sixteen."

"Chloe is Chloe that used to live here?"

"Yes, honey."

"So they did free her?"

"Oh, yes, honey. Parson Gillus was a good man, an' he freed Chloe when she was sixteen; but she staid wid him an' Miss Gillus till dey both died, and den she come to de city, an' married."

"And didn't they free the others too?" asked Tim.

"No, might as well not. De rest had to serve forever, I say—till dey was thirty-five year old, an' work to death, till de bes' part of 'em was gone."

"Well, Aunt Thula, are they free yet? Where are they now? Where was the place?"

"'Bout forty miles from here, honey—Mount Joy; we was all raised there. When Miss Mary and Miss Beulah died, de property was divided. Free? yes, dey's e'en jis' free, all of 'em. Oh, Lor'!" And a gush of grief overcame Aunt Thula again; but she soon went on—

"All de property went to two nephews; dey was brudders—Mass Jeams, and Mass Pete. Dreful bad. Mass Pete was a perfect torment in dis worl', an' I 'xpect he'll be wuss in de nex'. De chil'n didn't fall to him; dey went to Mass Jeams. He was better dan de ole one; bad enough, anyhow. He toted 'em all off to Tennessee. Hadn't ought to, no ways. Mass Gillus, Mis'r Gillus, said dey wan't never to be moved from de ole place."

"But, Aunty, how could he? 'Twas against the law."

"Law, child!—law ain't for de weak; law is for de strong. Law is for white men, not for niggers. He said he was on'y gwine to take 'em till things was settled; fotch 'em back ag'in in de spring. Nobody ever set eyes on 'em dere again."

"Oh, you poor, dear, darling Aunt Thula!—didn't you ever see them again?"

"Yes, honey; Prince, he got free eight years ago, an' he come on right off, an' I've had him under my nose ever since. Den Toby, he was sold. Mass Jeams he got short of money, an' he sold him to one of de neighbors."

"Was he a good master?"

"Ah, honey! most of 'em down dere is bad; ain't many good mas'rs. Dis one's a heap better dan de oder. He's tol'able. He let Toby come home once to see me, Toby worked, and got de money. He'd been gone nine years, and grow'd so I didn't know him. He stayed five months, and den went back. Oh, Lor'! and two years ago, he got free, an' was just gettin' ready to come home, an' he took de fever, an died."

"Oh, Aunty! that was too bad!" cried little Chunk.

"No, honey, not too bad, else 'twouldn't have been; but jus' bad enough. Den Peely, I an't hearn from her dis long while. I'se mighty oneasy. I reckoned dey wouldn't write for her; an' den p'raps she was dead; and las' week Miss Jeam she writ an' said Peely's time was out next March; but she ain't no ways well, an' he'd let her come now, if we'd send on de money to pay for de journey. But, oh Lor'! where's de money comin' from? If I'se well, I'd get it; but I've got de misery on my back, so I ain't good for not'in, and Prince's roomatis laid him up two months; he ain't jes' able to walk now, an' it takes all we can rake an' scrape, me an' Prince, to get along; an' my health is too bad for me to be knockin' round dis way."

"He's a miserable mean scamp!" cried Ivers, suddenly firing up. "Keep Peely, and work her to death, and then not give her money to come home with, after he'd stolen her away in the first place."

"An' after she'd done servin' all dis time. Yes, 'tis mighty mean. Mass Jeams al'us was meaner 'n dirt. Dat's de wus ting 'bout him."

"Aunt Thula," cried Muriel, after a pause, "how much money do you want to get Peely home?"

"Laws, honey, more'n I can get in a mont' o' Sundays. Nigh on thirty dollars." And Thula drew her gay shawl about her shoulders, and arose heavily.

"That's right, Aunt Thula," cried Muriel, clapping her hands; "I don't want you here; I want you to go." But though her words were unlovely, her voice and face were not. Evidently, she had been thinking, notwithstanding her morning inability to "think any more."

"Aunty Thula, 'go away, Come again another day.'"

When Thula was gone, Muriel came out with her thought.

"Now, I say, let's take our money, and give it to Aunt Thula. I'm tired to death of Christmas presents, and I'll give mine; and if you don't you are a mean set. That's all I have to say about it."

"I'll give mine," said Chunk, terrified by the tone.

"But we can't get thirty dollars, all told," said Ivers, who, by virtue of his age and sex was the financier of the kingdom.

"Yes, we can, if we all give up every speck and grain of our money, I know papa will give us the rest. I know him so well, I know he will."

What appalling fate would have annihilated papa had he refused, I do not know; but he did not refuse. He was rich enough to gratify his children—especially glad to encourage them in finding happiness in the happiness of others; and it was no small pleasure to him to see even Robby and Christie flushed with desire to give this great boon to the faithful old nurse. And when in the afternoon they all marched down to the cottage where Aunt Thula lived with Prince—a good two miles; but they were well and strong—each with two gold pieces in his pocket, you could not find a happier or a handsomer group in all the land.

Aunt Thula's New Year was gladdened by her long-lost daughter—the daughter who went away from her a buxom lass of eighteen—who came back to her weary, worn-out, almost an old woman, at thirty-five; but her daughter still, and well-beloved.

"So we did have our Christmas, after all," said Tim, as they sat on Christmas evening, cracking nuts around the library fire.

"And the best Christmas ever I see," added Christie, crawling out from under father's chair, where she had been in pursuit of a vagrant nut.

"Roll, Christie; don't creep. You'd get there sooner," drawled Ivers.

"I've got there," said Christie, in perfect good faith—"I'm just getting out again."

"It was a good Christmas, because it wasn't a selfish Christmas," said Muriel, with the dignity of an archbishop. "We are a great deal happier now with nuts and molasses candy—making 'em and eating 'em—than we should have been with all manner of nice candies and things, and toys, and know that Peely was a slave, and couldn't get out."

"Yes, we were good and kind, and gave our money, and that makes us happy, Bob," preached Christy, self-complacently, handing down her moral reflections to Bob, second-hand.

"But you would not have done it if I had not made you," interposed Muriel, severely. Christie's thermometer went suddenly down several degrees below freezing point.

"But you did it as fast as you understood it," said Ivers, punching her over and over on the floor—"and you were as noble as a queen, and as happy as a clam."

Thermometer goes up with a bound, into the summer heats.

"The Contraband"

Christie Pearl

The Student and Schoolmate 11 (February 1862), 45–48

"The articles called 'Contraband' stand greatly in need of clothing sufficient to protect them from the cold of the coming winter. Any garments for men, women, or children, however small, will be thankfully received. Old, cast-off clothing will be useful. The clothes can be packed in barrels."

So read the oldest boy, Hubert, from a daily paper. His mother paused in her knitting, and said, musingly,—

"Why could we not send a barrel?"

"Do!" said Hubert. "You may have my old vest, which is too short, and those stockings which always slip down, and my old hat. I want a new one, like Jim's."

"You may also have those dickeys which endanger my ears every time I put them on, and that coat lined with red silk which flaps open so in the wind," said the father. Corolla clapped her hands and laughed.

"I should like to see a negro with a dickey on, those negroes down South, I mean," said Willie.

"But they do wear dickeys and diamond rings," said Carl, soberly.

"Shan't I send my gold bracelet?" suggested Mary, smiling.

"Mother! mother! mayn't we send a barrel? I've lots of old things I want to get rid of. Say, mother!"

"Yes, yes, run along. I'll look over the things and see if they are not too good."

Away scampered the children.

"That is your spirit of benevolence, is it?" said Mary. "If they're not too good."

"I think you'd better send your bracelet," said Hubert.

"It's my spirit of economy," replied her mother. "There are many things which we can wear yet. What a noise!"

There was a noise, the sound of footsteps everywhere. Attic closets were searched, drawers were rummaged, boxes were turned inside out, and Bridget, unconscious of all the work of clearing up which was in store for her, sat calmly in the kitchen, chopping mince meat, and muttering, as she heard the loud reverberations in all parts of the house, "Och, and it's those children that have got a tantrum."

She was not long left in silence, for Willie burst into the room,—

"Bridget!" he screamed, in a voice like a railroad whistle. "Haven't you got any thing for the contrabands, any clothes, I mean?"

"The contrabands! and sure, who be they?"

"Why, the negroes down South, who haven't got clothes enough to keep them warm."

"Sure, and it's meself that hasn't clothes. Don't I want a new bonnet with red roses in it, and a blue and yellow silk dress, like Mary McCarty's?—but I've two night-caps, ye may have them. Ha! ha! may they keep their ears warm!"

"Poh! their wool will keep their ears warm! but I'll take them."

Willie didn't tell Bridget, that while she was gone for the caps "He put in his thumb, and pulled out," not only one plum, but six, from the mince-meat. But Emerson says, "Crime and punishment grow out of one stem. Punishment is a fruit that unsuspected ripens within the flower of the pleasure that concealed it." Willie has plucked the flower and must eat the fruit sometime.

The footsteps neared the parlor. They were heard pattering in all directions, the doors were thrown open, and piles of clothes, moved by some invisible power entered the room, but bright eyes and tangled locks appeared, as they were thrown upon the floor.

"What have you there? my blue silk dress! Carry it back this moment! And an embroidered handkerchief! Oh Lizzie."

"Let us see what you have," said the mother; and the whole family stooped to examine the treasures.

"See, mother," said Corolla, "here's my purple pumpkin hood, and my two muslin sacks that I don't want any more, and my old plaid dress."

"Muslins?—what do they want of muslins?"

"Keep still, Mary; if you can't send any thing yourself, don't make fun of us!"

"And here are my long-sleeved aprons. I'm too big to wear them now, and mother, I took the yellow blanket off my bed. Willie always pulls it off me, and it's too small," said Carl.

"How many little negroes will sleep under it? I should think six might."

"Mother, can't Mary keep still?—And here are my blue stockings, and my old shoes."

"A hoop skirt! well, Lizzie!"

"I don't care. I want a new one, and they'll be proud of it, and I've got some flannels, and my old cloak; I declare I won't wear it another winter, and here's that old pillow which hasn't got more than two feathers in it."

"Hurrah for the 'contrabands'! I believe my wardrobe will be empty! Long-tailed coats, white vests, silk stockings, boots, and collars!" shouted Hubert.

"Here's Bridget's night-caps, and my black trousers—I hate them—and my jacket with that patch on the elbow!" screamed Willie.

"What a tempest of voices!" said the mother.

"Isn't there a barrel-full?" asked Willie, anxiously regarding a skull-cap in his hand.

The father stood before the fire, and warmed his hands, and gave a loud "Ahem!" Then the children gathered around him, for they knew that he was going to say something important.

"What is it, pa!" they asked.

"My dear children, are there any things there that you want or need?"

"No! No! Not one!" chimed the voices.

"Then you have not given properly. Your clothes may keep the 'contrabands' warm, but they will bring no additional warmth to your own hearts. You must make sacrifices in order to reap the benefit of giving. Think if there is not something you can part with which will cost you a struggle."

Then all the children looked thoughtful. Mary spoke first,—

"I'll give my pretty green shawl which I like so well, and wear my brown cloak this winter, and my brown stuff dress."

"I'll give my red mittens," said Carl.

"I—I—I'll give my skull-cap," said Willie, with a sigh.

"My best kid [glove]s shall go to the 'contrabands,'" said Hubert mockingly.

"What a sacrifice!—We won't tell what we are going to do," said Corolla, after a whispered consultation with Lizzie.

"I'll give my new top, and if the negroes can't spin it, I'll write a letter and tell them how," said Carl, bravely.

The barrel was packed with good, warm, substantial things. Nicely wrapped in cotton was a large doll, with blue eyes, and a pink nose and cheeks, and gay dresses in abundance, to one of which was pinned the following note:—

"My dear little 'contraband':
Whoever you may be, we send you our doll with all her clothes. If she don't keep you warm outside, she'll make your heart warm, we guess.
—Lizzie and Corolla."

And in one toe of a little blue stocking, nestling beside a gaily painted top, was another note,—

"My dear little darkey,
I send you a top. It has a string with it. You must wind the string all round it and then take hold of one end of the string and let go the top ever so quick, and then it will spin. If you can't read this you must get your father to read it to you.
—Carl."

"The Two Christmas Evenings"
Lydia Maria Child
Our Young Folks 2 (January 1866), 2–13

It was a beautiful Christmas Eve. A light snow had fallen just before night, and made the city streets look clean. Icicles hanging from the roofs glittered in the moonlight, and the trees on the Common looked as if they had put on white feathers for a festival.

Mrs. Rich's parlor was brighter than the moonlight splendor without. The folding-doors were open. A clear flame rose from the cannel-coal as it split and crackled in the grate; the gas burned brilliantly in the chandeliers; at the upper end of the room was an Evergreen Tree, with a sparkling crown of little lamps, and gay with festoons of ribbons and trinkets; the carpet was like a meadow enamelled with flowers; the crimson damask curtains glowed in the brilliant light; and the gilded paper on the walls gleamed here and there, like the bright edges of little sunset clouds. Mrs. Rich was just putting some finishing touches to the Tree, when the great clock on the staircase struck seven, and the pattering of feet was heard. The door opened, and Papa entered with a group of children. There was Frank, in all the dignity of his fourteen years; earnest-looking Isabel, who was about twelve; Ellen, not much over nine, whose honest face had an expression of thoughtfulness beyond her years; and little Alice, whom they named Pet Poodle, because she had such a quantity of soft, light curls falling about her face. In her first stammering of this name she called herself Petty Poo, and they all adopted her infantile abbreviation.

The Evergreen Tree and the treasures with which it was covered produced but slight excitement in the minds of the older children. As they approached it, they said, "How tastefully you have arranged it, mamma!" and they quietly awaited the distribution of the gifts, like well-trained young ladies and gentlemen. But little Alice, who opened her blue eyes on the world only four years before, had not done wondering yet. She capered up to the tree, and, pointing to one thing after another, said, "Isn't dat pooty?" A large doll had been sent to her last Christmas, and when she spied one seated among the green boughs, she gave a little shout, and cried out, "Dare is nudder dolly for Petty Poo!" She was told Aunt Jane had sent it to her, and she received it with unalloyed satisfaction. "Tank Aunt Jane," said she. "Dis dolly's eyes is b'oo, and tudder dolly's is b'ack." Well pleased with this variety in her family, she hugged it up, and seated herself on the carpet to examine the little blue rosettes on the shoes.

When Mr. Rich handed his son a handsomely illustrated copy of "The Arabian Nights," he received it with a bow, and, turning over the leaves carelessly, said, "I wonder what Uncle Joe sent me this for! I have one edition, and I don't want another." Isabel took a gold bracelet that was offered her, and, slipping it on her wrist, remarked to her brother, "I don't think this bracelet Cousin Emma has sent me cost so much as the one I sent her last Christmas." "And see this gutta-percha watch-chain that Cousin Joe has sent me," rejoined Frank. "You know I sent him a gold one last year." "If you read what is written on the card," said his father, "you will see that it was made in the Hospital, by his brave brother, Captain George." Frank glanced over the

The Rich children find themselves bored with their family's typical Christmas celebration. From Our Young Folks.

writing, and replied, "Yes, sir; but I should rather have had the gold one." Mary received a handsome French work-box, filled with elegant implements for sewing. She said, "I am much obliged to Aunt Jane"; but she set it aside after a slight examination, and returned to the tree again. Many more presents were distributed,—beaded nets for the hair, books, photographs, bronze dogs, Parian images, and all sorts of things. But Petty Poo was the only one who seemed to take a very lively interest. She stood by the table hugging her doll, expressing her admiration of everything by little shouts, and holding out her hand now and then to receive a paper of sugared almonds, a china lamb, or a little horse on rollers. The last thing that was taken from the tree was a small basket, containing a doll's nightgown and nightcap. This furnished her with delightful employment. She seated herself on the carpet and undressed her doll, and when she had made her ready for the night, she said, "Now Petty Poo will go to bed, and take all her tings wid her; and dolly wid de b'ack eyes may s'eep in de drawer." When she had been kissed all round, she was carried upstairs, and mamma followed, to have another kiss from the little darling before her blue eyes closed for the night.

When Mrs. Rich returned to the parlor, Isabel said archly, "Are you sure, mamma, that you took everything from the Christmas Tree?" and mamma, who knew she was about to be surprised, replied, "I believe so; but I will go and look, dear." Among the boughs she found a rustic watch-case, an embroidered ottoman-cover, and a pretty worsted shawl, on which Frank and Isabel and Ellen had each written their names, and added, "For my dear mother." Mrs. Rich smiled lovingly, as she wrapped the shawl about her, and put her watch in the case, and spread the cover on the ottoman, and said the colors were beautifully arranged.

"We made them entirely ourselves," said the young folks; "and we had such a job to keep you from finding out what we were doing!"

"Thank you, my dear children," replied the happy mother. She kissed them all, and they clung about her, and asked again and again if she really thought the things were pretty.

"Perhaps you have not found all yet," said Ellen. "Please look again."

After a diligent search, which was purposely prolonged a little, a box was found hidden away under the boughs. It contained a set of chessmen, a crocheted purse, and a worsted comforter for the neck, on which Frank and Isabel and Ellen had written, "For my dear father," with the names of each appended; and again they said, exultingly, "We made them all ourselves, papa."

"Thank you, my children," replied Mr. Rich. "So, Frank, these chessmen are what you have so long been busy about at Uncle John's turning lathe." He smiled as he added, "I will not say I had rather have gold ones; for such neat workmanship done by my son is more valuable to me than gold could be. And Isabel, dear, I don't know whether this handsome purse cost so much as the skates I gave you for a Christmas present, but I certainly like it better than any purse I could buy." The brother and sister blushed a little, for they understood the rebuke conveyed in his words. But he patted their heads and kissed them, and as they nestled close up to him, he folded them all in his arms. "So my little Ellen has made me a red, white, and blue comforter," said he. "How grand I shall feel walking down State Street with this round my neck!"

"Then you will wear it, papa?" said Ellen, with a glad little jump.

"Wear it? Indeed I will," replied her father; "and proud I shall be of the loyal colors, and of my little daughter's work."

"Ellen is very patriotic," said her mother. "I think papa would like to hear her play 'The Star-Spangled Banner.'"

The little girl ran eagerly to the music-stool; for she had been practising the tune very diligently, in hopes she should be invited to play. Frank and Isabel kept their fingers moving to the music, and when it ceased, papa exclaimed, "Bravo!" He was really pleased with his little daughter's improvement, and that made her as light-hearted as a bird.

While they were deciding what Isabel should play, the door-bell rang, and one cousin after another came in to talk over the Christmas gifts. Isabel glanced shyly at her father, when she said, "I am much obliged to you, Cousin Emma, for the bracelet you sent me. It is very handsome." And Frank was as red as a turkey's gills when he thanked Cousin Joe for the gutta-percha chain, and said it would be a valuable souvenir of his brave Cousin George. Cousin Max, who always thought whatever he had was better than other people could have, remarked that their presents were very handsome, but he didn't think they were equal to what they had on their tree at home.

"The worst of it is, I have so many duplicates," said Cousin Emma. "Last year I had three bracelets, and this year I had two. When I put them all on, they reach almost up to my elbow."

"My aunts and cousins, and particular friends, all take to sending me books in blue and gold," said Cousin Jane. "I get so tired of seeing those little volumes, all just alike! There they are always standing on my shelf, like 'four and twenty little dogs all in a row.'"

"But they are not all alike inside," remarked Uncle Rich.

"I suppose not," she replied; "but I am so tired of 'em, I never read 'em."

"Here are some new charades," said Mrs. Rich, who wished to change the conversation. They were soon laughing over the charades, and then they sang some funny catches, and bade each other "Good night."

The next evening, when little Alice went away with her nurse, after kissing them all "Good night," she peeped into the door again to say, "Dolly wid de b'oo eyes is going to s'eep in de drawer, and dolly wid de b'ack eyes is going to s'eep wid Petty Poo." They smiled upon her, and threw her kisses, and when the door closed after her, Mr. Rich remarked, "Even with Petty Poo the novelty of Christmas gifts don't last long. What part of your Christmas evening did you enjoy most, my children?"

"When I was playing to you, and you liked it," replied Ellen.

"When you and mamma seemed so pleased with the things we made for you," said Isabel.

"And you, my son?" inquired Mr. Rich.

Frank replied, that was the only part of the evening he cared much about.

"I thought so," rejoined his father. "Have any of you thought what might be the reason?"

The young folks were silent, each one trying to think what their father expected them to say.

"I will tell you how I explain it," continued Mr. Rich. "I learned long ago that it is not the having things, but the *doing* things, which makes people happy. You enjoyed the presents you gave us, because you had expended ingenuity and industry upon them. Nothing you could have bought for us would have given either you or us half the pleasure."

"And they were working for *others*, not for *themselves*," added their mother. "That greatly increased the charm."

Her husband smiled approvingly, as he rejoined, "You have said the best work, my dear."

The children looked in the fire thoughtfully. At last, Isabel broke the silence by saying, "When we went to bed last night, Ellen and I said we didn't know what was the reason we felt so little pleasure, when so many had tried to please us."

Their father rejoined, "The trouble is, you have so many handsome things that the charm of novelty is lost. A poor child would feel as rich as Croesus with any one of the many things you think so little of."

Isabel looked up eagerly and exclaimed, "Papa, that makes me think of something. We will agree with our uncles and aunts and cousins, not to exchange Christmas gifts next year. We will do something else."

"What can we do?" asked Ellen. "I should admire to do something different."

"We'll give dolls and picture-books and tops to the children in the Orphan Asylum," replied her sister.

"That is a very good thought," said their mother.

"And, papa, you said it made folks happy to do things themselves," remarked Ellen. "So we'll make up the dolls and dress them ourselves; and we'll knit comforters and mittens and hoods for the poor children; and we'll make balls for the boys; and ever so many things. Won't we, Issy?"

"Where are you going to get money enough to buy the dolls' heads, and stuff to make the hoods and comforters of?" inquired Frank.

His sisters looked puzzled. Mr. and Mrs. Rich said nothing; for they wanted the children to work out their own plan and depend on their own resources. After a little reflection, Isabel said, "We could have a Fair. Not a public fair, mamma; but a sort of pleasant party for our uncles and aunts and cousins and particular friends. We've got ever so many things laid up in our drawers, that we might sell as well as not."

"O, but that would never do," rejoined Ellen; "for they were given to us, and we couldn't sell people their own things. But if they will agree not to give us any presents next Christmas, we can buy worsted and dolls' heads with our money, instead of buying bracelets and vases for them; and they have so many they don't want them."

"That's true," answered Isabel; "and we could do without many of the things that we are buying every week."

Their father looked highly pleased, and said, "That will be another good thing, to have a generous motive for practising economy. I will buy ten dollars' worth of whatever things you make yourselves."

"And so will I," said their mother.

"You might lend us the twenty dollars beforehand, and take your pay in the things we make," said Frank. "I will make some cups and balls for the girls, and some bats for the boys."

His father looked at him with a significant smile, and said, "One thing you may be sure of, my son. The poor boys will be too glad of their wooden bats to complain because they are not gold ones."

"Please, father, don't remind me of that again," replied Frank, coloring.

"And please, father," said Isabel, "not to tell me I shall have nothing given me that costs so much as what I give away; for that was a mean little speech of mine, and I am ashamed of it."

"Very well; I won't allude to it again," rejoined their father.

Ellen, who always liked to apologize for any fault of her brother or sister, remarked, "If they hadn't have said it, I suppose they would have thought it, and you and mamma say you like to have us speak right out before you whatever we think."

"That is true, my child," replied her mother. "We never want you to feel restrained before us. But I noticed that you made no complaint about your handsome work-box."

"That was not because I was any better than Issy," said the sincere little girl; "for I did think that I had two work-boxes, and I did wish it had been something else. I didn't say so, because I thought what Frank and Issy said made you and papa look sober."

"We do not blame any of you for your thoughts, or for speaking them openly before us," said Mrs. Rich; "though I cannot deny that Frank's and Issy's remarks seemed to me in a wrong and mean spirit. But your indifference to the presents you receive is not your fault; and certainly it is not the fault of the kind relatives and friends who take so much pains to please you. The trouble is, both with you and your cousins, that you have too many things to care very much about anything. I am glad you are going to try the experiment of giving without receiving."

It was a pleasure to the parents to see how the planning of things and the doing of things waked up the energies of their young folks. Almost every morning Isabel and Ellen would bound into the breakfast-room, with eager faces, saying, "Good morning, papa and mamma. We've got a new idea." The phrase became a family joke.

"Bless me!" exclaimed Mr. Rich, when they came jumping in as usual one morning. "What's coming on the carpet next? Some new idea I suppose. What a privilege it is to have a family so full of ideas!"

"Why, papa," replied Ellen, "you know Issy acts charades beautifully. Frank has written one, and she's going to act it at the Fair, and charge the visitors five cents apiece. Perhaps we shall get as much as five dollars; and that would buy a good many dolls' heads or picture-books for the orphans."

Another morning, Isabel was in great ecstasy over a plan Ellen had suggested. "O papa, it is such a bright idea!" exclaimed she. "We are going to have a Tableau of Europe, Asia, Africa, and America. Petty Poo is going to be Europe, with some pearl beads on her neck and arms, and Frank's miniature ship beside her. We are going to paint little Cousin Joe yellowish brown, and dress him up like a Chinese Mandarin, and seat him on a tea-chest. That's for Asia, you know. We are going to paint little John reddish brown, with a coronet of feathers on his head; and Frank is going to make a bow and arrow for him. That's for America. You remember that bright-looking little black girl, Kitty Jones? We're going to ask her mother to lend her to us, and we'll dress her up for Africa. Frank says she ought to be leaning on an elephant's tusk, but I don't know where we could get one."

"What's the child thinking of!" exclaimed Mr. Rich. "Why, you might as well give me a meeting-house steeple for a cane. What could such a little creature do with an elephant's tusk, five or six feet long; taller than I am?"

"Perhaps we can find a baby elephant's tusk," replied Isabel. "We shall have to charge ten cents apiece for the Tableau, it will be so much trouble."

The weeks passed on, bringing with them a succession of new projects. Many of them were nipped in the bud by adverse circumstances; but whether they ripened or not, they occupied the young brains of the children and gave their bodies healthy exercise. They were impatient for spring to come, that they might remove to their country-house in Dorchester. There they could pick up hen's feathers, and color them pink with cochineal, and blue with indigo, for ornamenting the dolls' hats. Sometimes the cockerel dropped a gaudy feather that needed no coloring, and great was their joy over the prize. Then they wanted autumn to come, that they might find moss-acorns; for mamma had given them some pieces of her brown silk dress, and promised to show them how to make little emery-balls, that would look like real acorns when they were fastened in the mossy cups. An unthought-of value was imparted to every scrap of pretty ribbon or calico, and to broken strings of beads that had long been rolling about. Even little Alice caught the prevailing spirit, and was every day bringing a doll's sash, or some other of her little treasures, saying, "Dis is for de orfins." The children of this wealthy family had never before experienced the great pleasure of turning everything to some good use; and the novelty was very delightful to them.

When relatives and friends heard the proposal not to exchange Christmas presents, they were very much surprised, and some were half disposed to be offended. The children soon reconciled them, however, by saying, "It is not because we are ungrateful for your presents, or unwilling to send presents to you. But we have thought of a new plan, and when you come to know something about it, we hope you will like it." They of course perceived that something uncommonly engrossing was going forward, but could not find out exactly what; and this little air of mystery added a new charm to the enterprise.

What with lessons in English and French, and music and dancing, and all their plans for the Fair, December came round again without the children's ever having occasion to say, "I wish I knew what to do." The large drawing-room was arranged for their accommodation on the eventful evening. At one extremity, English ivy was trained round a large hoop to form a framework for the Tableau. When the screen was removed, and pearl-white Alice, and yellowish-brown Joe, and reddish-brown John, and brown-black Kitty were seen grouped behind the ivy, they really made a very pretty picture. Little Joe looked very funny in his Chinese cap, with a peacock's feather in it, a little round button atop, and a long braid of hair tied on behind. Alice was charming in white muslin, with some small blue flowers and strings of pearl beads hanging among her flaxen curls. John had a coronet of turkey's feathers, and a short beaver-skin skirt, fastened round the waist with a gaudy belt of many colored wampum. Bead-embroidered moccasins covered his feet. In one hand he carried a bow and arrow, trimmed with red and yellow ribbon, and in the other a stuffed squirrel, to represent the fur trade. Kitty Jones wore a short skirt of yellow merino. Her arms and feet were bare, with the exception of strips of gilt paper on wrists and ankles. On her head was a crown of gilt paper surmounted by an ostrich-feather. Frank had fashioned a piece of wood into the resemblance of a small tusk, and painted it suitably, that she might represent the trade of Africa in gold and ivory and ostrich-feathers. The little ones behaved very properly, till Alice spied out her white poodle sniffing round the room in search of her. Then she forgot all the instructions she had received, and called out, "Poody! Poody!" That was a very improper proceeding for Europe, with a ship by her side to represent the commerce of the world. And it made Asia laugh out loud; which was an unheard of want of dignity in a

Mandarin upon a state occasion. America grinned rather too broadly for a sedate Indian chief. Africa was perfectly motionless in every muscle; and looked a little bit afraid; which Frank said was very natural, considering Europe was so near with her ship, and still carrying on the slave-trade; a remark which his sisters and cousins thought quite witty. After the little ones were dismissed with kisses and candy, Frank came tottering in, bent half double, with a white wig on his head, an hour-glass in one hand and a scythe in the other. He was followed by Isabel, handsomely dressed in the newest mode. Afterward Ellen and her mother appeared, dressed just as women and little girls dressed forty years ago. "O how funny they look! Did you ever see such frights?" shouted the young folks. They all agreed that it was very easy to guess the first, and the second, and the whole of the charade had been acted. When they had taken off their disguises, friends and relatives began to compliment them. Ellen, who was always ready to praise her sister, because she really thought her something uncommon, replied, "Isabel acted her part beautifully; flirting her fan, courtesying, and swinging her crinoline; but I didn't do anything only walk round with an old bonnet on my head. I never could act charades well."

"There is one thing she can do well," said Isabel. "She preaches beautifully."

"O Isabel! How can you say so?" exclaimed Ellen, blushing scarlet.

"It's nothing more than the truth," persisted Isabel. "I heard you preach a beautiful sermon at Carry Rice's party."

The company, amused at her confusion, began to say, "Ellen, you must let us hear you preach. We will give you ten cents apiece for a sermon."

This offer tempted her; she thought of the dolls and tops the money would buy. She allowed them to place her on a stool, but when she found herself there, with all of them looking at her, she felt very much heated, and said, bashfully, "Ladies and gentlemen, I don't know what to preach about. When I was at Carry Rice's, some of the girls and boys got into a quarrel, and I preached to them from the text, 'Return good for evil.' But you are not quarrelling. Besides, everybody preaches about the war now, and I do want the Rebels to be beaten; so that text won't do; and I don't know what text to take."

"'Proclaim Liberty throughout all the land, to all the inhabitants thereof,'" said her father, in a loud, clear voice.

"That's a good text," said Ellen, brightening up. "Liberty ought to be proclaimed to all, because it ought to be. They say they used to whip the slaves down in Dixie for trying to learn to read and write. That was very wrong. There's little Kitty Jones, that was Africa to-night; she's as bright as a steel button. She learns her letters a great deal faster than our Alice; and it would be a sin and a shame to whip her for it. The slaveholders wouldn't like to have their children whipped for learning, and they ought to do to others as they would be done by. Besides, it would be better for the white folks down there if liberty was proclaimed to all. They wouldn't be so violent-tempered, and go round stabbing folks with bowie-knives, if they hadn't been used to beating and banging slaves about when they were boys. And if they hadn't slaves to wait upon 'em, they would find out what a great pleasure it is to learn how to do things, and to help themselves. So you see, if we beat the Rebels, and proclaim liberty to all, we shall return good for evil; and that text would have done for my sermon, if I had thought about it. But then I think the greatest reason why we ought to proclaim liberty to all is because we ought to. And I don't know as I have anything more to say to-night."

As she descended from her eminence, all in a flutter, her friends came up to offer her money; and Uncle Joe patted her on the head as he said, "I've heard some sermons that were not so well worth ten cents."

There was a short recess, and Isabel played lively tunes while the guests walked about and ate ice-creams, which the girls had made under their mother's directions. Over the refreshment table Frank had printed, in large letters, "Home Manufacture." All the articles were sold before ten o'clock; for the secret was discovered, and everybody wanted to help on the good work. The children were impatient to have the guests go, that they might count their money. They were greatly surprised and delighted to find they had received more than two hundred dollars. They kissed papa and mamma, and kissed each other, and said, over and over again, "Didn't we have a good time?"

When they had sobered down a little, Isabel, looking up archly, said, "Papa and mamma, I've got a new idea."

"I dare say she has," said Ellen; "she's always having new ideas."

"And what is it now?" asked their mother.

"We have got so much more money than we expected," replied Isabel, "that I think we can do two things. You know that slave woman down South, who hid Cousin George when the Rebels were after him? He wrote to us that she had a very pretty, bright little girl. Seeing Kitty Jones tonight has made me think about her. I should like to spend half our money in picture-books and toys for the freed children."

"Good! good!" exclaimed Ellen, clapping her hands.

They all agreed with her, and when their articles were collected together, they were divided into two parcels, one of which was immediately sent off to the islands of South Carolina; the other half was reserved till the day before Christmas, when they were conveyed to the Orphan Asylum. Frank procured a pretty evergreen tree, and they all went to help the Superintendent arrange the articles upon it. The little inmates of the asylum were kept in the dark about the whole affair till evening, when they were marched into the room in procession, two and two. They were very shy in presence of the strangers. A few of them gazed with wonder on the lighted Christmas Tree, and some little laughs were heard; but most of them stood with fingers on their mouths, looking down. When hoods and mittens, and balls and bats, and tops and skates, and dolls and picture-books were distributed among them, a few jumped and laughed; but most of them made little formal bows and courtesies, and said, "Thank'ee, ma'am," "Thank'ee, sir," as they had been taught to do. When the articles were all distributed, the Superintendent conducted them to the play-room. She returned a few minutes afterward, and said to Mr. Rich and his family, "They were constrained before strangers; but I have left the door of the play-room ajar, and I should like you to have a peep in."

Such a merry scene! The orphans were jumping and skipping about, tossing up their balls and dancing their dolls. "See how high my ball goes!" shouted one. "See what a pretty dolly I've got!" said another.

"O mamma! this pays us for all our work," said Isabel.

"I thought you were paid in doing the work," rejoined her mother.

"So we were," said Ellen; "but this pays us over again."

While they were putting on their cloaks to return home, a chubby little orphan asked the Superintendent for a "fower." When asked what she wanted it for, she answered, "For de lady dat did give me de dolly." When she had received a geranium blossom, she went to Isabella and bashfully held up her flower. Isabella thanked her and kissed her, and she trotted off in a state of high satisfaction.

When the family returned to their elegant parlor, there were only ashes in the grate, the gas burned low, with a seething sound, and the gleams of the gilded paper were hidden by a veil of shadow. But the cheeks of the children glowed as they had not glowed under the brilliancy of the last year's Christmas Eve.

"O, what a pleasant world this is!" exclaimed Ellen.

Isabel took up a graceful Parian vase for one flower, and said, "Mamma, won't this geranium keep longer if I put salt in the water?"

Her mother smiled as she replied, "You are not apt to be so very careful of the flowers that are given you. But I see, my dear child, that you are learning by experience how much more blessed it is to give than to receive."

The water in the vase was changed every day; and when the blossom fell, the petals were pressed in a book, and under them was written, "The Little Orphan's Gift, on Christmas Eve."

The Fair and the visit to the Asylum furnished topics for household conversation for many a day afterward. When Petty Poo was asked what she did at the Fair, she answered, "Oo-up."

"O, but you naughty little puss, you made Asia laugh," said Isabel.

"And what did sister Ellen do?" asked her father.

"Made booful preach," answered Petty Poo; and they all laughed, as if they had not heard their little darling say it twenty times before.

"And where did you send your black dolly, with the two babies in her arms?" inquired her mother; and again they laughed when she lisped out, "To ittle conty-ban."

In a few weeks they received a letter from Cousin George, in which he wrote, "Dear cousins, your box arrived safely, and the teachers distributed the things on New Year's Eve. I would have given fifty dollars if you could have looked upon the scene. Such uproarious joy I never witnessed. Such singing and shouting are never heard among white folks. I wrote to you that the slave woman, who saved me from the horrors of a Rebel prison by hiding me under some straw in her hut, was here at work for wages. Her little Chloe is not much older than Petty Poo, and is as pretty, in a different way. Such glorious brown eyes you never saw. When the doll with two babies was given her, she jumped and capered, and danced and sung, till my sides ached with laughing. All these people naturally express their feelings in music; and little Chloe, small as she is, has the gift. She sings whatever tune comes into her head, and makes words to suit it as she goes along. It would have done your hearts good to hear her sing:

How kind de Yankee ladies is!
So kind I nebber see
How kind de Yankee ladies is,
To gib dese tings to me.

"I made a sketch of her merry little face on a leaf of my pocket-book, while she was singing, and if I had colored crayons here I think I could make you a pretty picture. It is a pity you could not have had her for your Tableau; though I have no doubt she would have laughed when the white poodle appeared on the stage, and in all probability she would have jumped down to catch him."

Not long afterward Captain George came home on a fortnight's leave of absence. And, hurried as he was, he found time to make a picture of little Chloe in colored crayons. The yellow cheeks and the great brown eyes made it look like a coreopsis blossom in the sunshine; and the face had such a happy, merry expression, that everybody laughed who looked at it. Isabel printed under it: "From Cousin George. A Souvenir of our Useful Christmas." It was framed and hung in the breakfast-room; and one day they found that Frank had pasted on the back the following inscription: "This is a commentary on the 'booful preach' Ellen made at our Fair, from the text, 'Proclaim Liberty throughout the land, to all the inhabitants thereof.'"

7

Times of Wretchedness and Brighter Days

Magazines for Southern Children

Southern publishers had never paid much attention to children, and youngsters of neither race had much reading material to choose from during the war. Of course, Southern whites would never have considered it necessary to publish anything for African Americans. It was, after all, illegal to teach a slave how to read. But among the multitude of sins attached to slavery by Northern abolitionists was its denial of the joy of learning. With thousands of blacks seeking shelter and freedom inside Union lines during the war, determined Yankees took it upon themselves to educate as many blacks as they could reach. Missionary organizations, private philanthropists, and even the U.S. Army opened schools in which eight-year-olds sat next to octogenarians in barns and churches and shacks. They learned to read from the Bible, from dog-eared schoolbooks rounded up from abandoned Southern schools, and from publications written especially for them.

The leading producer of educational materials for freed slaves was the American Tract Society, which had for years published didactic and religious-oriented pamphlets and even novels. Its "Educational Series," which included *The Freedman's Spelling-Book*, *The Freedman's Primer*, and *The Freedman's Second* and *Third Reader*, were modeled after antebellum spellers, primers, and readers but also featured biographical sketches of Abraham Lincoln and black heroes and heroines such as Paul Cuffe, Toussaint L'Ouverture, Frederick Douglass, and Phillis Wheatley. Other publications included a pamphlet called *First Lessons*; the *United States Primer*, which provided "elementary educational" information along with "scriptural instruction";

The Ten Commandments Illustrated; two dozen short *Tracts for Beginners*; and several sets of what modern children would call "flash cards," showing the alphabet, the Ten Commandments, short sentences, and other lessons in grammar and spelling. The American Tract Society sent hundreds of sets of cards and thousands of copies of the educational books South during the war.

Even as Southern blacks welcomed the output of Northern presses, white Southerners were trying to assert their independence from Northern publishing houses. But there was no Southern Oliver Optic or Charles Coffin or Lydia Maria Child, and Southerners produced only a few children's books or magazines. A booklet called *For the Little Ones* included "Dickie—The Boy Soldier" and "Willie's Political Alphabet," which offered rhymes drawn from military images and the names of eminent Southerners, such as "A's for the Army—now don't you forget—/And B's for the Banner, the 'flag of the free,'/For Beauregard, Bartow, Bethel, and Bee!"* Other cheaply made children's books devoted a few pages to the war, with the story of a fourteen-year-old Confederate capturing a squad of Yankees; lists of cabinet ministers, state capitals, and governors of the Confederacy as well as census figures for Confederate states; and an account of "Uncle Ned," an African-American Yankee-hater who helped guide Stonewall Jackson's troops over the mountains of Virginia.

Southern children may have been more likely to read about the conflict in schoolbooks written expressly for them. Tired of the nearly complete monopoly by Northern publishers of the antebellum Southern trade and hopeful of making large profits after the Union blockade had cut off the importation of luxuries such as books, Southern publishers instituted a crash program to produce texts intended to correct the misinformation appearing in Northern books. The page-long subtitle to John Rice's *System of Modern Geography* promised that the "Political and Physical Condition of the States composing the Confederate States of America are fully treated of, and their progress in Commerce, Education, Agriculture, Internal Improvements and Mechanic Arts, prominently set forth." His volume—"compiled by a Southern man, published upon our own soil"—would correct "every *yankee* work" that had "studiously concealed" the "actual conditions and resources" of the South. *Dixie Primers* and *Southern Grammars* were joined by *Confederate Arithmetics* in which students were asked, for

---

*For the Little Ones (Savannah: John M. Cooper, n.d.), 32–33.

example, if "a Confederate soldier captured 8 Yankees each day for 9 successive days, how many did he capture in all?"; or, if "one Confederate soldier can whip 7 yankees, how many soldiers can whip 49 yankees?" Mrs. M. B. Moore's *Geographical Reader* criticized Northerners who, once they found slavery unprofitable in their region, had begun to agitate against the Peculiar Institution. Even worse, Northerners had elected as president the weakling Abraham Lincoln, who, the South believed, "would allow laws to be made, which would deprive them of their rights." Since Lincoln had "declared war" on the Confederate states, the "earth has been drenched with blood."

Few Southern children's magazines spouted this kind of fire-eating rhetoric, but the handful of periodicals for youngsters that appeared at this time did try to make their readers aware of the costs and sacrifices of the war. More narrowly focused than Northern magazines, they made for rather depressing reading. Their grim reflections on the death and hardships faced by white Southerners provide a jarring counterpoint to the cheerful and forward-looking tone of *The Freedman*, a periodical produced just for Southern blacks by the American Tract Society. Yet readers could share one important bond: the strength that could be drawn, in defeat or in victory, from an abiding faith that whatever happened to them was part of God's plan.

TIMES OF HORROR

Evangelical-minded Southerners were perfectly willing to admit that the war had plunged their section into unprecedented suffering. By the end of the war, the Southern economy had been destroyed and hundreds of thousands of men had been killed and maimed (one of the largest items in the Mississippi state budget immediately after the war was an allotment for artificial legs and arms for crippled Confederate veterans). Civilians suffered, too. As one Confederate soldier emphasized in a letter to his children, "these are times such as one *sees only once*—when we are all dead & gone many lifetimes hence—they will be spoken of as the *'bloody age'*—the times of horror—of famine—misery—wretchedness." Yet a lesson could be learned from such trials. Children must imagine the diseased, cold, hungry, blighted soldiers living and dying in *"camps* all over the land," and *"resolve* never to *complain* of the little difficulties & troubles that come in your way." Editors made young readers aware of those members of their own communities who had suffered losses; they also believed that the war was an opportunity as well as a burden, but only if everyone, even those whose households had thus far remained untouched by war, realized its costs. Gen. William T. Sherman had not yet declared that "war is hell," but, as the selections that follow painfully demonstrate, Confederate children already knew it.*

"War"

The Child's Index 1 (September 1862), 2

While the little readers of *The Child's Index* are sitting quietly at home, or sleeping soundly in their cots, many of our poor soldiers are standing guard all alone in the far off woods, perhaps in the rain and cold. Though their tents are nearby, they dare not enter them; nor must they by any means sleep on their post.

They are put on watch to guard against surprises; and if they go to sleep when standing guard, it may prove the ruin of a whole army. Those soldiers who are placed on guard are called sentries; many sentries have been put to death for sleeping at their posts.

Not only do our soldiers suffer by standing guard in all kinds of weather, both by day and by night, but they suffer much from long and rapid marches, and from poor food, and sometimes because they have no food. They suffer from the hot sun and from the cold wind; and many get sick and die. But many are killed in battle by muskets and cannon. Cannon are large dreadful guns, on wheels, dragged by horses. They shoot terrible balls and shells, belching forth volumes of smoke and making the earth quake with noise louder than thunder.

Our soldiers frequently rush up to the very mouths of these dreadful cannon, and though many of them are killed, yet they dash forward, drive the enemy away, and take the guns. It requires great bravery to do this; but our gallant Southern soldiers often make such charges with success.

War is horrible, children, most horrible, because it causes so much suffering and sorrow and distress. So you all ought to pray for peace. But it is a great consolation to know that we are fighting in a just cause; that is, to save our country from ruin. We are but trying to drive wicked invaders from our land.

---

*Edward Pye to Matilda Pye, December 27, 1863, "Letters from the Confederate Medical Service," 381–82.

"What Children Should Do"
The Child's Index 1 (May 1863), 19

It is a sore trial to the father to leave home and loved ones, not knowing that he will ever see them again; not knowing but his little ones may want bread, and a friendly counsellor, while the leaves of a distant land cover his unknown grave. Often, my little reader, when your eyes are closed in sleep, your papa's pillow of straw is wet with tears while he entreats God to bless mother and you. Sometimes the father's heart is made glad by hearing that his little children are loving and kind to his lonely wife.

Little reader, whose father is in the war, do you make your mother happy? Will you every night, ask yourself, and mother too, what have I done to-day to make her happy? . . . If you love papa, make mother happy while he is gone. Some of you, my little readers, have your papas yet with you. How thankful your little hearts should be! But do you not pity the child whose papa is far away in the war? Do you not deeply sympathize with those whose papa now sleeps far away in a soldier's grave? . . . Go, my little reader, seek some child that has lost its father, and do it a kindness. If it be very poor, give it some clothes; ask it to visit you; give it some book to read; take it with you to church and to the Sabbath School. If it be not so poor as to need clothes and something to eat, it needs kind words, sympathy and encouragement. It needs some kind hand to point out the way where no father guides. . . . Can you not find a child that has no papa to send it the Child's Index? . . . Little reader, will you not do something? Will you not remember the advice of a SOLDIER?

[signed by a soldier from Jackson's Army]

"The Soldier's Orphans"
Child's Banner 1 (February 1865), 1

While I am preparing this paper, I remember that many little boys and girls will read it whose fathers have died or been slain in this bloody war. Perhaps your father fell on the field of battle, or died in the hospital, or far away in a distant Northern prison, and was buried there without you and your mother having the privilege of seeing him again or even visiting his grave. You are not so happy now as when from week to week you looked for letters from him, or expected him to get a furlough and come home. You would have felt it to be some relief to you if he had been brought home and laid in the old grave yard, where you could have planted some roses and evergreens around and scattered some flowers and shed some tears upon his tomb. Your home is lonely now and your tender hearts ache when you think that though peace may come, you cannot greet your father home any more. It may be that in your sadness and grief, you may feel discouraged because you have not only lost your father, but find the world disposed to overlook you and not to help you much through these times of want and trouble.

Let me, as a true friend, exhort you to cheer up. There are many people who warmly sympathize with you. They will always have kinder feelings for you because you are the children of a father who sleeps in a soldier's grave. And you have it in your power to make friends all around you.—Oh, if you will only be good, how much better it will be for you! You must feel while you read this, as if you and I were standing by your father's grave and I had hold of your hand, while both of us had tears in our eyes, and I was talking instead of writing. I would say to you "be good, and do good in every way you can." Then you will honor the memory of your father, and soothe and cheer the heart of your widowed mother. Then you will win the hearts of those who know you and they will be friends to you. Then life will be far happier to you than it seems now that it can be. Bow down in prayer and in the name of Jesus give your hearts to your Heavenly Father, promise to love and serve Him, and then He will bless you and take care of you in all things, and at all times. Perhaps your father was better prepared for death than you even had reason to expect, and is now resting from his toils and struggles in that beautiful world where the joys of the sainted are his portion forever. Be always good, upright, pious, and then you shall meet him again at last, and with your fond mother, join him in the sweet pleasures of Heaven forever.

"Early Fruit"
The Children's Friend (Richmond) 1 (February 1863), 26

My heart swells with sympathy and love, when I think of the dear children. I wish every effort to promote their good greatest success. May ten thousand, thousand blessings go with "The Children's Friend"! With this feeling I write the following for publication in its little columns. It will show how a very young child may love Jesus, and receive, through faith in his dear name, the sweetest gifts of the Holy Ghost. This account is literally true.

Not long ago, little L's father came home from the army to spend a few days in the enjoyment of his dear happy home. One night after his children were undressed, and had offered the evening incense of their prayers to the great and loving God, her father went to the bedside of L. to kiss and bid her good-night. She at once threw her slender arms about his neck, and bursting into tears, said to him, "Oh, papa, when will you come home to stay with us? It is so hard for you to be away from us." He soothed her grief by telling her it was the will of Jesus that they should be separated while the war lasted; that He would stop the war just as soon as it was best to do so; and, as long as He called us to suffer, it was very wrong in us to complain; that she especially had no reason to do so; for, while others had lost their fathers and brothers, her father had been kindly spared. She then clasped him the more closely, exclaiming, "Oh, papa, what would become of me if you were killed,—I know it would kill me too." He told her that was wrong; for if he were killed, Jesus, her Saviour, would take him to a happy and peaceful home in heaven, where, in good time, she might meet him, and be with him forever.—This comforted her somewhat.

She then asked, "Papa, will we know each other in heaven?" "Yes," he replied, "I believe it certain we shall know and love each other there." "But, papa, do you think we will love each other in heaven with a peculiar love, such as I now feel for you? I know we will love every body there, but will I love you with this same love?" He told her he had no doubt whatever on that point; that God bound us to one another in this world, with special ties, for a good purpose, and that these ties would not be broken in the eternal world, but we would there love each other with even a stronger, and purer, and happier love than was ever felt on earth. "Oh," said she, "how delightful that will be!"

"A Letter from a Little Boy Who Never Has Been to School in His Life"
The Children's Friend (Richmond) 2 (May 1, 1864), 85

Warm Springs, Bath County, Va.,

April 22, 1864.

Dear Mr. Editor:

As you say you like for children to write to you, I will try and write you a short letter this morning. I am a little boy of eight short years. I never went to school any. My mama learned me to write and read at home. I could read in the Testament tolerably well when I was only three and a half years old. I have three little sisters, one of them can read. My papa is in the army. I would like to see him, but I don't know whether I ever will see him again or not; and if I don't, I expect to meet him in heaven, for he is a good Christian. I pray for him several times a day. And dear Mr. Editor, I hope you and all the good little children that read my short letter, will pray for him too, and ask God to spare him till the war is over; so he can come back to us again; for my Bible says the prayer of the righteous availeth much.

I am a new subscriber for your paper. I like it very much. A little girl sent me one of the papers and that put me in notion of sending for it. Oh how I like that little girl. I have never seen her. She lives about twenty-two miles from here. And now I have that dear little paper for my own, I wish it would come twice a week in place of twice a month; it's so long I get tired waiting for it. I will try and get some more little boys to send for it. Our Sunday-school will commence before long. I will quit now for fear my letter will be too long. Respectfully, with much friendship,

—Martin Luther.

"Martin Luther," you have a good name, and I think from your letter, you must be a good boy. I am sure you have a loving heart, from the way you speak of your absent father. Dear little fellow! I trust God will hear those prayers you are offering to him so many times every day, and that He will bring back your beloved father safe and well, when this dreadful war is over, and that you may see him and he may see you again. You must have a very good and faithful mother, for she has not only taught you to read and write, but she has taught you to pray too, which is still better. You must ask God to give you a new heart, and then you will be certain to meet your dear father and all those who love our blessed Saviour in heaven.

"WHAT IS IT TO BE FREE?"

The closest thing to a magazine for black children in the United States was *The Freedman*, an American Tract Society publication that appeared in January 1864 and ran until early 1869. It was widely distributed, with 648,000 copies produced in 1865–66 alone. The four-page monthly borrowed the format as well as the overwhelmingly moralistic tone of other Tract Society productions. Although ostensibly printed for adults—one story featured black soldiers eagerly studying their copies of the little paper—the first issue suggested that when the grown-ups were finished, it "may be given to the children as a reward for diligence and good conduct, and thus become doubly useful." Indeed, letters from Tract Society agents and teachers indicated that their adult students did exactly that, while others ordered copies expressly for their younger students. The format of the paper resembled that of a juvenile periodical or Sabbath school paper: brief vignettes, writing drills, simple reading and arithmetic lessons, poems, prayers, and general information about geography, nature, and history. The Ten Commandments appeared in every issue, along with the occasional exegesis of a selected Commandment. Articles and stories and exercises hammered home the importance of values such as thrift, hard work, planning ahead, temperance, honesty, and perseverance.

 The Freedman—designed for adults, seemingly written for children—raises questions about the definition of children's literature. More to the point, it highlights whites' assumptions about race. Slave owners had long justified what they believed to be a "paternal" system of race relations by comparing grown slaves to children: emotional, short-sighted, imitative. Many Northerners, even those educators and abolitionists most sympathetic to the plight of African Americans, held the same opinions. Some, even as they fought to end slavery, opposed granting political equality to blacks. Even missionaries who came South during the war sometimes demonstrated racist ideas about the abilities and potential of their pupils, young and old. *The Freedman* seems to reflect the notion that the freed slaves were blank slates who, like children, had to be coaxed, guided, and prodded into living virtuous and productive lives.

 Many of the stories in *The Freedman* contained no reference to race and—especially those concerned with moral issues and the virtues of charity and loyalty—could have appeared in any one of the many periodicals for children published in the North or South during this period. Yet the editors followed a relatively inclusive editorial policy, with articles on Africa, the history of black soldiers in the American Revolution, the transition from slavery to freedom, accounts of the good behavior and courageous fighting of "colored" troops during the Civil War, and even a twist on a Confederate arithmetic problem: "If the freedmen should kill, or take prisoners, 394 of the rebels who numbered 462, how many would be left to run away after the battle?" Northern children's magazines had frequently cast African Americans as beneficiaries of Northern philanthropy, and a number of pieces offered sketches of Union heroes and stories of Northern whites who had contributed money, established schools, and risked their lives to emancipate the slaves. The sense of gratitude these stories were designed to invoke reminded the freedmen that although they had gained their liberty, freedom also carried responsibilities. As one writing exercise declared, "But what is it to be free? . . . I am free to be a good and noble man, and not an idle, bad, worthless fellow."

"The Fifth Commandment"
The Freedman 1 (July 1864), 28

"What does this commandment mean, boys?"* asked the teacher.

"We must mind when we are told to do any thing," said Sam.

"And when we are told not to do any thing," added Frank.

"There are two ways of minding," said the teacher. "You may obey at once, and cheerfully, or you may do it unwillingly, and with a pout and a frown. Which is the right way?"

"The first," they all replied.

"You may mind when your parents are looking at you; but when you are away from them take no pains to obey. Is this right?"

"No, indeed," said the boys.

"You may mind because you are afraid of being punished. Is this right?"

"I suppose it's right enough," answered Sam, "but it isn't the best way."

"What is the best way?" asked the teacher.

"To mind because we ought to," said one.

"Because God has told us to," said another.

"Because we love our father and mother," answered Frank.

---

*The Fifth Commandment, as it appeared in other issues of *The Freedman*: "Honor thy father and thy mother, that thy days may be long upon the land which the Lord thy God giveth thee."

"Yes; love and duty are the best motives—duty to God, and duty to your parents. Are you to do every thing they tell you to?"

"Yes, every thing," answered the boys.

"Every thing that is right. But, supposing your parents should tell you to do what is wicked; must you do it?"

"No,"—"I don't know,"—"How can we help ourselves?"—said several of the class together.

"No; you must do nothing wicked. The Bible says, 'We must obey God rather than man.' If a boy's father should command him to lie or steal or swear or break the Sabbath, he must not obey; no, not if he has to suffer very much. But every command that is not wicked you must obey, though it be ever so hard."

"I haven't got no father nor mother to mind," murmured one of the boys.

"Then," answered the teacher, in a kind voice, "you must obey those that take care of you, just the same as if they were your parents. And now, boys, there is a promise connected with this commandment. You may repeat it."

They did so.

"This is the first and only commandment with a promise. God will surely bless the affectionate, grateful, obedient child: and I hope every one of you will receive this blessing. A well-ordered home, where the parents are kind and the children obedient, is the happiest place on earth. Now, the parents take care of the children; by and by the children will take care of them in their old age. This is God's wise and good arrangement."

"Reading Lessons"
The Freedman 2 (June 1865), 22

The earth on which we live is a globe. Have you thought of the shape of the earth? It is round, like a ball. You would not think so, would you? When you look out of your door, when you walk up and down the road, it seems to you that the earth must be flat like the floor. Did you think so? And did you think that if you should walk a long way, you would come to the end of it, and could jump off? Where do you think you would jump to? In old times, long, long years since, men thought so; but at last they found that it was round. Now, why does it seem flat if it is round? It is so large that we can not see the curve of it from where we stand. The hills and the trees fill up all the space as far as you can see. But if you were out on the wide sea, where there are no hills or trees, and cast your eyes all round, by and by, it may be, you would see the masts of a ship rise up from the edge, just where the sky seems to come down to the waves. Then these masts would grow more and more tall, as if they grew out of the sea; and, at last, you would see the hull of the ship. Now why did you not see the hull of the ship first? Ah! this is one proof that the earth is round. You caught sight of the ship just on the curve, and the hull was far down out of your sight; and the high masts were all you could see, till it came more near to you. This is one way that men found out that the earth is round. The sun is a globe, too, and the moon, and the stars. If there are boys and girls who live in the stars, this earth of ours looks to them as the moon does to us. The moon is not so large, though, as our earth is. If it were not for the sun, we should have no light by day or by night; for the moon and stars can give no light but as they get it from the sun. The sun shines on them, and they shine on us; so that when the sun sets, they can give us some light. We do not see their light by day, for the light of the sun is so much more strong.

"Instruction for the Freedmen"
The Freedman 1 (January 1864), 1

It is with no small delight that the American Tract Society publish the first number of this little paper. They hope by means of it to share in the good work which is now going on in many parts of the country in teaching those who were lately in slavery to read and gain that knowledge which is to fit them to be good and happy.

God has wrought wonders on behalf of the colored people of this land. He has seen all the wrongs they have suffered, he has heard all their prayers, and in his own time has come down to relieve them from their oppressors, and open the door of deliverance. He is also sending them teachers, with schools and books, that they may learn to read God's Word and become wise unto salvation. Our picture shows a beautiful scene, where under the dark shade of the trees the children are taught by a lady who loves them, and has come from her home in the North to instruct them in useful knowledge.

It is our purpose to give in the Freedman lessons in reading, geography, arithmetic, history, etc., also such moral and religious instruction as will be suited to the wants of its readers. Some of these lessons will be very simple for those who are just beginning to learn; others will be for those who have already made some progress. They will serve often instead of books, especially when the books can not be had. The paper may be given to the children as a reward for diligence and good conduct, and thus become doubly useful. Those who can read must try also to teach those that can not.

We trust that there is before the colored people of our country a brighter day than they have ever before known. Their own good conduct in the time of war and trouble has gained for them much favor. Their readiness to enlist in the army of the Union and their bravery in the field of battle have done them great credit. Let them continue to show themselves worthy of freedom, and they will win the respect and esteem of the whole nation. Above all things, let them strive to become disciples of Christ, and heirs of eternal life. There is a slavery which is worse than that from which they have been delivered. It is the slavery of sin. The former only held the body, the latter binds the soul. Jesus alone can grant them freedom from it. All worldly things which they may require will be worth little without this. What shall it profit a man if he shall gain the whole world and lose his own soul?

"Home"
The Freedman 1 (March 1864), 11

See this home! How neat, how warm, how full of cheer it looks! It seems as if the sun shone in there all the day long. But it takes more than the light of the sun to make a home bright all the time. Do you know what it is? It is love. Love is the light of God's face.

Boys and girls, do you know that you can all help to make just such a home as this? Let me tell you how.

When the cock crows at the dawn of the day, you wake up. Once you had to catch your food and run as fast as you could to the field to work. But not now. Now you may wash and dress with care, and set your room to rights. You may spread the board with a clean cloth, and place the cups and plates and knives on it, and the chairs around it.

When the food is cooked, you may sit down and eat. But first, you must thank God for it, and ask him to bless it, that it may make you strong to work, and to serve him.

Now you may eat, but not too fast, nor with a noise like the pigs. If you want more food, ask for it in a low but clear voice, and wait till you are helped. If you do not want more, wait till the rest are done, too.

Then bring the Word of God, and let your father read some of the sweet lines, which tell you of the love of God, and of his good and just law. If you have time, it will be nice to sing just a verse or two, and then you may all kneel down, and bow your heads, and shut your eyes, and join in the prayer that is said, while you think all the time, that

"God does not care for what I *say*,
But I must *mean* it too."

Now you can all start for the work of the day. You may have to plow or dig or hoe, or you may have to wash, to scrub, and to bake. Or some of you may have a chance to go to school. Oh, what a grand thing it is to go to school, and learn to read and write and sew! But in all you do, God will be with you and bless you, if you love and fear him and try to do his will.

Now is not this the way to make a good home,—a home such as the Son of God will be pleased to see? And you can all help to make such a one. Each boy and girl, large or small, who reads this, say at once, I will do my part. I will not speak a cross word, or a bad word, or one that is not true. I will not do an act that is not kind, or that I would not like to have done to me. I will be neat and clean. I will have a place for each thing, and put each thing in its place. I will mind all that is said to me. My home shall be a home of love.

"The Little White Box"
The Freedman 1 (February 1864), 8

I wonder if our colored friends at the South know how many affectionate hearts of their own people are thinking about them there at the North. Oh, if they could but hear the fervent prayers which are going up every hour into the ear of our Father in heaven, if they could know of the warm sympathy and love felt for them by the colored people in the free States, I am sure they would be inspired with new hope and courage!

Yesterday there was a collection taken up in one of our large churches for the freedmen. The minister told the people, before the baskets were passed around, that he had two gifts to put in. A gentleman in England, whom he had never seen, had sent him two hundred dollars for the freedmen of our country, and one half of this rich gift he should put in the basket at that time. But he had another offering, far more precious than that.

Then he took up a little white box from the table before him, and untying a red ribbon which was around it, he told us that there were six dollars and forty-six cents in that box, in all ten and five cent bills and pennies. It was the gift of a small mission Sabbath school of colored children, who had sent it by their superintendent to be given to the freedmen. The minister took a note out of the box and read it. It was this:—

My dear Mr. B.:

You mentioned in the pulpit, a few Sabbaths ago, that you proposed to take up a collection for the benefit of the freedmen. Whenever you take up such a collection, will you be kind enough to add to it the accompanying pennies. This is their history:—We thought it time that the little ones of our mission school should be taught a new lesson,—that of *giving*. I therefore suggested to them that I thought it would be pleasant, on the last Sabbath of the year, for us to give a thanks offering to God. The children seemed pleased with the idea, and last Sabbath, when they brought their hoarded pennies, I was as surprised as I was delighted to find that they already knew the lesson we had proposed to teach them. The little ones could scarcely wait until we handed them the plate, but with all the eagerness of childhood held out their pennies at arm's length,—pennies that were earned before they were given, and had resisted the enticement of cake and candy. If we passed by heads of families,—feeling that as so many depended on them for bread we should spare them the pain of refusal,—they called back the plate, as if to scorn such a thought, and gave what they had, if the scanty sum was but a few cents, in the simple faith that God, to whom it was given, would value it aright. There is not a dollar in this collection but has been earned by hard work or self-denial, and we felt many times as if we ought to check the eager givers, when we thought of the scanty meal and empty stove that must be the result of the gift.

It is a heart offering, a grand gift, although small in the value of the world's coinage; and now, Mr. B., as they think it most fitting that their first contribution should be for the benefit of their own race, I take the liberty of sending it to be added to your collection as the readiest method of reaching them.

Our minister, when he had read the note, put the little white box, with its contents, into the contribution basket, remarking that if our blessed master, the Lord Jesus Christ, were here, he would say, "These poor little ones have cast more in than all they which have cast into the treasury; for all they did cast in of their abundance; but these of their want have cast in all that they had."

"A Brave Boy"
The Freedman 2 (January 1865), 4

While passing through one of the hospital wards, I caught the eye of a little colored boy, who looked just as if he wanted to speak to me. So I went over to him and said, "Well, my little fellow, what is the trouble with you?" "Oh, no trouble, sir; only I've lost a leg." "Why, you are a young hero to shoulder a musket." "I wasn't a soldier, sir; I was the captain's waiter." "Well, how did you come, then, to get in the way of a ball?" "I didn't sir; it got in my way. I wanted to let it pass, but it wouldn't; and so it took my leg off." "What are you going to do when you get well?" "Going back to the captain, sir; he will take care of me." Brave little fellow! only twelve years old, and yet a hero! Regardless of danger, he had followed his captain to the field; and fell, where his impulse led him, among the veteran soldiers of Grant. He has the stuff in him out of which soldiers are made; and had he been older and stronger, would have been quick to shoulder his musket in defense of the Union.

"What the War Has Done for the Negro"
The Freedman 1 (May 1864), 20

It was not, perhaps, to be expected, that in three years the war should do much for the individual negro. On the other hand it has done more for his race than the sanguine enthusiast could have expected.

For the first time, the black man has been officially acknowledged as an American citizen. In many of the separate States he has undoubtedly the full rights of State citizenship; but hitherto, the Federal government had scrupulously declined committing itself to any assertion that he was entitled to be regarded as an American subject. The war has brought this question to an issue, and decided it in favor of the negro; and this out of no popular caprice, but by the inexorable logic of facts. The necessities of war compelled the employment of negro soldiers; the employment of black troops entailed the adoption of measures for their protection; and these measures have obliged the President to declare authoritatively that the black soldier is of equal value with the white, and that his murder or enslavement is an offense for which retaliation must be inflicted just as it would in the case of a white free-born American.*

---

*To the extent that citizenship grants full and equal rights to citizens, African Americans did not become true citizens until the Fourteenth Amendment extended to them the same civil rights enjoyed by white Americans. The status of African Americans in the Union Army was somewhat controversial. First enlisted in large numbers in 1863, they were paid less than white soldiers. Black troops captured by Confederate forces could be sold as slaves. On some occasions, the most famous of which was a vicious battle at Fort Pillow, black soldiers were killed after surrendering to Confederates.

"Joy for the Conquering Right"

Mourning and Celebrating
the End of the War

A song published in *The Student and Schoolmate* commemorating the first Fourth of July after war's end asked the nation's children to "sing for the happiest birthday/The dear, dear land ever knew!" to "welcome . . . peace returning/With rebellion overthrown!" It called for young ones of all ages, of all classes, in cities and on farms, to join their parents in singing "for Columbia's birth-day!/Shout for Freedom, Peace." This joyous Fourth would be like Christmas in summer:

> Eyes lit up with the new-born glory—
> Cheeks flushed red with joy—
> Joy for the conquering Right that cheers
> Every girl and boy.

Northern children celebrate Union victory and the Fourth of July, 1865. From The Student and Schoolmate.

The spasm of joy that accompanied peace after four long, bloody years was tempered by the assassination of Abraham Lincoln, whose determination to win the war had gained him the admiration of many Americans who had initially doubted his ability to defend the Union.

Children's magazines spent the summer of 1865 celebrating victory and lamenting the passing of the commander in chief. By the end of the year, however, the Civil War had all but disappeared from children's stories. Oliver Optic continued to feature brief biographies of generals, *The Little Corporal* mentioned soldiers' orphans from time to time, and *Our Young Folks* ran a series of travelogues to battlefields around the South. But for all intents and purposes, the war was over for young readers within a few months of the joyous Fourth of July envisioned in the song.

A VICTORY "SWALLOWED UP IN DEATH"

The Little Pilgrim regularly featured short obituaries of child readers written as minisermons, almost parables, of youngsters living Christian lives and embracing God in emotional deathbed scenes. These were part of a long tradition in children's literature. Ever since Puritans tried to inspire their children with stories of youthful piety in the face of death, religious instruction had frequently featured the noble deaths of children as worthy of emulation. A fairly typical wartime obituary, introduced as "a very touching story of love and bereavement," appeared just after the war. "Dear Grace Greenwood," it began:

> I wrote you last August, from Providence, R. I., of the death of my only daughter, and a subscriber for your Little Pilgrim, Kate S. Slocum. She died the second of July, of scarlet fever. She was five in March. Her papa, Col. John S. Slocum, of the second R. I. Regiment, was killed at the first battle of Bull Run. Kate had been his idol—she remembered him, and never got over his death. She would say to me, she would rather be in the Happy Land with her dear papa, than to stay here even with me. She would ask me to bury her close beside him, and bring flowers and lay on their graves. She was ripe for the home she was called to so early. On the ninth of the same month, my dear little boy, but three in June, died of the same disease. They were all the children I had! I have given up in the last four years, father,

husband, and children, and I try to say, "Thy will, not mine,
oh God, be done!"*

It was hoped that readers of all ages would respond to
this triple tragedy with resignation—even inspiration—rather
than despair. The same could be said for the assassination of
President Lincoln less than one week after Gen. Robert E. Lee had
surrendered the Army of Northern Virginia, ending, for all intents
and purposes, the Civil War. Children reacted to Lincoln's assassination in many ways. Some, such as the Longfellow children,
called on their dramatic instincts and re-enacted the incident,
while others projected their grief in less theatrical ways. A New
England boy took to the hills near his home and shouted "Hurrah
for Lincoln," then listened as the salute echoed down the Otto
Creek Valley. And two Nantucket Island girls used scraps of material from their mothers' sewing boxes to cloak the windows of
their homes in mourning. As adults, Civil War children often tried
to make sense of Lincoln's martyrdom. In Chicago, for instance,
social worker Jane Addams used the memory of the sixteenth
president to inspire the immigrants who flocked to Hull-House
with the possibilities of life in America.

The two selections that follow both mourn and com-
memorate the slain president. Children were to be made aware
of the mortality of even the greatest of men. They would learn
to revere Lincoln as a great political leader and as a role model
whose character incorporated all the traits to which children
should aspire.

"Gone Home"
Grace Greenwood
The Little Pilgrim 12 (May 1865), 62

With these two words, so simple yet so full of tender comfort,
we have been used to preface our notices of departure of dear little friends; yet now we find them more fitting than any others
when we come to speak of the sudden and awful death of a man,
ripe in years and old in honors, of the great head of a great nation, of our beloved and revered President, Abraham Lincoln. It
is fitting that his death should be recorded in the children's
paper, because we are all children to-day in our common sorrow
for the father of our country, taken from us in a manner so cruel
and terrible. It is fitting, because he was so childlike in the

---

*Fenimore Chatterton, *Yesterday's Wyoming* (Aurora, Colorado: Powder River
Publishers, 1957), 15.

simplicity of his character, in the tenderness of his great, un-
spoiled heart; because in goodness he was "a child of God." It
seemed that *he* did not need to "become as a little child, to enter
into the kingdom of Heaven," for he had always *kept* himself as
one. O, surely he has gone *home!*—gone to the rest he so much
needed—gone to *meet* the peace he so longed and labored for.
The mighty care of the nation wore upon and wasted his life.
Now he has cast all his care upon God. He thought little of the
honors of his high station; the realization of its *duties* so filled his
soul. Now he has laid his earthly glory, which was to him like a
crown of thorns, at his Master's feet, but only to receive from the
dear hand once so cruelly pierced, the martyr's immortal crown.
Here, disloyalty, calumny and hatred pained his gentle, forgiv-
ing nature; he is now where treason, ingratitude, injustice and
deadly hate can trouble him no more. In "The green pastures, beside the still waters," in the white tents of Israel he is safe. The
heavenly guards are about him. No hand of brutal violence, of
cruel murder, can strike at the life that is "hid in God."

  We know that for *him*, "death is swallowed up in victory"; but for *us*, victory is swallowed up in death. We cannot rejoice that his work was so nearly and gloriously done, because *he*
is not here to rejoice with us. We *must* weep for our poor country, wounded to the heart in her hour of joy and triumph, for the
dear friends who so tenderly loved him—for the widow, fainting
under the mighty grief and horror of his martyrdom—for the
son, on whose bright young manhood such fearful gloom has
fallen—for the dear boy, who was like the small shadow of his
father—the pleasant little companion, who went with him almost everywhere—in walks, in rides, through hospitals, camps
and conquered cities—and at last, clung to him, as he journeyed
swiftly and unconsciously down the "valley of the shadow of
death," where, for the first time, that loving father was unmind-
ful of his presence, returned not the clasp of his little hand, felt
not his kisses, heard not his crying.*

  We must weep, because for a time wickedness has tri-
umphed over such goodness, treason over such loyalty. We must
grieve most of all to know, that in a world for which Christ died,

------

*Abraham Lincoln and his wife, Mary Todd, had four sons. Robert, the oldest, was born
in 1843 and was the only one to live to adulthood. After brief service as a staff officer in
the Civil War, he was a successful businessman and secretary of war. He died in 1926.
The second, Edward, died in Springfield, Illinois, in 1850 at the age of three. Willie died at
the age of eleven in 1862. The famously spoiled Tad—"the small shadow of his father"—
was eight when the war began. He frequently interrupted White House meetings and accompanied his father on his visits to the Army of the Potomac. Tad died in 1871.

such monstrous sinners as the murderer of our President yet live. Yet we have all sinned. For the great transgressions of the nation this unspeakable sorrow and humiliation have come upon us—and yet also for its purification and salvation. Our homes are under a cloud of mourning—our very souls are darkened—our hearts are chilled and silent; but the April skies are blue, flowers bloom, birds sing, and God's love is over all.

"Extract from a Speech on the Death of President Lincoln"
Park Godwin
The Student and Schoolmate 15 (June 1865), 184–85*

The great captain of our cause—ABRAHAM LINCOLN—smitten by the basest hand ever upraised against human innocence, is gone, gone, gone! He who had borne the heaviest of the brunt, in our four long years of war, whose pulse beat livelier, whose eyes danced brighter than any others, when

> "The storm drew off
> Its scattered thunders groaning round the hills,"

in the supreme hour of his joy and glory was struck down. One who, great in himself, as well as by position, has suddenly departed. There is something startling, ghastly, awful in the manner of his going off. But the chief poignancy of our distress is not for the greatness fallen, but for the goodness lost. Presidents have died before: during this bloody war we have lost many eminent generals—Lyons, Baker, Kearney, Sedgwick, Reno, and others;[†] we have lost lately our finest scholar, publicist, orator. Our hearts still bleed for the companions, friends, brothers that sleep the sleep "that knows no waking," but no loss has been comparable to his, who was our supremest leader,—our safest counsellor—our wisest friend—our dear father. Would you know what Lincoln was, look at this vast metropolis, covered with the habiliments of woe! Never in human history has there been so universal, so spontaneous, so profound an expression of a nation's bereavement.

---

*Although this was originally published as a declamation piece, the gesture numbers have been deleted.

---

†Gen. Nathaniel Lyons, the fiery Republican killed at Wilson's Creek in 1861; Gen. Edward Baker, Illinois politician and commander killed at Ball's Bluff in 1861; Gen. Philip Kearney, highly respected division commander killed at Chantilly in 1862; Gen. John Sedgwick, a longtime senior officer in the Army of the Potomac, killed at Spotsylvania in 1864; and Gen. Jesse Reno, a competent corps commander killed at South Mountain in 1862.

Yet we sorrow not as those who are without hope. Our chief is gone; but our cause remains; dearer to our hearts, because he is now become the martyr; consecrated by his sacrifice; more widely accepted by all parties; and fragrant and lovely forevermore in the memories of all the good and the great, of all lands, and for all time. The rebellion, which began in the blackest treachery, to be ended in the foulest assassination; this rebellion, accursed in its motive, which was to rivet the shackles of slavery on a whole race for all the future; accursed in its means, which have been "red ruin and the breaking up of laws," the overthrow of the mildest and blessedest of governments, and the profuse shedding of brother's blood by brother's hands; accursed in its accompaniments of violence, cruelty, and barbarism, and is now doubly accursed in its final act of cold-blooded murder.

Cold-blooded, but impotent, and defeated in its own purposes! The frenzied hand which slew the head of the government, in the mad hope of paralyzing its functions, only drew the hearts of the people together more closely to strengthen and sustain its power. All the North once more, without party or division, clenches hands around the common altar: all the North swears a more earnest fidelity to freedom; all the North again presents its breasts as the living shield and bulwark of the nation's unity and life. Oh! foolish and wicked dream, oh! insanity of fanaticism, oh! blindness of black hate—to think that this majestic temple of human liberty, which is built upon the clustered columns of free and independent states, and whose base is as broad as the continent could be shaken to pieces, by striking off the ornaments of its capital! No! this nation lives, not in one man nor in a hundred men, however eminent, however able, however endeared to us; but in the affections, the virtues, the energies and the will of the whole American people. It has perpetual succession, not like a dynasty, in the line of its rulers, but in the line of its masses. They are always alive; they are always present to empower its acts, and to impart an unceasing vitality to its institutions. No maniac's blade, no traitor's bullet shall ever penetrate that heart, for it is immortal, like the substance of Milton's angels, and can only "by annihilating die."

THE RESPONSIBILITIES OF PEACETIME

Over two million men served in the Union and Confederate armies during the Civil War, and over 600,000 died. The rest marched home soon after, as the Union Army quickly demobilized the vast majority of its soldiers. After a final, symbolic parade in

Washington, DC, and smaller, local celebrations, the veterans faded into their families and communities. But none could forget being "touched with fire," in the words of Oliver Wendell Holmes, Jr., and some failed to adapt quickly, or at all, to civilian life.* Some entered the National Homes for Disabled Volunteer Soldiers established in 1867—the precursors to modern Veterans' Administration hospitals—and a few lapsed into drug abuse and the unemployment that plagued the American economy during the depression-wracked 1870s.

When they mentioned veterans at all, children's magazines pleaded with their readers to give them respect and understanding. In addition, getting nearly a two-decade jump on adult literature, a few stories, poems, and playlets urged the North and the South—and, as in the final reading, the West—to reconcile their differences and unite to help the United States realize its economic and moral potential. The war had to mean something; Americans' sacrifices must not have been in vain. Paying tribute to the veterans who had survived the war and reminding readers of the great promise of the United States might help children justify the high costs of the conflict and accept their roles in rebuilding their shattered country. As "Uncle Sam's Boys after the War" argued, Americans shared a common set of values—the honesty, frugality, work ethic, and religiosity that children's authors had always promoted—which would propel the United States to greatness. But first, its citizens had to overcome the sectional tensions and stereotypes that had flooded the land with blood.

"The Last Review"
The Little Corporal 1 (August 1865), 28

Twenty-one miles of boys in blue,
Sixty abreast in the last review,
How grandly the columns stretch away,
In the cloudless light of this sweet May day.[†]
Onward, in rank and file they come,
To the cheering beat of the victors' drum.

---

*Quoted in Mark de Wolfe, ed., *Touched with Fire: The Civil War Letters and Diary of Oliver Wendell Holmes, Jr., 1861–1864* (Cambridge: Harvard University Press, 1946), v.

[†]The Army of the Potomac under Gen. George G. Meade and Gen. William T. Sherman's Army of Georgia and Army of the Tennessee—145,000 veterans in all—marched in review for thousands of spectators down Pennsylvania Avenue in Washington, DC, on May 23–24, 1865.

Wearied, and scarred, and worn they be,
But a *prouder* host you will never see,
Their faded banners, riddled with balls,
But floating triumphantly after all,
Never again in the world's sunlight,
Shall the Nations look on a grander sight.

No more, till the Christian army stands,
Whose warriors shall gather from every land,
For a *last* review on the other shore,
Their *life-long* battles and marches o'er,
Will a marshaled host like this appear,
Crowned with the glory that victors wear.

Let the heads of the nation bow as they pass,
And scatter with flowers the dewy grass,
As their gleaming weapons flash in the sun,
Remember the deeds of valor done.
How that solid column of human breasts,
Was bared to the storm, for the nation's rest.

Then beat the drum for the last reveille,
The echoes of strife are growing still,
With a conquering tread the heroes come,
Back to the dear delights of home.

But alas, the army of countless dead,
We shall list in vain for their coming tread,
Full forty miles of our noble braves
Sixty abreast, are in their graves,
As your cheers ring out for the living host,
Remember the heroes loved and lost.

And think of the maimed, and wasted band,
Seeking the homes of this stricken land,
For whom the brightness of life is o'er,
Whose feet are nearing the other shore,
Remnants of manhood *once so* strong,
These cannot march in the gala throng.

Then hail, all hail to the boys in blue,
Gathered to-day for a last review.
Marching with floating banners back;
Scatter with flowers their joyous track.

Their brows perchance are dark with scars,
And their worn feet seamed with crimson bars,
But *kings* and *victors* we crown to-day,
The war-scarred host, on their homeward way.

And I wonder, if down from the sweet repose
Which the soul of the martyred hero knows,
The Commander-in-Chief looks down and sees
Those banners float in this earthly breeze,
And if in the calm of that world of bliss,
His spirit would thrill at a scene like this.

"The Returned Veterans"
Park Benjamin
The Student and Schoolmate 13 (April 1865), 120–21*

I saw the soldiers come to-day
From battle-field afar;
No conqueror rode before their way
On his triumphal car,
But captains, like themselves, on foot,
And banners sadly torn,
All grandly eloquent, though mute,
In pride and glory borne.

Those banners, soiled with dirt and smoke,
And rent by shot and shell,
That through the serried phalanx broke—
What tales of sudden pain and death
In every cannon's boom,
When e'en the bravest held his breath
And waited for his doom.

By hand of steel these flags were waved
Above the carnage dire,
Almost destroyed, yet always saved,
'Mid battle clouds and fire.
Though down at times, still up they rose
And kissed the breeze again,
Dread tokens to the rebel foes,
And strength to loyal men.

---

*This is another declamation piece, published here without gesture numbers.

And here the true and loyal still
Those famous banners bear;
The bugles wind, the fifes blow shrill,
And clash the cymbals, where
With decimated ranks they come,
And through the crowded streets
March to the beating of the drum
With firm though weary feet.

God bless the soldiers! cry the folk
Whose cheers of welcome swell;
God bless the banners, black with smoke
And torn by shot and shell!
They should be hung on sacred shrines,
Baptized with grateful tears,
And live embalmed in poetry's lines,
Through all succeeding years.

No grander trophies could be brought
From patriot sire to son,
Of glorious battles nobly fought,
Brave deeds sublimely done.

"Uncle Sam's Boys after the War"
The Student and Schoolmate 16 (December 1865), 151–57

CHARACTERS—UNCLE SAM; BUCKEYE, JONATHAN, PALMETTO, *Nephews of Uncle Sam*; DIJAH CRAB, *from Virginia*; TOM PIKE, *from Oregon*; HEZEKIAH CRANE, *of Pigeon Hollow, Conn.*

[Uncle Sam is seen, seated at a table, near a recess, examining papers. Enter Palmetto and Buckeye, talking busily.]

Buckeye: It's no use talking—one might as well try to move one of the mountain crags in his own barren land.

Palmetto: And that could be done more easily than you could get a penny from his pocket.

Uncle Sam: What is the trouble now, Buckeye? Who is the object of your displeasure, Palmetto?

Buckeye: Why, Uncle Sam, we've been talking with cousin Jonathan. You've no idea how narrow-minded and set he is. I've been telling him about our great western country, and the improvements we're making; but you ought to have seen his contempt—he thinks no improvement is worth anything, which does not have for its object that little strip of rock and sand, New England, and which was not invented in that hub of all creation, Boston.

Palmetto: And of all the stingy people I ever saw, he is the closest. He has no idea of hospitality. Then you never saw any one so vain as he is of his part of the country; but I've been there, and all I found was rock in the summer, and ice in the winter; still, the people export both those things, and cheat so outrageously, that there's scarcely a person who doesn't live in comfort, and even luxury.

Uncle Sam: Jonathan has been a pretty good boy—perhaps you might find some good traits as well as these disagreeable ones you have mentioned. (*Enter Jonathan.*) Your cousins are making a hard case against you, Jonathan. They think your ideas are so closely confined to your own section, that it is impossible for you to have correct ideas of the world in general.

Jonathan: Well, I'm sure I don't know what ideas they have at the South, that would pay going after—

Palmetto: Pay, of course; that's indispensable!

Jonathan: So long as they would all be second-hand, for all the young men there come to our colleges and schools for everything they know; that's what Palmetto came North for,—and—

Uncle Sam: Well, here's Buckeye who considered you quite narrow and "set" in your notions of the West.

Jonathan: I know—he didn't like my objecting to their way of doing things—to their cities that grow up like Jonah's gourd in a single night, and collapse as suddenly—for my part, I think what is worth doing at all, is worth doing well. He was quite disgusted with my ideas of progress; very "slow," he considered them.

Buckeye: That's so; his country must be favorable to longevity; the people there don't live fast enough to reach the age of seventy in six times as long as we.

Palmetto: Well, New Englanders improve plenty fast enough for me. They work hard enough, even if they don't improve in the bustling, hurrying way, that Buckeye likes. Why, they work all day long, and when that's over, they sit down and rock as hard as ever they can, reading a newspaper, and fanning themselves with all their might. That's their idea of rest! Mercy on us! I'd as soon be fastened to the train of a comet as to either of your two sections. And now the war is over, the Northern people will be swarming down upon us, seeing nothing in our beautiful rivers but good water-power. The very Goths and Vandals are these Yankees!

Uncle Sam: And is there not one of you who loves the honor of his country more than the glory of a single state or section? Have all these years in which the blood of our braves has been so freely shed, been for no purpose but to bring us together again to engage in petty bickerings among ourselves? We have come forth from our trial purified and strong, have agreed to let bygones be bygones, and now we are ready to take the lead in the world's grand march to the highest civilization, were it not for these contemptible wranglings among ourselves as to who shall be greatest. Each of you accuses the other of sectional prejudice, and with reason, for you all have it. You feel that your different sections are united under one government, while the interests of the people are not so much in the whole nation as in part of it. But we are not a Union of States—we are a Union of people. Each state has something in which it surpasses the other. Why can you be not only willing, but glad, that this should be so? Why can you not throw away your pride and jealousy for a state, and substitute for it a pride and love for our whole country? Our path is onward; you have no time for strife. The people demand your help that our nation may become great and good.

Jonathan: What do you mean by saying that we must help make the nation great and good?

Uncle Sam: Here are other nephews of mine. They are talking very earnestly. Let us remain unobserved, and perhaps you may discover something to be improved. *(They retire to the recess.)*

(Enter Hezekiah Crane and Tom Pike.)

Tom: You talk as if you knew the place—ever been in our part of the country?

Hezekiah: Wal, I have traviled some there. I left hum when I was fifteen year old, and was raound in them parts considable. Ye see, dad allers wanted his children to have a good eddication. So I went to school and studied 'rethmetic, so that nobody couldn't never cheat me; than dad said folks ought to know somethin' of the world they live in, and I must know jography. But he said the beatinist way to larn jography was to travil; so he sot me up with a tin trunk full of needles and thread and sich groceries, and I went aout peddlin'. That was the fust thing I knew about your west country.

Tom: Wal, you see it saved me a sight of trouble about larnin' jography, because I was born thar, and didn't have to travil. *(Enter Dijah Crab.)* Hello, stranger! What might your name be? Where do you hail from?

Dijah: I'm Dijah Crab, an' I'm on my way hum. I'm e'enamost gin out, for I've been traviling ever sence sun-up, an I've had a right smart chance of plunder to tote. Is thar any place where I ken stay all night?

Tom: Wall, I reckon.

Hezekiah: You look like a clever sort of a chap; there's places enough tew put up if you ken fork over the dimes, but I guess you ain't troubled with an awful lot of 'em. Yeou'd wanter stay over Sunday, tew, I s'pose.

Dijah: Sunday? What's that?

Hezekiah: Land! don't you know what Sunday is? Where under the sun do you live?

Dijah: Down on the edge o' Massa Wheaton's plantation. I was raised thar.

Tom: Whar's your plunder?

Dijah: Right cher by the branch. *(Exit Tom, Dijah, and Hezekiah. Uncle Sam, Palmetto, Jonathan, and Buckeye come forward.)*

Uncle Sam: Do you see anything that needs to be done for our people?

Jonathan: Uncle, there's work enough to be done to prevent the English language from going to destruction.

Palmetto: We must educate all our people.

Buckeye: Yes; and just think of Dijah Crab helping to choose a President of the United States!

Uncle Sam: Universal education we must have to be a true republic. Each man must have education sufficient to judge for himself about the rulers needed, and discipline sufficient to submit, when his will is not that of the people. But here are our friends again. You may find that some other improvements are needful. *(They again retire.)*

(Enter Hezekiah, Tom, and Dijah.)

Tom: I tell, you, boys, it's a splendid country—you never saw nothin like it. And Dije, if I war in your place, instead of staying down on that ole sandy plantation, I'd pull up stakes and travil to new diggins. Why, on that quarter section whar I squatted fust, I planted a part to pumpkins. Well, they growed all summer, and in the fall I had the powerfulest crop you ever see. The pumpkins lay so close together on the ground, that if I jest struck one with my foot, it jarred the whole field.

Dijah: Dew other things grow as big as the pumpkins you tell on?

Tom: In course they do. I bought a new piece o' land and thort I'd grow pertaters thar. Wall, I planted 'em, and didn't go near 'em agin till one day in the fall. When I'd got to the place whar my land orter be, I see a lot of mounds that looked jest like the great Injin mounds that you come across sometimes. I couldn't think at fust what they was, but in a minit I knowed they was pertater hills.

Dijah: I should think the men thar would hafter be bigger than us to tote such things.

Tom: Wall, they be bigger, some on 'em—and them that ain't no bigger is a good deal smarter and spryer than folks here. Thar's some things above my bend, but then, I'm considered putty smart. It's the easiest thing in the world for me to swim the Mississippi, or jump the Ohio, or to chase a streak of blue lightnin' up a thorn tree without gettin' scratched.

Dijah: Wal, you be a smart un!

Hezekiah: I van! what whoppers! you dew beat all creation to blow!

Tom: Do you mean to tell me I lie? Reckon you'll find out whar thar's some grit if you ain't careful! *(Makes threatening motions with fists.)*

Hezekiah: Wal! Flare up and get mad if you're mineter! I ain't a goin' er take back what I said. I calkylate you'll find some other folks has pretty considable spunk as well as you! You needn't s'pose I was brought up in the woods to be scart by your bluster!

Tom: Come on then! I'm ready for you! I'll make an end of you, shortly!

Hezekiah: Wal I'm blowed if I don't make mince meat of you in less than no time!

Dijah: Pitch into him, Kiah!

Uncle Sam: *(Coming forward, followed by Jonathan, Palmetto, and Buckeye, and speaking authoritatively.)* You can make up and be friends as soon as you choose. You will not fight. *(They stand astonished.)*

Hezekiah: Wal I vum! Uncle Sam, if that ain't you! I'm plaguy glad to see ye, but I wish yeou hadn't come till I'd larnt this feller a lesson!

Tom: I tell ye, Uncle Sam, he orter have a reglar maulin'. *(Uncle Sam seats himself, studying a written paper attentively.)* He said I lied, and everybody knows that if thar's one feller on the face o' the earth that hates fibs and whoppers, Tom Pike is that feller! It's too bad to hafter flunk out so!

Buckeye: *(To Hezekiah.)* An'n't you Dick Moon of Pumpkin Hook, Connecticut? If you are, you deserve a "maulin'" for your cheating, as richly as Tom ever deserved one for lying.

Palmetto: No, he isn't Dick Moon. I've seen him before. He is Job Spooks, of Spoonville. He has cheated as much as Dick Moon ever did, though, I'll warrant.

Hezekiah: Wal, you're all mistaken; my name's Hezekiah Crane, of Piggin Holler, Connecticut.

Palmetto: Well, whatever your name may be, you're the Yankee peddler who very kindly stole a counterpane, some time ago, from the bed a cousin of mine allowed you to sleep on.

Buckeye: And he's the very one I met in the country, not very long ago, too, selling Young's Night Thoughts. It seems he bought an old edition very cheap, and was selling them off as bad books for five dollars apiece.

Hezekiah: Land o' Goshen! I should hafter be in forty places tew onct, tew dew all the things you tell on! Neow, anybody in Piggin Holler will tell ye that I've got a manufactory tew hum, that I'm carryin' on full chisel, where I'm plaguy cute at makin' all sorts of curus notions, and could n't possibly leave tew dew anything else!

Palmetto: Manufactory! Of course you have! Or where could all those wooden nutmegs come from to bother the cooks?

Buckeye: And I've examined some of the Pigeon Hollow garden seeds, and Tom Pike didn't plant his field of pumpkins with seed that he bought of Hezekiah Crane, I'll be bound. If he had, he would most likely have had a goodly crop of pine trees. Pine timber is the best material for making the "very best cucumber and pumpkin seeds," eh, Kiah?

Hezekiah: Wal, if I do make sich notions, I guess I know where to find a market for 'em.

Tom: Wall, I'd ruther tell big whoppers, than dew sich little, mean, cheatin' buzness as that ere!

Jonathan: Uncle, there's one thing that all our people need more than education.

Uncle Sam: And what is that?

Jonathan: Honesty; it's a rare virtue, I believe. Everywhere I see the same want of truth and honesty in dealing—the same fraud and deception. Everybody likes to tell a good story of his own achievements. Everybody from lowest to highest, wants to overreach his neighbor, and get the best end of a bargain, so that cheating is a part of business itself.

Uncle Sam: (*Rising.*) And when honesty is lost, honor is also lost. A man had better lose his life than his sense of honor. Then to be a nation that is just, and honest, and honorable, it is the work of each man to see that he preserves for himself his own truth and honor. With these for foundation-stones, our country shall rise, a glorious temple, firm and fair, sacred to Truth and Liberty. These must be our strength, and even now we have need of that strength, for the foes of liberty throughout the world have shown themselves our enemies. The British Lion, with terrible roar, threatens us. The Gallic Cock would stride through Mexico over our Southern border.*

Buckeye: Just say the word, Uncle, and we'll change the roar to a pitiful howl. We'll silence the crowing of the barn-yard fowl. We haven't been training ourselves to war, to be insulted or threatened by any nation on the globe. If England can't be our friend, she shall at least fear us. We have nothing to fear—we can defy any power. Let us compel the world to respect our flag!

Dijah: Let anybody tech our flag if they dar!

Palmetto: The long ears of the donkey have cropped out through the skin of the British Lion for a long time. The coward deserves an effectual fright.

Jonathan: 'Twould be capital amusement for our navy to annihilate the British fleets. E'en now the threatened supremacy of the "green over the red" has thrown the nation into convulsions.

Uncle Sam: And how long is it since you declared one of the grave faults of American citizens is self-conceit—the love of boasting of your own achievements and prowess? The lessons of the past years have been sadly lost upon us, if they have not taught us better things than these. When the rich, precious life of our noble, our young, our brave, was taken from earth, leaving countless forms of clay—when the nation bowed in sorrow, but would not withhold the holy sacrifice—when he, the great and good Lincoln was slain, basely murdered,—even then, when every heart bled in sorrow, did you not learn to lay aside all boasting, and "to take for your motto, 'In God is our trust?'" With all this experience will you again so soon, can you begin, to boast?

Jonathan and Palmetto: Never, again!

Buckeye: By all the lives that left their bodies on the battle-field, No! Like them, we'll work, or we'll fight, and like them, we will let our labor speak for us.

*Wartime controversies over Britain's neutral stance and its involvement in blockade running continued into the postwar period. French troops and their "emperor" Maximilian, who had invaded Mexico in the early 1860s, remained there until well after the Civil War ended, thereby causing the United States to mobilize thousands of troops along the Texas border.

Jonathan: Our people shall be enlightened—

Hezekiah: We'll be honest—

Tom: We'll stick to the truth—

Dijah: And to the flag—

All: The old flag forever!

Uncle Sam: Yes! and then, with a Union not simply of states, but "A union of hearts, a union of hands—"

All: Hands round! *(They clasp hands.)*

Uncle Sam: *(Pointing with one hand to the flag above them.)* We'll support "The Flag of our Union forever"!

Epilogue

"This Cruel War"

No one knows exactly how many children were touched by the messages of Civil War-era magazines. But a tiny window into the minds of the most likely readers among children of that time does exist. A handful of youngsters published their own magazines, offering the same combination of humor, sentimental poetry, and human interest stories found in juvenile magazines. Some were professionally printed, with long runs and lengthy subscription lists, while others were hand printed, lasted only an issue or two, and were read only by parents and a few best friends. Yet the editors of these "amateur" newspapers replicated the great political and social debates of the day, using the arguments and styles of adult newspapers as well as juvenile magazines. Few other sources show so clearly how children explained the war to themselves.

A typical effort was *The Sunbeam*, produced by the children of two Providence, Rhode Island, printers named Weeden and Barnes. The children, who ranged in age from seven to fifteen, took turns as editor, printing stories originally written as compositions for school. A majority of the articles dealt with school subjects, especially history and natural science. The paper's motto—"There is no sunbeam but must die or shine"— reflected the cheerful, modest, and pious tone of many juvenile magazines.

The realities of war, however, intruded even on the lives of these privileged children. The October 1863 issue acknowledged that while "we are made comfortable and happy, thousands of children are deprived of friends and homes, by this cruel war. We do not forget them, but often wish we could do something for their comfort." A later article on "The Holidays" reminded readers that while they may look forward to a happy holiday season with their families, "There will be a great many broken circles this year" because so many soldiers had been killed or captured and many more would have to stay with their units. "We must not forget them," *The Sunbeam* urged, "while we are enjoying so much, with our friends." The New Year's editorial for 1864 gratefully reported that "health, and happiness have been bestowed upon us: the lives of our friends have been spared, and each day has seemed to bring some new source of comfort and enjoyment." However, "How different the lot of many about us. This cruel war has brought sorrow and sadness into many homes. Fathers and brothers have been taken, and many children, who, at the commencement of the last year, were as happy as we, are now left orphans."

Other pieces provided the kind of trivia and interesting facts common to periodicals such as *Our Young Folks* and its competitors. Two of the children penned slightly different versions of a visit to a fort near Newport, where they saw Confederate prisoners in balls and chains and "caught a glimpse of Maj. Anderson, the hero of Fort Sumter." Another composition on "A Soldier's Life" contrasted the "gay sight" of men on parade with the "not . . . very pleasant" life of a soldier in the field, where he experienced pain, cold, danger, and loneliness. *The Sunbeam* even included an obituary for a young soldier named Peter Hunt—a relative of the Weeden children—reminiscent of the obituaries that appeared in *The Little Pilgrim*: he was "a good son, a kind brother, a faithful friend, and a brave officer. His end was peaceful, for his hope was in Jesus."

Several papers focused on the serious as well as the humorous aspects of the military and political scenes. *Once a Fortnight*, a Worcester, Massachusetts, biweekly, offered a straightforward "War News Summary" in each issue, while *The Union*, out of Pawtucket, Rhode Island, ridiculed a line from the Charleston *Mercury* that called the Yankee troops now threatening the South "tin pedlars." "It is true," said *The Union*, "that the Yankees have generally in their visits South peddled tin, but we guess they mean to peddle lead this time." The Worcester *Monthly Chronicle* chuckled over the inexperienced colonel who, "exhibiting less recollection of 'the tactics,'" deployed his unit by yelling, "Get up there on the hill, & scatter out as you did yesterday."

The adolescent Oliver Optics in New Jersey who published the long-running Newark High School *Athenaeum*, a hand-written monthly, offered serious editorials as well as humorous stories only obliquely connected to the war. One young patriot somberly argued that the moral courage of Northerners had to match their physical courage, while another related the farcical tale of "Uncle Zeke at the Fair," in which an old "down easter" battled the crowds and high prices of a local fund-raiser for the Sanitary Commission. A number of authors submitted pleas to remember the soldiers and to overlook their shortcomings. "It becomes us not to censure the soldier who has enlisted under the banner," wrote one boy, "to keep it sacred from vile traitorous hands, or give his life as an alternative!" A December 1863 editorial reported that the soldiers would "not look with joy" on the coming of winter. "There will be no Christmas dinner or New Year pleasures for them," only hardship and, possibly, death. One curious piece traced the "career" of a leather boot, from the slaughterhouse and tannery through bloody campaigns, Libby Prison, and a dramatic escape, to its final resting place in a closet as a war "memento."

Few amateur newspapers were illustrated, although the *Athenaeum* usually featured an original pencil sketch on the last page of each issue. The drawing for January 1864 depicted a band of angels unfurling a scroll that read, "In Memory of Our Soldiers and Sailors Who on Land or at Sea Have Fallen for Liberty and Law." Another showed a Union cavalryman plunging his sword through the breast of a Confederate opponent over a caption proclaiming, "A Blow for the Flag." The wistful September 1864 title page included a small picture of a Rebel shaking hands with a Yankee, framed by the word "Peace," an angel placing laurels on each of their heads, and the paper's motto.

That motto—"United We Stand, Divided We Fall"—indicated its student editors' political principles. Like these high-schoolers, child journalists throughout the Northeast professed their political creeds in the confident, purple rhetoric of nineteenth-century editors, reflecting the pro-Union, pro-Lincoln, and antislavery passions of most children's magazines. "Don't give up the ship, boys!" urged the Concord, Massachusetts, *Observor* early in the fall of 1862. "Stand by her to the last hour." The *Once a Fortnight* also threw its support behind the Lincoln administration, declaring that a defeat at the polls would bring "a disgraceful and dishonorable peace, a divided Union, and the re-establishment of the Slave Power in more than its former strength."

Just like the adult-published children's magazines, the homemade journals often printed correspondence that promoted their principles. *The Sunbeam* offered a letter from an army chaplain in Georgia who detailed his rough quarters, some of his battlefield adventures, the exotic Southern landscape, and the numerous African Americans he had encountered. Although the bulk of his two-part missive was descriptive, he concluded with his impression of the meaning of the war: "How wonderful is this war in its origin," he exclaimed. "Slavery stabbing Freedom! How wonderful in its results: Slavery prostrate, and gasping in its grave!"*

Their choice of topics, as well as their faithful re-creation of the themes and styles of children's magazines, indicate the extent to which these young editors and writers had taken in the forms and attitudes of the professionally produced juvenile magazines. There is no way of determining how many of these children subscribed to or even read them, but it is clear that their patriotic and moral messages had infused the middle-class child culture of the North.

Most of the Civil War-era secular magazines survived the conflict by only a few years. Oliver Optic founded *Oliver Optic's Magazine* in 1867; *The Student and Schoolmate* lasted only a few more volumes. One of the most famous postwar children's periodicals, *St. Nicholas*, absorbed both *Our Young Folks* and *The Little Corporal* in 1873 and 1875, respectively. The style of writing—perhaps influenced by Oliver Optic's adventures and the escapism of the wildly popular dime novels—would begin to change soon after the war, as part of the long transition in children's literature from messages that would inspire boys and girls to save themselves and form "heaven on earth" to the gently moralistic humanism of the late nineteenth century. A Tom Sawyer, rarely repentant despite frequent moral lapses, a hero despite his narcissism, could not have survived in the fictional world created by antebellum children's authors. Suddenly aware of urban poverty and the complexity of the postwar economy and society, authors replaced the rational child with a much more romantic view of childhood.

Few of the men and women who edited or wrote for midnineteenth-century juveniles are recalled today, although some, such as Louisa May Alcott or Thomas Wentworth Higginson or Horatio Alger, are remembered for their other writings. Yet for a time, they provided words and images that helped explain the Civil War to a generation of children. From

---

*The *Athenaeum* is held by the New Jersey Historical Society. The other amateur newspapers can be found at the American Antiquarian Society, Worcester, Massachusetts.

the stories and editorials, games and illustrations, and adventures and parables published in their magazines, Civil War children could piece together the causes of the conflict and determine their roles in it. Promising readers that the war could be won if they demonstrated the necessary piety and determination and assuring them that no contribution to the war effort was too small, children's magazines politicized and inspired young Americans to act on their loyalty.

Suggested Readings

ON CHILDREN'S MAGAZINES AND LITERATURE

Avery, Gillian. *Behold the Child: American Children and Their Books, 1621–1922*. Baltimore: Johns Hopkins University Press, 1994.

Billman, Carol. "McGuffey's Readers and Alger's Fiction: The Gospel of Virtue According to Popular Children's Literature." *Journal of Popular Culture* 11 (Winter 1977): 614–19.

Blum, John Morton, ed. *Yesterday's Children: An Anthology Compiled from the Pages of Our Young Folks, 1865–1873*. Cambridge: Houghton Mifflin, 1959.

Crandell, John C. "Patriotism and Humanitarian Reform in Children's Literature, 1825–1860." *American Quarterly* 21 (Spring 1969): 3–22.

Darling, Richard L. *The Rise of Children's Book Reviewing in America, 1865–1881*. New York: R. W. Bowker, 1968.

Demers, Patricia. *Heaven upon Earth: The Form of Moral and Religious Children's Literature, to 1850*. Knoxville: University of Tennessee Press, 1993.

Elson, Ruth Miller. *Guardians of Traditions: American Schoolbooks of the Nineteenth Century*. Lincoln: University of Nebraska Press, 1964.

Ford, Paul Leicester. *The New-England Primer: A History of Its Origin and Development*. New York: Dodd, Mead, 1897. Reprint, New York: Teachers College, Columbia University, 1962.

Keller, Holly. "Juvenile Antislavery Narratives and Notions of Childhood." In *Children's Literature*, edited by Francelia Butler, R. H. W. Dillard, and Elizabeth Lennox Keyser, 24:86–100. New Haven: Yale University Press, 1996.

Kelly, R. Gordon, ed. *Children's Periodicals of the United States*. Westport, CT: Greenwood Press, 1984.

———. *Mother Was a Lady: Self and Society in Selected American Children's Periodicals, 1865–1890*. Westport, CT: Greenwood Press, 1974.

Kiefer, Monica. *American Children through Their Books*. Philadelphia: University of Pennsylvania Press, 1948.

Lystad, Mary. *From Dr. Mather to Dr. Seuss*. Boston: G. K. Hall, 1980.

MacLeod, Ann Scott. *American Childhood: Essays on Children's Literature of the Nineteenth and Twentieth Centuries*. Athens: University of Georgia Press, 1994.

————. *A Moral Tale: Children's Fiction and American Culture, 1820–1860*. Hamden, CT: Archon Books, 1975.

Marten, James. "For the Good, the True, and the Beautiful: Northern Children's Magazines and the Civil War." *Civil War History* 41 (March 1995): 57–75.

Stone, Jane Clement. "The Evolution of Civil War Novels for Children." Ph.D. diss., Ohio State University, 1990.

Tebbel, John W. *From Rags to Riches: Horatio Alger, Jr., and the American Dream*. New York: Macmillan, 1963.

Westerhoff, John H. III, *McGuffey and His Readers: Piety, Morality, and Education in Nineteenth-Century America*. Nashville: Abingdon, 1978.

Winship, Michael. *American Literary Publishing in the Mid-Nineteenth Century: The Business of Ticknor and Fields*. New York: Cambridge University Press, 1995.

GENERAL STUDIES OF CHILDREN

Boylan, Anne M. *Sunday School: The Formation of an American Institution, 1790–1880*. New Haven: Yale University Press, 1988.

Butchart, Ronald E. *Northern Schools, Southern Blacks, and Reconstruction: Freedmen's Education, 1862–1875*. Westport, CT: Greenwood Press, 1980.

Calvert, Karin. *Children in the House: The Material Culture of Early Childhood, 1600–1900*. Boston: Northeastern University Press, 1992.

Censer, Jane Turner. *North Carolina Planters and Their Children, 1800–1860*. Baton Rouge: Louisiana State University Press, 1984.

Demos, John. *Past, Present, and Personal: The Family and the Life Course in American History*. New York: Oxford University Press, 1986.

Formanek-Brunell, Miriam. *Made to Play House: Dolls and the Commercialization of American Girlhood, 1830–1930*. New Haven: Yale University Press, 1993.

Heininger, Mary Lynn Stevens, et al. *A Century of Childhood, 1820–1920*. Rochester: Margaret Woodbury Strong Museum, 1984.

Hoffert, Sylvia D. *Private Matters: American Attitudes toward Childbearing and Infant Nurture in the Urban North, 1800–1860*. Urbana: University of Illinois Press, 1989.

Kaestle, Carl F. *Pillars of the Republic: Common Schools and American Society, 1780–1860*. New York: Hill and Wang, 1983.

Kett, Joseph. *Rites of Passage: Adolescence in America, 1790 to the Present*. New York: Basic Books, 1977.

Marten, James. *The Children's Civil War*. Chapel Hill: University of North Carolina Press, 1998.

Morris, Robert C. *Reading, 'Riting, and Reconstruction: The Education of Freedmen in the South, 1861–1870*. Chicago: University of Chicago Press, 1981.

Nasaw, David. *Schooled to Order: A Social History of Public Schooling in the United States*. New York: Oxford University Press, 1979.

Nylander, Jane C. *Our Own Snug Fireside: Images of the New England Home, 1760–1860*. New Haven: Yale University Press, 1992.

Pollock, Linda A. *Forgotten Children: Parent-Child Relations from 1500 to 1900*. Cambridge: Cambridge University Press, 1983.

Schorsch, Anita. *Images of Childhood: An Illustrated Social History*. Pittstown, NJ: Main Street Press, 1979.

Sommerville, C. John. *The Rise and Fall of Childhood*. Rev. ed. New York: Vintage, 1990.

Stevenson, Louise L. *The Victorian Homefront: American Thought and Culture, 1860–1880*. New York: Twayne, 1991.

West, Elliott, and Paula Petrik, eds. *Small Worlds: Children & Adolescents in America, 1850–1950*. Lawrence: University Press of Kansas, 1992.

Wishy, Bernard. *The Child and the Republic: The Dawn of Modern American Child Nurture*. Philadelphia: University of Pennsylvania Press, 1968.

Youcha, Geraldine. *Minding the Children: Child Care in America from Colonial Times to the Present*. New York: Scribner's, 1995.

Annotated Bibliography*

Children's Friend. Dayton, Ohio, 1860?–1863. Published semi-monthly by the Gospel Herald and edited by J. Ellis. Promoted temperance, Sabbath schools, obedience, and preparing for death; urged children to become self-reliant and independent. Letters from young readers tended to celebrate the opening of Sunday schools or mourn their absence in remote regions. Games and puzzles drew on biblical as well as more secular ideas for clues and answers.

Children's Friend. Richmond, Virginia, 1862–1915. Published monthly by the Presbyterian Committee of Publication and edited by the Rev. William Brown as "an evangelical Sabbath School journal." Four pages long, it was devoted exclusively to religious topics, with no games, illustrations, or fiction. Articles related Bible stories, described missionary activities, depicted obedient children, discussed appropriate reading material for Christian children, and described positive Sabbath school experiences.

Child's Banner. Salisbury, North Carolina, 1865. Short-lived, four-page magazine published by the Rev. A. W. Mangum as a Sunday school paper.

Child's Index. Macon, Georgia, 1863–1865. Published as a Baptist paper for children by the Rev. Samuel Boykin, editor of the *Christian Index.* The four-page monthly included illustrations, music, and some stories. Circulation reached at least four thousand. Authors included fifteen-year-old Joel Chandler Harris, who wrote "Charlie Howard; or, Who Is the Good Boy?" for the July 1863 issue.

Forrester's Playmate. Boston, 1854–1867? One of several magazines edited by Mark Forrester from the 1840s through the

---

*From R. Gordon Kelly, *Children's Periodicals of the United States* (Westport, CT: Greenwood Press, 1984), 543–52; and Sarah Law Kennerly, "Confederate Juvenile Imprints: Children's Books and Periodicals Published in the Confederate States of America, 1861–1865" (Ph.D. diss., University of Michigan, 1956), 250–312.

1860s. Like the others—*The Youth's Casket and Playmate, The Boys' and Girls' Magazine and Fireside Companion, Forrester's Boys' and Girls' Magazine*—it presented fairly typical selections on nature, history, and biography, along with encouragement to live moral, hard-working lives. Forrester's monthly column—"Chats with Readers and Correspondents"—was, perhaps, more extensive than similar sections of other magazines. Although war-related material appeared rather irregularly, the editor did urge former readers in the army to keep him informed of their experiences.

Little American. West Point, New York, 1862–1864. Published semimonthly by Susan Warner and edited by the author of "Wide, Wide World" and "Dollars and Cents," according to the masthead. It offered Bible stories, travelogues, natural history, and short stories reflecting Christian principles.

The Little Corporal. Chicago, 1865–1875. Published by Alfred L. Sewell and edited by Sewell and Emily Huntington Miller, a well-known author for children. Inspired by the devotion to duty and sacrifices of Union soldiers during the Civil War, Sewell conceived *The Little Corporal* as a way to sustain the wartime spirit exemplified by the children who had helped him raise $16,000 for Chicago's Northwestern Sanitary Fair in 1865. The monthly, which supposedly reached a circulation of 80,000 by the late 1860s, featured serialized fiction, success stories, poems, songs, "Indian stories," games, and letters from readers, all loosely devoted to the magazine's motto "Fighting against Wrong, and for the Good, the True, and the Beautiful." Somewhat inevitably, considering the magazine's martial origins, the stories slanted toward male readers, as in Horace Greeley's late 1860s column, "Counsel to Boys."

The Little Pilgrim. Philadelphia, 1853–1868. Published by Leander K. Lippincott and edited by his wife, Sara J. C. Lippincott, under the name Grace Greenwood. It was named as a juvenile version of the title character in John Bunyan's *Pilgrim's Progress* and dedicated to promoting a genteel Christianity and high moral purpose. Authors featured in the monthly included Greenwood, Lucy Larcom, and other writers for children, but also John Greenleaf Whittier, Hans Christian Andersen, and Charles Dickens. Selections included European stories, pious obituaries of readers, "Anecdotes and Sayings of Children," morality tales, and, during the Civil War, commentary on political events and the war's effects on society.

Our Young Folks: An Illustrated Magazine for Boys and Girls. Boston, 1865–1873. Published by Ticknor and Fields, publisher of *The Atlantic Monthly* and *North American Review*. Edited chiefly by Lucy Larcom. Perhaps the best and most popular of the wartime magazines for children—Theodore Roosevelt was an enthusiastic reader—its circulation reached upward of 75,000 in the years following the war. Its sixty-four pages per month offered a balanced menu of fiction; articles on nature, art, science, and geography; and games. Less religious in its orientation than many earlier magazines, it nevertheless focused on proper middle-class behavior such as obedience, modesty, generosity, and hard work. During the Civil War, it featured a number of articles and stories revolving around sympathetic African Americans; in other stories, Native Americans and Jews are also portrayed. Authors included Louisa May Alcott, Harriet Beecher Stowe, and Mayne Reid; drawings by Winslow Homer also appeared.

The Student and Schoolmate. Boston, 1855–1872. Created by the merger of *The Student and Tutor* and *The Schoolmate*. Several publishers produced the magazine, but its dominant editor was Oliver Optic (William T. Adams). Its subtitle, "A Monthly Reader for School and Home Instruction," reflects its editor's didactic bent. Optic frequently espoused political and moral causes from his column "The Teacher's Desk"; and, among all the editors of juvenile magazines, he was the most vociferous supporter of the Union during the Civil War. Along with typical fiction and nonfiction selections, *The Student and Schoolmate* offered patriotic songs, declamations (speeches to be given in school or public settings), and dialogues (short plays on patriotic subjects). Optic wrote a large portion of each month's issue, but he also published pieces by other authors, including, on occasion, Horatio Alger.

OTHER CHILDREN'S MAGAZINES OF THE CIVIL WAR

The Child at Home. Boston, 1863–1873.
Children's Guide. Macon, Georgia, 1863–1865.
The Child's Paper. New York, 1852–1897?
Child's World. Philadelphia, 1862–1871.
Clark's School Visitor. Philadelphia, 1857–1875.
Deaf Mute Casket. Raleigh, North Carolina, 1861–1865.
Little Joker. New York, 1863–1866.
Merry's Museum. New York, 1841–1872.
New Church Magazine for Children. Boston, 1862–?

Portfolio. Charleston, 1861.

The Standard-Bearer: An Illustrated Magazine for the Young. New York, 1851–1863?

Sunday School Advocate. New York, 1841–1921.

Sunday School Times. Philadelphia, 1859–?

The Wellspring: For Young People. Boston, 1844–?

Young Reaper. Philadelphia, 1857–1908.

Youth's Instructor. Rochester, New York, 1852–?

The Youth's Visitor. Boston, 1864–1872?

Youth Temperance Visitor. Rockland, Maine, 1863–1870?

Index

ISBN 0-8420-2654-1